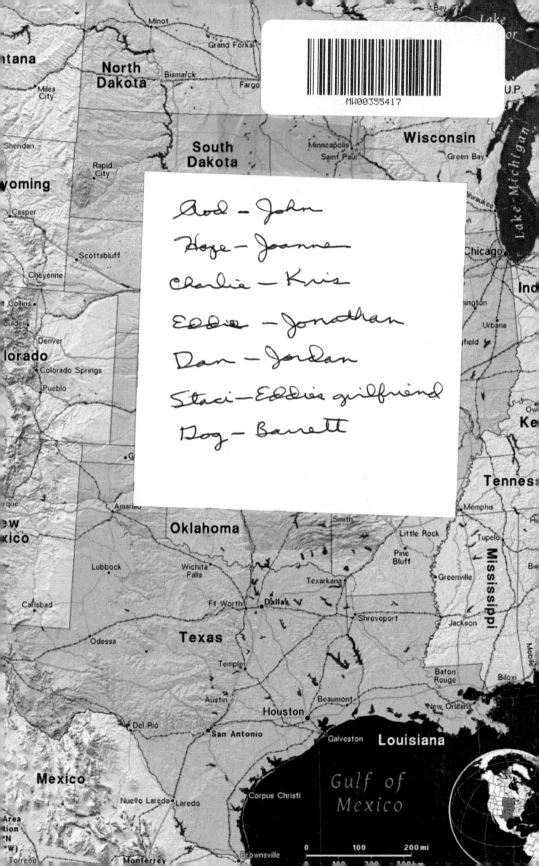

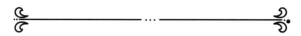

The year was 2010. Private First Class (PFC) Charlie Martin, was getting ready for the ride of his life. He was about to deploy along with some 4,000 other Iowa and Nebraska National Guard troops to the pit they call Afghanistan. His days were numbered. In other words. He was leaving soon….maybe forever. How would he handle war? Would the first suggestion of bullets whizzing by his head cause him to duck and run? Not likely. Martin had been planning for this day for a long, long time.

But his deployment wasn't just about him, indeed the whole family was involved. Charlie's brother, Private Second Class (PV2) Eddie Martin idolized his older sibling. So much so, he followed in his brother's footsteps joining the Guard a year after Charlie had. And then there was younger brother, Dan. He was watching the whole thing way too up close and personal. Both of his brother's would soon be gone…off to military life. Then came Mom and Dad. Hope and Rod Martin were part of the process too. How would they navigate the coming year? Would the family be able to handle all of the stress and uncertainty? They were all about to find out. In order to do that though, they needed something to arm themselves with. They found the perfect weapon. One that didn't use ammunition.

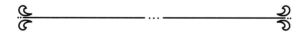

The Truth of it All...

These are a few things that will be helpful for the reader to know.

Although this book is written as a work of fiction, it is surely based on a very real story. The characters names have been changed and some embellishment has been added to the message of the story.

All blog posts were written during the deployment of 4,000 Iowa and Nebraska National Guard Troops in 2010 and 2011. The blog can be found at my-fathersvoice.blogspot.com

About the photos. All pictures are actual, original and true to the story.

Our purpose in the writing of this book is to shape a story that will encourage you. Through that encouragement, our prayer is that you too will find that hope is a weapon. Without it, we can fall into a darkness so deep that we despair even life itself.

HOPE
IS A
WEAPON

JOHN KELLING

Book Baby Publishing

Pennsauken, NJ

Names, characters, places and incidents other than those used from actual news reports and the author's blog stories are the product of the writer's imagination or are used fictitiously.

Print ISBN: 978-1-54398-382-1

eBook ISBN: 978-1-54398-383-8

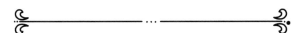

To my Delectable Darlooney, (my wife Joanne), who endured many, many hours of my writing and who proved a valuable editor and key contributor in this journey with me. And most certainly to my awesome sons (Kris, Jonathan and Jordan). Love you guys to pieces......

HOPE
IS A
WEAPON

CHAPTER 1

Eddie Martin was lying awake in his ruffled queen-sized bed staring off into never-never land. Sheets were pitched this way and that. Pillows were at the bottom and sides of his resting spot. But for Eddie, it hadn't been a night of bliss. He had tossed and turned, put pillows over his head and under his rump. But sleep hadn't come peacefully.

"Whatever", said Martin disgusted with the situation. Eddie, a thin 5 foot 11 inch, sandy haired dude was deep in thought. He'd joined the Iowa National Guard in 2010 in his senior of high school at Johnston High. Not because he felt pushed by anyone in doing so, but he'd felt directed to follow in the footsteps of his older brother, Charlie, who enlisted roughly a year earlier. Eddie loved Charlie. He idolized him in so many ways and treasured the ground he walked on. But he was scared or maybe conflicted. He wasn't sure which. At 18, what do you know for sure? So he signed up.

As Eddie looked out the windows at the big blue summer sky above he was trying to decide how the day would unfold. It was drill weekend at Camp Dodge and Martin was supposed to report for duty. Martin, though, had other ideas.

"Eddie", time to get up and head to drill" yelled his dad, Rod, from the first floor living room. Silence. "Eddie", he repeated. Again no reply. Eddie was hoping the notions of his dad would go away. But not so. Seconds later, Rod entered the bedroom and stared at his middle son. He sensed there was trouble and the looks of the situation spelled it out. Eddie was laying cross-wise across the bed in his underwear and it was quite apparent he wasn't planning on leaving the house anytime soon. "Dude", said Rod. "You need to get up and head to drill". Confidently, Eddie responded, "not going Dad."

"And why not?", said Rod. "I'm just not going. I don't feel all that great, anyway", said Eddie. Rod took a deep breath and slowly let it out. This wasn't good but his thoughts suggested there was much more to it than Eddie's lack of desire or illness.

"Okay", said Rod. "We've told you before, you have free will but if you don't make the right decision, you'll have to accept the consequences....so you need to call the base and tell them you're sick", he added. But the words weren't acknowledged. Already Eddie had made up his mind. He had no intention of telling anyone, anything. Whether it was the body language or the glazed look, Martin's dad held his tongue which was a surprise considering the spike he was feeling in his blood pressure. Just then, older brother Charlie sauntered into the bedroom. Charlie, 19, was set to deploy along with roughly 4,000 other National Guardsmen to Afghanistan in October. Charlie would be among the 2nd Brigade Combat Team, 34th Infantry Division comprising soldiers from Iowa, Nebraska and another 100 from other states. It was to be this group's largest deployment since World War II.

"What's going on?", said Charlie. "Your brother thinks he's going to skip drill this weekend and not tell anyone", said Rod. Charlie stopped in his tracks. Immediately disgust swept over his face. "Bro, not a good idea. Things don't work like that", fired Charlie. Eddie equaled Charlie's disgust with an attitude of his own. "I don't care. I don't care what they do to me, I'm not going", said Eddie. Charlie and Rod looked at each other certain they weren't going to change any decision Eddie had made. "Alright then", said Rod. "Just be aware that whatever you do will affect Charlie. Your last name is the same and everyone who's anyone knows that you're brothers."

Rod and the 6' 2" barrel-chested Charlie retreated to the living room. Their conversation was in agreement. What Eddie was doing was stupid and selfish. As they continued their discussion, Hope Martin entered the room. A mother's female senses quickly kicked in. Something was not right. "Eddie's not going to drill", offered Charlie. "And his idiotic idea is going to impact the both of us."

Just then, the ring of Eddie's cellphone from upstairs brought everyone to attention. From the exchange taking place it was apparent his drill sergeant was wanting to know where he was. The Sgt., was known as a no-nonsense type of guy. He had very little if any compassion and was a distinct double for Jim Taylor, the Green Bay Packer fullback of the '60's. Square jaw, the look of a bulldog and the presence of Rocky Balboa. Crap was not in his makeup. He dished out a butt load of attitude and for obvious reasons got none back. The talk lasted about three minutes. Then the cursing started, littered with a multitude of four-letter words. And the throwing of pillows, tennis shoes and anything else he could get his mitts on. "I told them I was sick", Eddie yelled. "And in addition to that, I told them my recruiter lied to me about my ADD not being an issue with the military. I told the sergeant I wanted out", he continued. "He asked me if my folks were home...and I said yeah, why?" "Then he said you'd better round everybody up and be at the base in the next half an hour. Or else", he said defiantly. Little did Eddie know, crew cut man had been updating his superior officer during their dialogue regarding the reason for Martin's absence. The military wheels were now in motion.

Back in the Martin's living room, Hope and Rod shared glances. The deep brow on Rod's forehead was showing more clarity and Hope's nervous twitch of her eyebrow started up. As Eddie hit the bottom of the landing in his military gear there was a much less confident person than a short time ago. Then like in a little swarm, the three hit the two-stall garage and fired up the Martin's black 2009 Yukon. Inside the house, Charlie was explaining the morning ruckus to the youngest Martin, Dan. A burly high school junior, Dan was seeing military life all too personal. Probably wasn't his cup of tea. The garage door creaked as it began its downward run. As the truck backed down the drive, mom and dad were in agreement. They hoped their middle son hadn't shot himself in the foot. Eddie had indeed dug himself a big hole.

CHAPTER 2

There were some definite weather changes taking place as the Martin's headed down the street from their two-story home at the end of the cul-de-sac. The sky which a little over an hour ago was a deep rich blue now looked more ominous by the minute. A storm was on the horizon in more ways than one. Hope Martin, a woman approaching age 50 with mid-length blonde hair swept behind her ears and who could have easily passed for someone half her age, piped up. "Guys, I don't like the looks of this", she offered. "The sky's getting so dark. The weather system is moving so fast." As Hope turned to her husband she observed someone lost in his thoughts, yet a person she admired for his persistence in enduring many different trials in his 60-year life. Although a tad bit overweight, Rod handled his 5 foot 10 inch frame with ease. His brownish-black hair showed a few signs of gray and his face was adorned with a thick full beard. "Rod. Rod", said Hope. Rod was completely lost in his own thoughts although the radio might have had something to do with it. Blaring through the dashboard was a song from Skillet, entitled "Hero". The lyrics no doubt were making their impact.

"It's just another war. Just another family torn. Falling from my faith today. Just a step from the edge. Just another day in the world we live."

Far, far away Rod was hearing his name being called again, "Rod. Rod." "Did you hear what I said?" echoed his wife. "Can you turn down the radio so we can pray?" Being the spiritual person Mrs. Martin was, she turned to prayer each and every time she knew her own power wasn't enough for a situation. Addressing his wife's request, Rod turned down the sound and looked in the rearview mirror at his middle son. The reflection mirrored a young man that looked as though he was headed to the electric chair. It was obvious, Eddie's choice of trying to skip out on drill was not a good one. As Hope began her prayer you could see some relief come to the youngster. "And we also ask you Father God for a compassionate man for us to meet with. Please provide a man that can see all sides of a situation and provide a proper direction for us all." As she ended her words, the Yukon arrived at the south gate to the post and a huge hulk of a solider stepped up to the Martin's window and asked for identifications. "Can I help you folks?", said the gate man. Somewhat sheepishly, Rod's words came out, "we're here to see Major Fritz Jenkins." As the guard took account of the three individuals in the vehicle, he no doubt wondered why a family would be seeing Major Jenkins. But that wasn't his issue. Safety was. After checking everyone's identification, the guard sneered, "Okay, you can go on through, first building on your left after the circle."

Entering Camp Dodge was a step into military history. When Charlie had joined the Guard his family had googled Wikipedia to educate themselves on the base. "Original construction of the post began in 1907, to provide a place for the National Guard units to train. In 1917, the installation was handed over to national authorities and greatly expanded to become a regional training center for forces to participate in the First World War. Along with the numerous National Guard units located at Camp Dodge, the post is also home to the Sustainment Training Center (formerly the National Maintenance Training Center), Joint Forces Headquarters, Iowa's Emergency Operations Center, a MEPS installation, and the State Police academy. The camp is the home of the Iowa Gold Star Military Museum, a member of the Army Museum System. Formerly the town of Herold was surrounded by the Camp. But in 1990 the U.S. Army Corp of Engineers purchased the town and it is now known to reside in Johnston." Many soldiers had come here over the years. Each with a story unto their own.

The sleek truck came to a quick and complete halt in front of Building 1285. And then it hit. Buckets of rain poured down from the skies. The kind of moisture that beats right into your brain. Along with that the northwest winds began to howl in dog like fashion more than 30 miles an hour. The Martin's made a mad dash up the sidewalk and into the new red and cream brick structure. Shaking off the droplets from their clothes, Hope, Rod and Eddie began their slow walk to Major Jenkins office. As they entered the room, the Major, a man about 6'2" and perfectly proportioned, who no doubt had been anxiously awaiting his visitors, stood up and greeted the three. "Hi', I'm Major Fritz Jenkins, what seems to be the story here?"

Everyone's eyes went to Eddie and the nervous appearance fully apparent on his face. The big bulge in his Adam's apple said even more. This wasn't going to be an easy story to tell. But he was clearly on center stage. And the curtain was up. Action!

CHAPTER 3

The Sarge, aptly known as Carter, had a disdainful look as he ushered the Martin's in to the Major's office. Carter had heard Eddie's remarks about ditching his Guard commitment. He wasn't all that happy about those who showed weakness. He had his own thoughts on the subject. What angered Carter the most was being left out of any of the conversation that was going to take place. The major dismissed the sergeant and he closed the door rather abruptly and with a little show of disrespect. In the room, there were four accounted for. The walls were a drab off-white and as Eddie sat there he sensed they were taking on a life of their own. Slowly, ever so slowly they were closing in on him. He shot a glance at his Mom and Dad to see if they were truly with him. His dad was attempting to smile, but the nervous twitch of his lower left lip was something he was trying to keep in check. His mom was alert and anxious as to what was to come. Eddie performed a quick check of his own body language as his mind began to wander. Words only he could see hung in mid-air directly between him and the major. First came, Deceit.....then, Anger, followed by Not Ready and the one that lasted the longest, Scared.

Eddie's life to this point had been relatively secure. He'd lived in four different towns in his lifetime and each was a bubble in itself. That's where his comfort zone was. He could see the future and that meant leaving a bubble. He was beginning to have thoughts he wasn't ready to leave that bubble. Not now, maybe not for a long time. Maybe not ever. But as quickly as the words showed themselves, they disappeared. They were replaced by the look of the Major's staunch demeanor. Eddie could see the major's lips moving. Was he all of the sudden deaf?' Eddie wondered. He couldn't hear a word of what the Major was saying. Eddie's thoughts were clearly out trumping the Major's language. The knot he felt in his stomach when they first entered the room was getting tighter by the second. He had to utilize all his physical well-being to keep from doubling over in pain. Then the bubble burst. And he heard it. "Private Martin", I understand you have some concerns of your recruitment. Is that right?", said the Major.

Martin remembered back to the day he'd signed his commitment papers. At the time it seemed like a perfect place to support his older brother, Charlie. The other thing that was intriguing to Eddie was learning the mechanical trade and the Guard was a good way to get training and experience at the same time. When Eddie had first looked over the job description of the program he wanted to join he'd thought...that could be me. Why not? I can do that. Martin's intrigue had settled on the wheeled vehicle mechanic area. He was to maintain wheeled vehicles, their associated trailers and material handling equipment systems by inspecting, servicing, maintaining, repairing, replacement, adjusting and testing of wheeled vehicles and material handling equipment systems, subsystems and components. It also included the servicing of automotive electrical systems including wiring harness, and starting and charging systems and lastly perform wheeled vehicle recovery operations. No problem with any of that, Eddie thought.

Raise your right hand and repeat after me. That's pretty much what it took. That and a number of signatures on the dotted line. He was now in. Or there. At Camp Dodge. The Dodge was to be his home one weekend a month for the next few months before he headed to Basic Training at Ft. Knox, Kentucky in August. As the monthly drills continued they became a little more difficult for Eddie. In fact, he was downright dreading them. Maybe it was the clock ticking down to his departure or knowing that his brother was about ready to ship off to Mississippi and then off to California for some advanced training before deploying to Afghanistan. He was no doubt obsessing. The ADD was taking over.

"Yes, sir", a timid Eddie replied. "Alright, let's see where this takes us", shot back the Major. Eddie looked around the room. There were some pictures on the wall of some military people he'd never heard of. Dwight D Eisenhower for one. General George Patton for another. Maybe he'd heard of Eisenhower. He wasn't sure. Wasn't there an Eisenhower that was President of the United States?, he thought. Martin returned his focus on the Major. He tried sizing him up. What kind of a man was he? Did he go by the book? If he was, Martin was clearly cooked. He wasn't sure what his take was on the man behind the desk. Eddie began to feel some sweat forming on his brow. Eddie knew from the look on the Major's face he was likely doing some sizing up of his own.

Major Fritz Jenkins had been in his position a little over two years. The word on him was he was fair, firm and committed. Committed to the Guard. And committed to making a difference in people's lives. In an earlier life, the Major had been a police officer in Eastern Iowa. He'd seen a lot. And done a lot. It was those life experiences he had that he wanted to bring with him when he made his decision to join the National Guard full-time. At the time, he wasn't thinking of making a career change. But life has a way of making its own course when you least expect it. Sitting across from him was a young man clearly at a crossroad. These kids look younger every year the Major thought. Maybe that played into some of the issues with making a decision and sticking to it. What impressed Jenkins right off the bat with Eddie was his ability to talk. Eddie had always had the gift of gab, something he must have inherited from his mother.

Hope and Rod Martin were doing analyzing of their own. They saw the same pictures Eddie had. Only difference was, they knew the names and the background of both of the Generals. True Americans. Both of them. Hope took a deep breath and slowly let it out. Rod cleared his throat which was full of something. It felt like a frog. With the look overs commenced, the time had come for serious conversation. Ready or not....

Unbelievably for the next two hours, the Major, Eddie and his folks talked. Clearly, Jenkins was a compassionate man. The prayer initiated by Hope on the way to Camp Dodge was also at work. The clock seemed to be of no consequence to the Major. It was hard to fathom the time the Major was spending with them considering this was a drill weekend and he had tons of paper on his desk. His attention was clearly in the moment in front of him. He was in the business of saving lives and in many situations, helping reshape lives. Right now, that was the business at hand.

Eddie offered his feelings that his recruiter had misled him. When he had mentioned his Attention Deficit Disorder, the man looking to make quotas had said, "don't tell anyone about your ADD, we'll be alright". Looking back, Eddie realized he should have done more research before agreeing to enlist. Water over the dam...maybe. Was the ADD manageable? That was the subject matter the four discussed for some time. And then...

"What do you want to do with your life", the Major asked Eddie. Eddie thought for a minute. A long minute. "I really don't know, sir", he replied. "Guess I haven't thought all that much about it. Kind of living in the moment." Jenkins had heard this same response more than once. In fact, it was becoming a pretty standard comeback.

"Is that what you want? To just live in the moment", challenged the Major. "Private, let me tell you about some of the people I used to come across when I was a police officer", he started. "There were druggies, alcoholics, thieves and then of course the ones that like to beat up people. Each of those individuals lived in the moment." Eddie was beginning to get restless. He had never thought about it like that. The redness of his cheeks told a lot of the embarrassment he was feeling. Mom and Dad were silently cheering. Keep going sir, they thought. "I can't tell you what to do Eddie. This has to be your decision. I just know this. When I decided to transition from the police force to the Guard, it was the best decision I ever made. Hands down", finished the Major.

Eddie looked down at the floor and his boots. They were clearly looking more like clown's feet. Eddie shook his head. He had to get rid of that image. Jenkins knew he had hit a nerve. How dead on, he wasn't sure. But there was a flicker. "Private", the Major said. "This isn't going to be a question. Just a statement. I think you need a little time to think this thing through", added Jenkins. "Take the rest of the weekend off. No drill. I want you to think about what we've talked about and I want you to get back to me in five days with your answer. In or out? Okay?" Eddie couldn't believe what he was hearing. Not only did he not have to go to drill, the Major was letting him go home. Sweet. Eddie had dodged a bullet. Or so he hoped he had.

CHAPTER 4

Charlie Martin was dodging some bullets of his own. He was days away from the beginning of his deployment. Martin's Brigade would be going to Mississippi and then on to California for weeks of training. Then on to.... Afghanistan. It was all happening way too fast.

In front of him was a real pistol. Demanding some serious face time was his girlfriend, Staci. The 5'3" cuter than heck brunette was clearly making some demands known. Or was it desires? Charlie wasn't sure which. He was though, clearly overdressed for the occasion. Staci was three years younger than Charlie. Sexually she was his equal. They'd spent weeks, perhaps months, enjoying what they could of each other before Charlie was to deploy. More often than not, it meant time in Charlie's bedroom in the basement. When they weren't coming up for air, which was seldom, they spent their time locked in one sexual position or another. Martin's folks didn't approve of the rompings. They voiced their opinions more than once. Charlie, as often was the case, acted clueless. They liked Staci, but the goings on under their roof was not a good lesson for the other two Martin young men to learn from.

Staci and Charlie had met two years ago in Indianola, Iowa when the Martin's lived on a 10-acre lot outside of town. She had come from a different background. To say the family was dysfunctional would have been an understatement. Staci had plans to do something with her life. She wasn't going to spend it rotting in Iowa. She hoped Charlie would be part of that life. That thought would have to be shelved for now. It was time to get between the sheets again....

Fifteen minutes later, Charlie was clearly exhausted. Spent might be another way to put it. He looked up at the ceiling and the various markings in the tiles. His mind wandered to his brother Eddie. Wonder how his talk with the Major went? What an idiot, he thought. You can't just not show up to drill. Anyone knows that. But you couldn't tell Eddie anything. He'll learn. He'll learn to keep his mouth shut. Staci leaned into Charlie's chest and with her dark brown eyes afire, flashed a devious smile. "A penny for your thoughts", she inquired. "Nothing really. Just thinking of Eddie", Charlie offered.

"Are you kidding?" she shot back. "We've just had some sack time with each other and all you can think about is your brother? Unbelievable." On the last syllable. Staci sprang out of bed, tossed her black Tularosa Tay Fringe halter top over her head, pulled on her Calvin Klein denim shorts grabbed her white Gucci web sandals and said, "see you later, buddy." Left behind was her designer underwear. Most likely on purpose.

Before Charlie could offer a response she was up the stairs and out of the house. Gone. Martin knew it wouldn't be any good to run after her. She'd have to calm down on her own. And he'd have to think of the right thing to say. Clearly, he hadn't dodged when he should have. He hoped his little brother had fared better.

CHAPTER 5

Hope and Rod shook the hand of Major Fritz Jenkins. And they shook. If Eddie hadn't interceded by nudging his dad's arm, the two of them might be shaking the Major's hand yet today. The meeting with the Major couldn't have gone any better than it did. At least by most definitions. "Thanks so much for taking the time to talk with us, sir", said Rod. Jenkins had been firm, listened to Eddie's complaints and issues, offered some suggestions and put the decision to continue with the Guard back in Eddie's court. "Just curious sir", said Hope. "Where do you go to church? You're clearly a compassionate man and I sensed something about you." "Thanks", offered the Major. "Cornerstone of Hope in West Des Moines. You?", he rattled off. "Interesting", Hope countered. "So do we." Mom and Dad and the Major all hoped Eddie had gotten something out of the discussion. Without saying, Private Martin had a lot to chew on. Thursday was a long way off. For now, he took in a big breath from his small physique and released a long sigh of relief.

The three Martins turned to leave the Major's office area, but Jenkins' voice stopped them in their tracks. "Private. One last couple of thoughts", he suggested. "If you don't change direction you will end up where you're headed. But most importantly, your attitude determines your direction." Let those thoughts bounce around in your noggin. Talk to you soon."

The walk to the truck took a little over two minutes. Eddie was leading the way. Mom and Dad were lagging behind conversing in whispered tones. As they reached the vehicle, Eddie asked his dad to toss him the keys. "Why don't you let me drive, dad?", he asked. "That's the least I can do for the two of you coming with me today." Hope slid into the slick leather front passenger seat. Rod jumped in on the same side of the truck as his wife but in the back.

As the Martin's headed off the base, Rod was deep in thought. He had never been in the Service. When he was around his boys' ages, he had a deferment from his draft board due to attending college at Mankato State University in Mankato, Minnesota. Vietnam was the focal point of the military during those times. And because of that, the military's reputation was pretty bad. If Rod had lost his deferment and gotten called up, he wondered if he would have fled to Canada. Fortunately, he didn't have to cross that bridge. What readily came to Rod was the ugly demonstrations that took place on the Mankato campus and the streets and bridges of the southern Minnesota town in 1970. Fires were set. Cars rocked and windows broken out. At first the scene was exhilarating, then embarrassing. It was a time when as an American, you felt so un-American. Soldiers were spit on. Cursed. Called unimaginable names like Baby Killers. It was not pretty. Times have changed though. When the Martin family had traveled to Oklahoma to see Charlie's graduation from Basic at Fort Sill in 2009, Rod saw his country's military up close. Without question, he had come to a deep appreciation for the country's servicemen. Rod was proud his two boys had decided to join the Guard. He couldn't have thought of any better way for each of them to learn the meaning of responsibility. Now one was waffling. Rod wasn't happy. His wife was somewhere in between. The Lord knew what he was doing when he made man and woman. Yes, he sure did. A smile came to Rod. It had to have been the only smile he'd had all day.

Shaking his head, the cobwebs were beginning to disappear. The opening of the truck doors signaled an arrival at the Martin's home.

And then came a flash of light followed by a loud Craaaaack, a helpless scream and then a deep low rumble. "My God", wailed Hope Martin. "That was way too close. I hope no one got hit or hurt. It sounded like it was right next to us." This was the mother of all summer storms. Sensing it was now or never, the three dashed out of the SUV into the house. Then the clouds opened up…..again. It had been that way most of the day. Rain, a smattering of some fluffy clouds and then dark and ugly again. This was at least the third time a front had moved in by Rod's count.

"Crap", suggested Charlie who was trying his best to make a grilled cheese in the galley kitchen. Charlie was just learning some culinary skills but his messes looked better than his finished product. At his feet was the family buddy, a beautiful, docile Golden Retriever by the name of Mason, a rescue dog from the Iowa Golden Retriever Rescue. Mason was freaked out by the storm which Charlie was apparently completely oblivious of. However, the dropping of a big piece of cheese momentarily provided the Golden with a distraction. And a reward of sorts. Only thing was, that was the last piece of cheese in the house. Charlie looked at the three returnees. "Well, how'd things go?", he announced. "Did they kick you out? Or are you going to spend some time in the brig?" Charlie half-smiled. He had a vested interest in the outcome of Eddie's meeting and he wanted his little brother to know that. "Come on dude, what did they say?"

Eddie tossed a disgusted look at his brother Charlie. But said nothing. "Well?", said Charlie again. "Okay, okay…everybody settle down", Mr. Martin demanded. "Charlie, we have some things to talk over. When we finish up, then you can ask all the questions you want." With the discussion closed, Charlie smacked his right leg with his hand signaling Mason's attention. The two headed downstairs to isolation.

"Eddie", said Rod. "Let's grab a couple of minutes to talk. Shall we?" There was no response. The expression on his face and the body language said he wanted nothing to do with more conversation. "The last several hours you've had people trying to help you with the dilemma you're in, son", said Rod. "You're acting like there is nothing for you to be alarmed about." Nonchalantly as can be Eddie replied, "should I be?" With that response Rod stood and fired the orange nerf ball he was holding right above the young man's head. It was a perfect spiral. Tom Brady would have been proud. In response, Eddie stood rather slowly. He started to say something, but his thoughts didn't form spoken words. He turned, left the living room and headed down the hallway and out the door into the garage.

Squinting to see anything in front of his hand, it was apparent to Martin that the afternoon had been swallowed in darkness. It was only 3 p.m. but it looked like 9. Somewhere in the distance there was a noise that Eddie couldn't make out. Then it hit him. It was the city sirens. A tornado was nearby. The sirens were doing their best to alert everyone. Eddie hustled back in the house and headed for the basement along with the rest of the family....and the cats. Despite the raw feelings, the Martins would have to wait the storm out together. And considering pass happy Rod's display that backfired with Eddie, tensions were on an uptick. More than a little awkward.

CHAPTER 6

The previous hour had been stressful. The Martins and all the family pets were crammed into the downstairs family room. There was a feeling of uneasiness in the room considering the recent exchange between Eddie and Rod. Dan could've cared less. The intrusion had cost him a chance to hook up with some friends…and a chance to party. "Damn weather", he uttered under his breath. Since Direct TV had been knocked off the air, AM 1040 WHO Radio was the sole source of information on the storm and its whereabouts. "We've had reports of funnel clouds in the Grimes vicinity", said the newsman. "This coincides with the previous touch down near Van Meter a little over a half an hour ago. It looks like this storm is moving north, northwest to the Johnston, Ankeny and Bondurant areas. Anyone in those areas should take cover immediately."

Shortly after the sirens began blaring, it turned eerily quiet. Then the winds pummeled the neighborhood. Shingles were turned into flying saucers. Tree limbs were scattered like snarled twigs. Anything not tied or staked down was yards from its original location. The rain came down in troughs, not buckets. There might have even been a little hail too. And it lasted for a good hour. Then it went silent again. Slowly a sliver of light started to come through the basement windows. Little by little the clouds rolled on out and some specks of blue sky showed itself. "Thank God", said Hope. "See prayer does work guys. I asked for the Lord's cover upon us.

And he sure did. Didn't he?", she added. The boys began picking up their cell phones and magazines to head upstairs. On Mom's question though, they each stopped and shook their heads in agreement. Hope sat back on the sofa and took a little more time than everyone else in returning to the world. She was mulling a thought. She'd hoped they'd be safe in the basement during the storm. A worldly definition of that fear was a desire not to have something happen. But there were other definitions too. She'd remind them of that when the time was right. Satisfied with the outcome of the squall, she picked up her favorite cat, Big Bubba Bruise, and started the climb to the first floor. Back to life which quickly dissolved to tired minds and bedtime.

Tick-tock. Tick-tock. The Quicklook White Station Wall Clock sang in its continuous tune. Tick. Tock. Tick. Tock. It was becoming a song to the wide awake soul. Rod was laying on the right side of the comfortable Serta king mattress. Hope was quietly snoring on his left. It was comfortable but far from restful. Rod had nodded off quickly when he put his head on the pillow at 10:30 p.m. It was now 1 a.m. Sleep was not in the cards. He was now wide awake. He'd been playing through the entire day over and over before bedtime. His mind must not have completely shut down because it was active again. His right hand was stretched across his chest laying directly on his heart. He could feel his heart beating. Lub-dub. Lub-dub. It was nearly in time with the clock. Martin wondered if he could put the two in perfect harmony if he slowed his heart rate down. Slow down. Slow down. Together now. He attempted the possible stereo effect for a couple of minutes. Lub-Dub. Tick-Tock. Lub-Tick, Tock-Dub. It wasn't working. Maybe if he turned on his stomach it would work. Tossing the covers away, he took off his Hawkeye t-shirt and gray and green running socks. Hopefully that would make a difference. But the harder he tried the less it seemed to work. After a 5-minute workout he realized it wasn't going to happen. He removed the hand from his heart. The tick-tock continued loudly. The heart beating went somewhere in the background. The encounter with son Eddie might suggest to some he didn't have a heart anyway. There were always two sides to a story.

The longer Rod racked his brain, the more he was convinced. At first he reasoned with himself that throwing the nerf football at Eddie had been a perfect reaction. Why not? The kid had been as apathetic as possible. Not only didn't he show any appreciation for all that was done for him that day, Eddie had shown he could have cared less. Or did he? Eddie had always been a tough one to figure out. As a little guy, he was as competitive as they came. Sport after sport, game after game, he sought to beat his Dad. He always came up short. The topping on the cake was after a wiffle ball contest around the age of 9. Eddie led the entire game, but in the last inning Rod had rallied for a come from behind win. Eddie lost it. In more ways than one. He started screaming at the top of his lungs and ran into the woods behind the Martin home. The screeching eventually turned to tears. To this day, he's called Screech. Mom and Dad had to venture into the back forty to console and rescue their middle son. It took days for the defeat to wear off. Someday. Someday. He was going to beat his Dad. And when he did, it was going to be sweet. No, better than sweet.

But there was also his compassionate side. The previous spring, Eddie had seen two little furballs struggling to find their way along the county road near his Grandma Martin's lake house. The two couldn't have been any older than three weeks. There was no mother around. Eddie looked everywhere but he couldn't find one. No one else around his Grandma's wanted the kittens. So, naturally, at least in his mind, he brought them back to his house. For over two weeks he kept them in the basement closet feeding them by bottle and keeping his fingers crossed that they would live. Hope knew they were there. Rod didn't. At least not until the day he said, "what the heck is that noise?", after hearing the sounds of some little meows coming up the air vents. Rod went to the basement to investigate.

Sitting next to the beat up cardboard box was Eddie bottle feeding the little varmints. "We don't need these damn cats. Where did you find them? And when are they going?", said Rod. Dad wasn't happy with the situation. After a big family debate, the vote came in. Rod was outnumbered 4-1. The cats stayed.

The bad? In his sophomore year of high school in Indianola he joined the ranks of a criminal. Saddling up with a couple of other kids with little direction and a mind made for mischief they master-minded a break-in. A cycle shop on the south end of town was the target. Eddie had been in the shop several weeks prior and there were a number of things that had caught his eye. He passed the information on to his buddies. And the plan was forged. A couple of nights later they knocked out some windows and stole the place blind. They not only broke in once, they went back the next evening and robbed the place again. Their haul was cycle parts, riding gear and about anything else on the premises that didn't have tires.

Indianola was a town of about 10,500. The police force wasn't top notch, but they weren't idiots either. Little by little the pieces came together. One burglar said one thing to some friends. Another said something else. The word got out and the cops came into play. Stories didn't match up. Alibis crumbled and after a month long investigation, Eddie and his other cohorts were charged. It wasn't all that unexpected Rod recalled, because Charlie had been in some trouble of his own two months previous to Eddie. At the time, Dad mentioned to Eddie. "If you don't wise up, you'll be just like your brother." What a prophetic statement that came to be. Eddie's reaction. Total apathy. He was totally unassuming and uncaring about his predicament. Kind of like his Guard issue.

It was now 2:30 in the morning. Rod still couldn't get back to sleep. He flipped over and peered out the window. The full moon was as big and round as he could ever remember. A smattering of little clouds floated by. Its effect was grandiose.

As Rod stared at the heavenly planet, it hit him. The image he had was of an old Chuck Barris show in the late 70's called the Gong Show. Each show presented a contest between amateur performers of often dubious talent along with a panel of three celebrity judges. The program's frequent judges included Jaye P. Morgan, Jamie Farr, Arte Johnson, Rip Taylor, Phyllis Diller, Anson Williams, Steve Garvey and Rex Reed. If any judge considered an act to be particularly bad, he or she could force it to stop by striking a large gong. Rod deserved to be gonged. Maybe, maybe Eddie would forgive him. It would have to start with that. The ringing of the gong was music to the ears. Rod finally nodded off.

CHAPTER 7

When Rod woke up the next morning it was approaching 8:30. It was a bright, sun drenched Sunday morning. The kind that warms your innards and makes you glad you're alive. Hope had gotten up before him. He could smell bacon cooking downstairs and listening closely, he could hear the sizzling in the pan. Nothing like a nice breakfast before church he thought. He hoped there were over easy eggs, wheat toast, hash browns and a strong cup of coffee on the menu too.

As he got out of bed, he noticed his t-shirt and socks lying beside the bed. He had ripped them off during the previous night's wrestle for sleep. Rod strolled over to the chest of drawers and took out a new T, a pair of black Nike gym shorts and a new pair of orange running socks and then slipped on his favorite Adidas tennies. Satisfactorily clothed, he headed for the kitchen.

He could see Hope was working furiously. She didn't have an apron on, but was clothed in her typical summer bedtime attire, a white Raglan top and black and white striped shorts. Her kitchen was in order. She had a procedure in place for food prep and the buffet line. Any member of the family could eat when they felt like it. "Smells great", elicited Rod. "I could eat a.....". Before he could finish his sentence he could see Eddie outside through the set of double hung windows. He was tossing a football in the air. Regulation size. Not nerf. Sensing an opening, he looked at the dog. "Come on Mason", he quickly remarked. "Honey, we'll be back in a little while. Mason and I are headed outside. Keep that delicious breakfast warm. Maybe Eddie and I can.....", his words became inaudible as he turned to go out the door.

"Come on big boy", Rod shouted. Mason didn't have to be asked a second time. Any time he had a chance to take his perfectly proportioned 90 pound Golden body outside, he was in heaven. Dog Heaven. Rod opened the door and Mason flew by, literally and figuratively.

"This was going to be an impeccable time for him to mend fences with Eddie", Rod thought. Throw the ball a little and start talking. Something good would come of it he was sure. But, hold on. Maybe now, wasn't so perfect. The repair work between the two of them shouldn't come off as manipulated. It needed to happen the right way. With the right results. Rod's retaliation for Eddie's apathy the previous day hadn't been proper. It was human however.

Rod thought back to last week and a potential ugly encounter he had with a complete stranger. Rod had been hungrier than a bear most of the morning. He needed to fill his belly so he decided to pull into the first fast food/heart disease place he could find. McDonald's won out, that is, if he could get in the dang lot. He was in the southbound left turn lane waiting for a beat up 2002 red Toyota Tacoma heading northbound to turn in front of him. He waited. The truck didn't move. "Come on", he yelled. "Turn". "Turn". Rod felt he waited long enough and started to wheel to the left. Just then the pickup moved forward almost causing the two to collide. Rod darted across the two lanes of traffic into the Home of the Big Mac's lot. "What an idiot", he muttered while maneuvering his SUV to the back of the lot where the drive up was located. Maybe some food would help him forget the close encounter. "Could I have a double cheeseburger, a small fry and a cup of coffee?", he offered to the box next to the menu display. A sweet young female voice came over the loudspeaker and confirmed his order and cost. He moved ahead in the line of cars completely oblivious of anything around him. One vehicle at a time he moved closer to the window. As he reached the area to pick up his order, he looked in the rear view mirror and saw the old red pickup behind him. Actually, he mostly saw one beast of a man, with a head the size of Bigfoot. He could see the words coming out of his mouth. And they weren't good either. Rod's knack for reading lips told him that. The man-monster was locked in a dispute with his wife. She was tossing out unfriendly words of her own. Rod imagined she was the one telling her husband what to say. "$4.77. Please", interrupted Rod's thoughts. "Aaahh. Okay", he sputtered. Rod was in a kerfuffle. He had to think quickly. Ignore the red truck and its inhabitants or grab the food and run. As if prompted by a higher being, Rod heard these words come out of his mouth. "Can I ask you for a favor, miss? "Sure, I guess", said the little peanut Latino. "Can you tell me how much the bill is for the people behind me because I want to buy their meal", he asked. The dark brown eyes peered at Rod with question. "Do you know them?", she said. "Never seen them before", Rod offered. Little Ms. Inquisitive shook her head sideways but agreed to the unusual request. "Just one favor", Rod replied. "I want you to tell the people their food is paid for and that God Loves Them. And So Do I. You have to make sure you tell them that, okay?", he concluded. Rod paid the bill and sped off. If it wasn't for spilling his coffee down the front of his khaki slacks as he sped off, he would have come through unscathed. At least it wasn't Armageddon. An argument was avoided. Yep, McDonald's home of the Happy Meal.

The next morning Rod returned to McDonald's and asked the manager on duty about his "paying forward" lunch the day before. The pimply- faced toothpick of a young man reiterated what took place after Rod's breakaway. "Sir, those people were speechless. It's like someone had taken a pin and pricked a balloon. They both started laughing and I heard the big guy say, "Amen".

The lesson Rod gained was, retaliation isn't always the best medicine. There are ways to diffuse a situation and there are times to ask for grace. Someone had been looking after Rod that day. Paying it forward was so much better than a payback.

Rod's thoughts returned to the action in the Martin's backyard. Rod chased after Man's Best Friend. Mason had stolen the ball when it hit the ground and the dang dog had no intention of giving it up. That was until he was blindsided by Eddie. A big fumble occurred. Arms and legs went this way and that way, small swatches of fur were hanging in air and dog saliva flew upward. GAME ON. Mason was livid. He wanted that ball. Part of his offensive attack was to steal the ball from Eddie's hands as he got up off the turf. He jumped and he jumped and he made one more attempt to recreate Air Bud antics. The movie star dog had nothing on Mason.... that was for sure. The fun-loving boy was ready. It was as if he was saying to his two-legged buddies, "are you ready for some football? Bring it on".

Fifteen minutes later the game concluded. Rod and Eddie were covered in grass stains. The dog's tongue looked ten feet long. He was panting to beat the band. Rod and Eddie were clearly exhausted. But there were a whole lot of smiles to go around. Now, they were ready for a man-sized breakfast. From all appearances, they were in the right place. There was no decorum as the plates were loaded with some great looking vittles. If you got in someone's way you might get your arm eaten off. It wasn't dog eat dog, though. Mason was thankful for that. He laid in the corner with the water bowl between his front paws. Clearly wasted.

Sometime later it was apparent that breakfast had been a hit. Every family member had made their way to the table, ate and wiped their plate clean. It was now time to talk. The conversation was light until someone mentioned the national news of the day. Talk centered on the heavy monsoon rains in the Khyber Pakhtunkhwa province of Pakistan which caused widespread flooding. Over 1,600 were killed, and more than one million were displaced by the flood. "How blessed we are", Hope offered. "You know guys, I've thought many, many times how fortunate we are to have been born in the country we live in. Have you ever stopped to think about that? Think of all the other places God could have placed us on this earth and he chose this one for us", she interjected. The men had to agree. They had never stopped to think about their fortunate situation. If you want to call it luck, so be it. You'd never hear that word from Hope's lips. "Oh, my gosh, look at the time", volunteered Mrs. Martin. "We're going to be late for church if we don't beat feet. Who's in?"

CHAPTER 8

Hope and Rod flew around the downstairs Master bedroom and bathroom. If one wasn't in the way, the other one was. They were pushing it as fast as they could trying to make the 11 a.m. service at Cornerstone of Hope. They were both dressed casually, but certainly ready for the message of the day. Hope had on a pair of denim Lady Levi's, a red Batiste blouse and a pair of white Worishofer sandals. She had on some medium-sized gold hoop earrings which gave a pretty effect to her brushed back behind the ears hair. Blonde hair. Yes, the same blonde hair that had gotten her into a pickle a time or two because of her naiveté. Like the time she ordered the 10-pack of albums from Columbia House for $1.99 with commitment that she'd buy ten more albums in the coming year. When it came time for her additional order, she contacted the company and told them she wanted a specific album. Days later, the postman tried to deliver the package but no one was home. He placed a note on her mailbox that the album was undeliverable, marked "Dog Out." I didn't order any Dog Out album she thought. The next day the postman tried again. Same results. On arriving home, Hope saw the same kind of message with the same reason for not delivering. This time she was miffed. She motored to the local post office and proceeded to show the man behind the counter her slip. "Sir, I don't know what this is all about", she snorted. "I ordered an album and your mailman continues to try to deliver this one marked, "Dog Out". I didn't order any "Dog Out" album." The mailman smiled and slowly responded, "Maam, he didn't try to deliver an album by that name. Our carrier was saying he couldn't deliver the package because the neighbor's dog was out." Hope responded sheepishly, "I'm so sorry." A true blonde moment.

Rod's wet brown hair was swept back off his brow from his quick shower. He had on a pair of tan Docker shorts, a white polo shirt and a pair of black Nike tennis shoes. They made a quick inspection of the Martin household. It was apparent, none of the boys would be going with them. "Don't know what you guys are going to miss today", shouted Hope. "If you change your minds, you know where we're sitting. See you later."

The two sprinted to the SUV. Rod fired up the engine and they were off. He looked over at his wife and smiled from the inside out. Hope Martin was about as good as they come. In fact, she might have been too good to be true. The old expression, "you've married up my good fellow" surely fit here. Hope could have done any number of things and been successful in the business world. She could have been a news anchor, Rod often thought. Or a sales buyer for any woman's line. But that wasn't part of her makeup. She craved motherhood and all that went with it. Bottom-line, Rod was indeed fortunate. And he knew it. Hope's family, the Dawson's had come to Des Moines from the Brantford, Ontario area in the early 1960's. Brantford's claim to fame was the hometown to one Wayne Gretzky, the one of hockey fame. The Dawson's recall Wayne and his brothers, Kim, Brent, Glen and Keith spending time on their backyard ice skating rink. It all started there. The Great One. But there was someone else. We shouldn't forget Alexander Graham Bell. Two giants in their professions. True Brantfordites.

One of the town's largest employers was Massey Ferguson, where Frank Dawson, Hope's father was employed as an engineer. In 1966, Massey moved a big portion of their operations to Des Moines, Iowa. The Dawson's packed up and headed south. Hope's family was Catholic, something she struggled with in her late teens. She'd always imagined an intimate relationship with God. Not a hunger the Catholic Church she attended could seem to satisfy. In her early twenties, she sensed she needed something else. She didn't walk away with any animosity. But it changed her life bigtime. As a little girl she used to make cookies for Jesus on Christmas Eve. Her love ran deep for the Good Shepherd.

The Martin's married late in life. Hope was 30 and Rod 38. Rod had seen a number of his high school and college friends marry but he couldn't seem to pull the trigger. Bottom-line, he didn't want to ever have to go through a divorce. So he waited for a Christian young lady to come along. Being Christian didn't assure a marriage was going to last, but in Rod's mind it had a whole heck of a lot better chance than not. Their marriage on 9-9-89 was quickly followed up with a change in family dynamics. They welcomed their first child Charlie in August of 1990. Then came anotherand then one more within a 3 year period. The Martin's were blessed or saddled, however you want to look at it, with three little boys under the age of four. Hope was now in position to challenge for Mother of the Year with Beaver Cleaver's mother.....

June Cleaver. That's a character Hope closely associated with. June was always impeccably dressed. She was the director of the family household. Her job or career was as a housewife. Something done very little these days. She was...always there for the boys. She wasn't going to settle for someone else raising her children. There were times when money had been an object between Rod and her. But Hope had stuck to her guns and Rod eventually came alongside. Her memories of the three boys were much different than her husband's. Rod had been on the run free-lancing for a whole bunch of sports networks in the Midwest. ESPN and FOX needed associate producers for their live broadcasts. Rod was all too willing. It was fun and it made some additional dollars at the same time. Then came a break in the local Des Moines market. Rod launched a regional sports network in 2003 for Mediacom, a position he clearly loved. It was his chance to operate a production business without the risk of owning it himself. Six years later he got his walking papers when new management deemed him expendable. Such was life. Taking the good with the bad, Rod surmised.

The Martin's made the fifteen minute jaunt to West Des Moines in a little under twelve. Rod wheeled into the first available parking spot and the two of them made a mad dash to the sanctuary. Rod and Hope had started going to Hope some ten years ago when they were in the church that was in a little building down Franklin Road. The new digs were something to behold. The main service area sat around 2,500 people. The man behind the fast growing church was Jim Morgan. Morgan was a tremendous speaker. Gifted for sure. He challenged the congregation each and every Sunday. The lone problem? People were going out the back door as quickly as they came in the front. The mega-church was simply that. Too big for many people.

Hope and Rod were connected at Hope. They'd gone through Alpha, an evangelistic awakening. The course sought to introduce the basics of the Christian faith through a series of talks and discussions. It's described by its organizers as "an opportunity to explore the meaning of life." Months after completing their introductory course Rod and Hope became Alpha hosts. Their purpose was to direct the small group aspect of the night after the initial 90 minute conference. They didn't lead any of the 10-week group, simply "directed" the participants to openly discuss the message of the night. The Martin's got as much out of it as the attendees themselves. There was always someone who offered a unique perspective which was educational and informative at the same time. More often than not, the Alpha group was made up of couples. Who was leading who here? Was it the man or the woman who sought a spiritual connection. For instance, there was a report done around that time period asking whether men or women affiliate with a religion, more women than men said they identified with a faith group (83.4 percent versus 79.9 percent). Rod had been right in looking for that good, down to earth woman. In Hope, he'd found it.

Hope also participated in some one-on-one prayer times with people. And Rod launched a small group ministry at the church called Hope@Work. The classes were for those who were unfulfilled in their job or who were looking to gain employment. Such, Hope@Work, became a title that can be taken in so many ways. That's just what Rod envisioned when he put God's idea of helping those in the swamp called the "workplace". It's not any different today than it was then. Everyone needs Hope at Work. Rod emphasized "using your passion" in the Monday evening meetings. "Do whatever you do with passion" he said. "God will direct your path". That's most likely why his favorite verses in the bible were Proverbs 3:5-6. "5-Trust in the Lord with all your heart and lean not on your own understanding; 6-in all your ways acknowledge Him, and he will make your paths straight."

When the message of the week concluded, the Martin's headed out to the parking lot full of conversation concerning the pastor's message of the week. The sermon focused on fears. The pastor mentioned the shear definition of the word is the desire for something not to happen combined with an anticipation of it happening. Inherent in every hope is a fear, and in every fear a hope. To hope for something is to desire that thing, and to believe, rightly or wrongly, the probability of it happening. Pastor Morgan had caused a buzz. Just what he hoped to do.

The temperature had been on an upswing most of the morning. It was now approaching 95 degrees. The humidity was another thing. It was the kind that made your pants stick to the groin and your shirt or blouse to your back. Typical Iowa summer. Ugly humidity which can make one a little grumpy. Rod and Hope were focused though. "Honey, I know what we just heard was so important. I wish the boys had come today", Rod suggested. "Me too", said Hope. "We just need to keep praying and asking for God's direction in their lives". Funny or maybe seriously, that's something they'd been doing for a long, long time. And most likely would be doing for as long as they lived. AAAAHHH Parenthood.

CHAPTER 9

Rod was driving fairly fast down the tree lined Lakeview Circle road to the Martin's home. He was on a mission to get into his director's chair to watch his beloved Chicago White Sox take on the Oakland Athletics. Game time was 1 p.m. The Sox who were 53-43 on the season were throwing a young right hander by the name of Daniel Hudson. Oakland was 49-48 and tossing lefthander Dallas Braden. It was a game Rod was looking forward to watching. As the two approached the driveway they could see a little red 2002 Chevy Cavalier. That meant only one thing. Well actually two. Staci was back and she and Charlie were probably rolling in the sheets or arguing.

The young people's intimate activity was wearing thin, especially on Hope. This wasn't the type of behavior she approved of. It wasn't the demeanor she hoped for of her children. She hadn't slept around in her younger years and it wasn't setting a good example of what should be accepted, at least in the Martin household. The one kicker though, was the fact Charlie was only five days away from beginning his deployment. Would these days be the last the Martin's would see of him? And the same for Staci. So, sometimes the things you wouldn't accept, you make exceptions. That wasn't alibiing. It was just easier to ignore some things and focus on making as few waves as possible. Rod shook his head in disbelief. "My gosh", he offered. "Don't those two ever come up for air?"

Charlie heard the garage door begin to raise. It interrupted a perfectly good interlude. Staci had come knocking on the front door within minutes of Rod and Hope's departure for church several hours earlier. She must have been waiting on a side street for her opportunity. "What's the matter babe", cooed Staci. "I haven't experienced anything like that before with you. It was awesome." Charlie was unimpressed with her comment. He had other things on his mind. Staci hoped it wasn't his brother again. They'd been down that road before. "Hello? Hello?", she repeated.

Charlie stood up and put a towel around his mid-section. He left the bedroom heading for the 1/2 bath on the lower level. Within seconds, he was hugging the porcelain. Something hadn't agreed with him. It was either the Miller Lites from the night before, the big breakfast he enjoyed early that morning or the nerves of his upcoming departure. Five days were all that was left. Then off to Mississippi and California for 11 weeks of training and then to that country on the other side of the planet…..Afghanistan. The remainder of the afternoon and evening Charlie was in and out of the bathroom. Nothing seemed to settle him down. Not Pepto Bismol, not 7-up, not a heating pad and not an old fashioned remedy of Ginger either.

The next few days flew by. Friday morning came all too soon. It was 7 a.m. at the Martin house and a full scramble was on. Charlie was making sure all of his bags were filled and all his needs were in their proper location for the long bus ride. He was taking his time getting dressed, a sure sign of apprehension. Hope was functioning but that was about it. She was going through all the womanly chores, but was uncertain how she was getting them done. When she stepped back from the mirror she was surprised how good she looked. If only she felt that way. Her hair was firmly in place and her apparel was exquisite. A black jumpsuit and white sandals were her pick for the day.

Rod had been up since about 5 o'clock. He wasn't going to be late for any of the day's festivities He was dressed in a United States Flag polo shirt, a pair of denim jeans and his Odlee sandals. The youngest Martin, Dan, who could have passed for a pulling guard for the Johnston High School football team, had on an Army t-shirt, a pair of tan shorts and some white high top Adidas. He gave the impression he was going to a funeral, seemingly bored with the whole ordeal. However, that masked what was really going on inside him. He was losing one brother and a week later, he was going to lose another. The three boys had always been close. Dan was going to be in for a big transition. Now was not the time he wanted to think about that. What he was doing for much of the morning was fiddling with his cellphone. A common practice for most young people. The text chime was going off every two minutes or so. The lines were definitely abuzz.

Eddie had decided one day earlier to continue his Guard involvement. It wasn't a monumental decision from a standpoint of bells and whistles. Just the same, when he had called Major Jenkins with his decision, it had been met with a "Congratulations son" from the Major. "You'll never regret your decision." Eddie had wrestled for several days as to what he should do with his life. He had designed a plan to make it through Basic. And that same plan was going to help him weather the whole darn ordeal. "Yup, I can do this mom and dad. I can", he reported. "The Major made some good points and I'm going to take his advice." Eddie was dressed in his Guard attire for the day. He wanted Charlie to know he was in full support of what he was about to undertake. At 8:30, the little red Cavalier pulled down Lakepoint Circle. Staci got out and joined the remainder of the family on the lawn outside for a family photo. A few pictures later the six were off to Boone to join 110 other families for an emotional sendoff. No one knew what to expect. Definitely uncharted waters.

The date Friday, July 30th will forever be etched in the minds of the Martin group. At 10 a.m. the band began playing at the Des Moines Area Community College (Boone campus). 2nd Brigade Combat Team (approximately 110 Soldiers) were getting the celebration of their lives. The crowd was busting with pride when the Star Spangled Banner was played. What happened after that was pretty much a blur. The Governor of the State of Iowa Terry Branstad spoke as did some other military personnel. Tears were flowing. An hour later when soldiers began boarding busses it was general chaos. Hugs galore....cries of sheer desperation and an outpouring of love. These men and women were giving their ultimate sacrifice. The whole world should know. Imagine dropping your child off for their first day of school or that said, their first day of college. Magnify that by ten, actually by 100 or perhaps a thousand and you'd have an idea of the gut wrenching feeling that was present. As the busses began to leave the parking lot, the large crowd appeared paralyzed. Maybe this freeze frame would disappear and life would return to normal. The new tears forming said otherwise. And what about the soldiers who made up the 2nd Brigade Combat team? A penny for their thoughts. The men and women who were undertaking one of the biggest moments of their lives. Yes, women. Daddy's little girl. It all seemed so surreal. A general uneasiness prevailed amongst most. Would they come back wounded or come back at all? One thing was for sure. Nobody, nobody was ever going to be the same. There would be a whole slew of people tossing and turning in bed this night. And many, many more to come.

Tender Moments Before Deploying

CHAPTER 10

Somehow the Martin family made it through the night. Whether Charlie had or not, they weren't sure of. And they wouldn't be certain for several weeks. Communication would probably be limited during the next 11 weeks while the Guard trained in Mississippi. Rod was the first to rise. He semi-rolled and semi-fell out of bed. And then ambled to the bathroom to catch a shower. As the droplets of warm/too hot water fell on his face and body he kept having this reoccurring song run through his head.

"Oh What a Night. Late December back in sixty three. What a very special time for me. As I remember, what a night".

The catchy tune by Frankie Valli and the Four Seasons didn't have all the lyrics that had impacted Rod pertaining to his situation...but the "Oh What a Night" sure had. Hope hadn't slept much. She tossed most of the evening and into morning. Rod dozed off and then awoke no more than five different times. Both parents had heard Eddie and Dan up several moments as well. But the sun did rise. In pure majesty like a big fireball. Saturday was going to be a hot, hot one.

As Rod dried off from his shower, he looked for his green jockey underwear. He tried slipping them on yet something didn't feel right. Looking down, he saw that he'd put them on backwards. "Wow", he thought. "I'm glad no one saw that." Considering the trance most of the Martin's were walking in it's a wonder Rod hadn't put them on over his head. He was thankful for that.

Eventually he got fully dressed and headed downstairs for a cup of hot coffee. Hope joined him moments later. She slid onto the couch and snuggled up closely to her husband of 21 years. It felt good. They needed each other. And the other boys still at home did too. "Honey, did you have any nightmares last night", questioned Hope. "I had some real strange ones. Charlie was out in the desert and his armored truck hit an IED. It was terrible. I saw all this carnage and I was trying to look through the smoke to find him, but he was nowhere. I kept yelling his name and there was no response. Then I started freaking out." "I'm scared", choked Hope. "I don't know if I'm looking into the future or imagining things. Whatever it is, this is way tougher than I thought it was going to be and he hasn't even left U.S. soil." Rod nodded in total agreement.

Just then Eddie and Dan entered the living room. They looked like the Bobbsey Twins as each had on a white t-shirt, black Nike gym shorts and blue flip-flops. They were evidently headed out. "How you guys doing", asked Rod. "Did you guys sleep at all, because your mom and I sure didn't. Both guys shook their heads sideways. The look on their faces showed some anguish. "I don't want to talk about it right now", replied Eddie. "Maybe later. Dan and I are going fishing. We're going to hook up with Sal Jordan and head out to the Saylorville Dam spillway. We gotta run. Or we're going to be late", finished Eddie.

When the two young men had closed the door to the garage, Rod began talking. "Sal, huh?" "What a lost dude. I wish they wouldn't hang around him. He's definitely bad news. If he's not stoned out of his mind, he's running away from home."

It wasn't more than two months ago Sal's Dad, Ernie, had been on the warpath looking for his lost son. The two had gotten into a big argument and Sal walked out the door of their home and just kept walking. He hadn't taken his car or any clothes other than what he had on his back. He just disappeared. Ernie had called the Martin's house more than once trying to pinpoint his son's whereabouts. Apparently the words had rung hollow with Mr. Jordan because he showed up later that one evening about 11:30 thinking he'd find him camped out with the Martin's. You could tell Jordan was beside himself, but you could also tell why Sal might have jettisoned his family home. Ernie was a loud, stubborn man of about 50 years of age. His slim 6 foot 2 inch frame indicated either his lack of desire for food or a humongous metabolism. His language was coarse and his demeanor even worse. It took three days for Sal's dad to find him and another week to convince him to come home. The convincing came in the way of a new Honda XR650L black motorcycle and a blue 2008 Subaru Impreza. Hardly a remedy for discipline and accountability. Different strokes for different folks, the Martin's thought. Eddie and Dan saw through the Sal Jordan facade. Anything the Martin boys got, Jordan one upped them on. All at daddy's expense. It was relationships like this Rod and Hope were happy to have at least two of the boys leave behind.

Rod looked at his yellow and black IPhone 3 to check on the time and then glanced over at the calendar hanging on the kitchen wall. Seven more days and Eddie was going to be leaving the nest. He looked at his wife and hesitated asking the question. Somehow it worked its way from his lips. "How are we going to do this again next week?", he uttered. Hope didn't have an answer. You could see the scan taking place in her brain for a reply, but nothing showed. "I. I don't know", She stammered. "God help us."

Sunday, Monday, Tuesday and Wednesday shot by. There weren't many days left before Eddie left for Basic. Rod and Hope were beginning to come out of their funks. Ever so slowly. They had connected with some military support groups and the key "helper" suggestion was to stay in a routine. They both agreed they could do that. In other words, the morning walk Rod took with Mason, should continue. Not only for the dog but for

Rod. Keep doing what they were doing each and every day was the suggestion. Eddie was experiencing some routines of his own. He was partying late into the night and sleeping late into the morning. That was going to change. But that would be good for him. In the long run, Rod knew this would be a difference maker for Eddie. "Ten hut" would be something Eddie would be hearing very, very soon. That too would become routine.

CHAPTER 11

Friday arrived all too soon. It wasn't Good Friday. It was more like Sobering Friday. Not to say a drink or two couldn't have eased some of the pain that was about to be unleashed. Hope liked her wine and an occasional Blue Moon or Miller Lite. Never to the point of extreme. Just as a means to relax a little. Rod was pretty much the same way. Maybe even to a lesser degree.

As another scorching hot Iowa summer day turned to a beautiful orange clad dusk the Martins could be seen in the driveway near the back door of the SUV. They were getting ready to load Eddie's backpacks. Once all his luggage was onboard, Mrs. Martin hurriedly made a dash into the house and a last time look for anything left behind. Convinced that everything was accounted for, she returned to the truck. Joining Mom, Dad, Eddie and Dan was a lifelong friend of the Basic bound guardsman, Mike Mallory. Mallory had known Eddie since third grade and the two were pretty tight. At one point the two had thought of joining together, but when push came to shove, Mallory chose to stay behind. As disappointed as Eddie had been at the time, it was probably the best for both of them.

The trip to the Holiday Inn near the Des Moines International Airport took about 20 minutes. Much of the ride consisted of small talk between the three young men in the backseat. The parents listened for a while but then tuned to other thoughts of their own. Within the hour, their second son was leaving the state to begin duties in the U.S. Military. And more amazing, Eddie was their second child to leave within a week. How cool is that? Or maybe the overriding thought, how scary is that?

"Well, here we are guys", stated Rod as they pulled into the Holiday Inn lot. "Eddie why don't you go on in and see what you have to do. We'll wait in the truck until you get back", he pronounced. For years, the Holiday Inn on Fleur Drive had served as a headquarters for those who were getting ready to ship out. Sometimes it was meant for those who were headed to Camp Dodge and other times for those off to Basic Training in various parts of the United States. Eddie's orders had him headed to Fort Knox in Kentucky.

A little history on Fort Knox. The 109,000 acre base covers parts of Bullitt, Hardin, and Meade counties. It holds the Army Human Resources Center of Excellence to include the Army Human Resources Command, United States Army Cadet Command and the United States Army Accessions Command. For 60 years, Fort Knox was the home of the U.S. Army Armor Center and the U.S. Army Armor School (now moved to Fort Benning), and was used by both the Army and the Marine Corps to train crews on the M1 Abrams main battle tank. The history of the U.S. Army's Cavalry and Armored forces, and of General George S. Patton's career, can be found at the General George Patton Museum on the grounds of Fort Knox. The fort is best known as the site of the United States Bullion Depository, which is used to house a large portion of the United States' official gold reserve.

Private Martin was not ready to be transported quiet yet. Telepathically or any other way. "Hey, I can take my bags into my room and come back out", remarked Eddie to the occupants of the SUV. "You guys can get out of the truck and help me into the hotel, but then I'm on my own for a few minutes." As the tailgate swung open, Dan grabbed his brother's two duffle bags. Dan, Eddie and Mallory scooted off to the entrance into the hotel leaving Rod and Hope behind. Rod turned to Hope and asked a very pertinent question, "you gonna be alright?" She nodded her head in agreement, but her look said otherwise. "It's kind of like going to the dentist's office. As much pain as you're in, you don't want to go there, but once you're there you want to get it over with", she added. Before Hope could say anything else, the three young men could be seen coming back out of the building. The Martins hopped out of the truck.

For the next ten minutes the five recounted stories involving Eddie. Some Rod and Hope were hearing for the first time. Neither was sure if it was confession time on their son's part. Then came the awkward part. Goodbyes were to begin. Mike, Dan, Rod and Hope each got their own hug and whisper time. As Hope was concluding her interlude she slipped in a little ditty. "You know son, for every goodbye, God also provides a hello", she exclaimed. "Know that we love you and we'll see you in ten weeks." And just like that, Eddie disappeared into the hotel and the others sped out of the hotel parking lot.

Driving back north on Fleur Drive, Rod was replaying the last few minutes they'd had with Eddie. The video clips moving through his mind were not at full speed, but slow, slow motion. Martin couldn't quite put a word to what he saw, but he knew his son was entering foreign turf. It reminded him of 41 years ago when his parents had taken him to college at Mankato State. After they had said their goodbyes, Rod had stood looking in the mirror. He saw something looking back he'd never seen before. It was that same look on Eddie's face just a little while ago. Was it the human body morphing into manhood? Rod wasn't sure. He was certain though, humans don't do a good job of remembering when one thing stops and another starts. Maybe that's for a reason. Eddie's Grandma Martin used a phrase for times like these. When they called for extra effort or follow through. Rod hoped Eddie was thinking of those words right now. "Get 'er Done". "Just Get 'er Done", she'd say.

CHAPTER 12

Eddie made the slow walk to his room at the hotel. As he navigated the hallways the distinct smell of chlorine was in the air. Not only was this hotel a destination point for military comings and goings, it was a week-end haven for many young families. The pool area was often overrun with kids of all ages, nationalities and sizes. Tonight, the pool apron was nearly vacant with only a few brave, overweight souls taking advantage of the scarce number in the area. Eddie was beginning to drown in his thoughts when he felt the buzzing in his pants pocket. The text message that came in was from Mallory. Mike's message to Martin was he'd be back at the hotel in about an hour. It was obvious the two had something up their sleeves. Eddie was not going away quietly....and Mallory was all too happy to oblige.

Minutes later, Eddie reached the door to room 223. This is where his Basic journey was going to start. Private Martin's thoughts were so loud he thought his roommate heard them when he opened the door. "It's actually happening", he thought. "Life was not going to be the same anymore."

The next hour went by ever so slowly. Finally, Mallory showed back up. He tried to remember what the name of the Latino dude sharing his room was. Paco or Pablo. Something like that. Really it didn't matter. This would be the only time the two would spend any time with each other.

Eddie and Mallory spent the next two hours talking about their childhood memories and what their futures might look like. They shared a few beers and Mallory had some smoke with him to take the edge off any anxieties his buddy had. It was a short night for their partying and any sleep time Martin was to get. Eddie finally slipped into bed at 2:30 a.m. Around 4 a.m. he and his roommate got the first wakeup call of their military life. There wasn't any bugle sounding. The loud knock at the door made them both spring out of their beds. Attention!!

The breakfast that was to be served to the new recruits was non-descript in color, taste and satisfaction. A buffet line was spread out consisting of eggs, dry wheat toast, some scraggly hash browns, dried up burnt sausage links, orange juice and some strong caffeinated black coffee. Eddie had little to eat that morning. His stomach was in knots and food wouldn't have helped the matter. He pushed his food around the plastic plate with his plastic fork forming a pile here and a pile there. The silence was interrupted by some military type. "Alright men, it's time to hit the road and catch your flights", he pronounced. "Let's move." Quickly the twenty some men and women jumped out of their chairs and grabbed their duffles and hustled out the hotel doors to pile on the bus for the short, two-block run to the Des Moines International Airport.

About an hour later, after the group had gone through check-in protocol and boarded the United Flight to Chicago, Eddie sat in seat 18A staring out at the bee hive of activity taking place on the tarmac. Darkness was slowly giving way to daylight. The various gradations of orange were visible as the sun began to peek over the eastern skies. "Wow", Eddie uttered. The remainder of his language was kept internally and that's probably just as well. If he'd shared it with anyone else on board, who knows how much tearing up would have taken place. "No matter what, this is the right choice", Martin thought. "Nothing is going to take me back. I know it's not going to be easy but...."

Eddie looked around the plane at his fellow Basic bound group. He wondered what others on board were experiencing. He'd been part of the

RSP (Recruit Sustainment Program) at Camp Dodge and that had given him a great look-see what Basic might be like. In essence, Eddie had taken part in four or five drill weekends. That time had been tremendously helpful. Bottom-line, he was going to miss his parents and his little brother, Dan.

A little after 7 a.m. the plane lumbered down the runway and lifted itself into the sky. Hopefully the Friendly Skies thought Eddie. Next stop. O'Hare Airport in Chicago, Illinois. A little over an hour later the group scurried off the plane and made a mad dash to the carousels to pick up their duffle bags. To the naked eye, none of these looked the part of enlistees. They were dressed in civilian attire. But if you looked closer you could sense each was not looking like their destination was going to be a vacation retreat. What was to lie ahead with their respective trips could very well have been a replication of Planes, Trains and Automobiles.

Eddie's group had now been split to eight. These lucky ones drew Fort Knox...the others were headed to various other parts of the United States. They never did tag a name to the bunch but they certainly could have been called, Eight is Enough or Eight Legged Freaks. Each would have been accurate.

Hurry up and wait. That seemed to be the theme of the day. After a four hour wait in O'Hare the plane departed for an hour long flight to Louisville, Kentucky. Home of Muhammad Ali and Louisville Slugger. And of course the Kentucky Derby racetrack. Then there was another long wait this time for a bus that would take them to Fort Knox. Hours later a shiny one without a logo on its side, showed up. Over 30 other men and women were already on board so it became sardine time trying to wedge everyone in. Travel time was minimal to Fort Knox. A little less than an hour. Their arrival time was to be midnight. Eddie quickly did the math. Since he had gotten his rude awakening at 4 a.m., the total prep and travel time had taken 20 hours. What a way to get broke in. Then he saw the gates in the distance.

"Welcome to Ft. Knox", said the squatty little Sergeant not really meaning it. "Get your stuff and everyone get off." Immediately people began a wild scramble to the command. No one wanted to be called on the carpet. Outside the bus another military type threw a chair into the welcoming station grounds. The purpose was to get everyone's attention. Which he did. Others were shouting, "get in formation". That was perfectly understandable for those who had been in the RSP program. Those who hadn't were completely clueless as to his instructions. Eddie looked over at the couple of the guys he'd traveled with curious how they were reacting. That move was quickly halted. "You got a problem son?" yelled the Sergeant who had greeted them. "You think this is some picnic time. Get in line."

Eddie was here and in the moment. He hoped he could survive. What was it his Grandma Martin had said? Oh yeah. Before he could finish that thought the sergeant looked his direction. Uh Oh!

CHAPTER 13

Fortunately the Sergeant's look went elsewhere. Somebody else had caught the big guy's eye so for the meantime, Eddie was home free. The question was how long could he be invisible to the man? Private Martin had done a little research of what to expect at Basic and most importantly the drill sergeants. Here's what he found out through the wonders of Google. "Basic Training drill instructors aren't really psychic. They've seen a thousand kids just like you, and they know how you feel. They know how you think, and often they will head you off at the pass. If you're hungry, they know it. If you're tired, they know it. If you're scared, they know it and will take advantage of it for their purposes. What's their purpose? You may be tempted to believe that their purpose in life is to make you miserable. While they do a very good job at this, that's not their goal. Their goal is to "knock the civilian out of you". What you say, how you think, how you act, is no longer your business. It's now the business of the United States Military, and — through them — your drill instructors". Although Martin didn't agree with all of what he'd read it at least let him know what he was going to deal with. Even though it wasn't verbalized, it was obvious the real message was "okay, you're mine maggots."

People were on the move. Lines forming here and there. Men and women alike were being separated by the locations they would be assigned at the Fort. Eddie penned the first of some hundred signatures he gave that day. His social security number was burned into his noggin. He knew if he forgot his number he'd be in real trouble. There was more yelling and screaming and directing of bodies to get in line for physical training uniforms. Civilian clothes would be a thing of the past. Next, the duffles were emptied of personal belongings and processing began to take place. More lines, more signing of forms and more waiting until everyone was finished and dressed for the next routine. An old song floated through Eddie's head as the 60 some enlistees fell in line to march to a building they'd spend night number one in. "You're in the army now, you're not behind a plow, you'll never get rich. Oh, who cares about the rest?", he thought as they started the long trek. "Left, left, left, right, left", barked the drill instructor. "Left, left".

"Cabrera. Cabrera", get over here yelled another DI. "You're bed's here. Castro. Here. Martin. Martin, double time. You're here", barked the Sergeant. And so it went in putting a face with a bed. The whole process took a little over fifteen minutes when the leaders told everyone to go back outside and reform lines for a march to the mess hall. The enlistees were about to experience their first military meal and even as hungry as many were, most would have gladly passed on the food for the just issued beds and some shut-eye. For many it had been over twenty hours since they'd had anything substantial in their guts besides Skittles, Starburst, Hot Tamales and junk food.

Private Martin was concentrating as best he could. Perhaps that alone might keep him out of trouble. The schedule he and his buddies were under was pretty doggone taxing, but not unexpected. After the bunch had thrown some food down their throats, they marched back to the building where they were to sleep this first night. Thirty minutes after falling off, they were woken and told to hustle outside to formation. The next several hours were that way. Back to bed, up again and get into formation, back to bed and so forth. Sleep was nowhere to be found on the DI's radar. At six o'clock it was back to the mess hall and what looked to be breakfast. As the enlistees quickly found out, meals were not to be enjoyed….but snarfed. Woof, woof, woof, eat as much as you can as quickly as you can and be ready for the next order which in this case was back to formation to begin the march to get all the issued military gear. You name it and they got it. Boots, camo gear, gloves, socks, underwear, t-shirts, pants and anything else imaginable. And then the roll call began to split the soldiers into either, Alpha, Bravo, Charlie or Delta Company. Eddie got Bravo 146.

Then it was march to your individual company, dump all your gear (3 duffles full) out on a concrete pad and account for everything that you'd been issued moments earlier, Every article had to be held up and accounted for. The Sergeants continued their assault yelling rude, crude orders. "Come on, hurry up", more than one DI snorted. Paranoia was in the air. Each soldier was trying to perfect the melt into the woodwork method. Some were more successful than others. Eddie watched sheepishly as a rail thin, freckled face dude from Montana got taken to the woodshed. Literally not figuratively. All he could think of was he was glad it wasn't him. But in the back of his mind, he knew his time would be coming. "Melt, melt", he mulled as he put everything back into its proper bag. That thought was soon interrupted by a loud voice, "on your feet", Sgt. Foster announced.

The August 2010 version of Bravo Company entered their barracks for the first time on Sunday morning. The other Sergeants attached to the company scrutinized each individual with a once over. Most of the time they were correct in observations but occasionally they were wrong. However, you'd never hear them admit to it. Once inside everyone was assigned their rooms and introductions were made of the ornery men that would make their life a living hell the next ten weeks. One of the last duties performed at this time had to do with the cutting off from the outside world. Each soldier took his cellphone out of their bag, labeled it and watched as they were put into a huge bag. "Goodbye world", Eddie conceded. "Ten weeks from now I hope to get my phone back. That is, if I live through this."

This is what Eddie's world had turned into. He was some 625 miles away from family. Who knows what they were doing right now but he knew it wasn't anything like what he was going through. He conjured up images of his dad, mom and two brothers. These were pictures he locked into memory. He knew it would be some time before he'd talk to anyone from the outside world so he started his own little chant. "Stick to the plan, stick to the plan, stick to the plan", Martin muttered. "Stick to the plan." He looked over at the closest soldier to him to see if his words were overheard. Thankfully they weren't. This was going to be his journey and no one else's. "Stick to the plan."

CHAPTER 14

Hope Martin wasn't one to watch much television. She'd thought the box was an intrusion into her life. And for a matter of fact, all families lives. "Way too much time spent in front of that thing", she'd say. That was a complete contrast from Rod's former profession as a production executive. There had been times when there were disagreements between the two of them regarding Rod's viewing habits. The only thing that would make Hope happy was to eliminate the idiot thing once and for all. But today was different. She'd sensed a nudge early in the afternoon to catch the local evening news. So there she was sitting in front of the 55" RCA HD set in the family living room. The anchor on Channel 8 KCCI in Des Moines had delivered several of the news stories of the day in a machine-gun like fashion. Her name was Tonya Burns, a petite 5'3" twenty something bombshell who was considered eye-candy to most of channel's men watchers. She was more than a prompter reader though. Her newscasts were full of insightful, compassionate reporting and she'd won several local awards for her work. "When we come back from break, we'll take you to Mississippi where hundreds of the 2nd Brigade Combat Team are undergoing maneuvers prior to their deployment to Afghanistan. Only on News Channel 8", she smilingly offered.

The door from the garage into the Martin's house opened then closed with a loud bang. Rod was returning from a run to the neighborhood

Hy-Vee grocery store. He seemed agitated and his aura was not anything pleasant. Bottom line he was pissed off at the stupidity of the human race. "Honey", you won't believe what I ran into at the store", yelled Rod. "I just can't, just can't believe." His words were cut off mid-sentence. "Quiet", she said. "Quiet. They're doing a news story on the troops. Come here and sit down for a minute." Rod looked at his wife and then the screen as Ms. Burns's words led to a news piece from a local station in Mississippi. "The troops are indeed getting prepared" she said. "Jenny Jackson from Channel 13 in Biloxi has the story."

Hope and Rod sat transfixed at the feature. Ms. Jackson had done a great job of offering a glimpse of what the 2nd Brigade was training to do. At one point, the Martin's had thought they'd seen Charlie in the background of a shot. But they weren't sure. That would have been awesome to see, they thought. Near the end of the piece the reporter asked Major Rod Thompson the impact the October deployment would have on the state of Iowa. He offered these thoughts. "When we deploy a battalion, we touch anywhere from 270 to 290 communities. This brigade will deploy, and they will cover almost every community in the state of Iowa," Thompson said. "We call this Fort Iowa," he added, explaining that everyone has an important role to play. The will behind this fight, he said, includes the men and women back home, the families, the employers and the communities."

"Nice", Rod said. "That was nicely done. We need to send Channel 8 some type of appreciation for the work they did on that. It sure helps keep us in touch with them" he added. Hope nodded her head in total agreement but the little drip of moisture around the corners of her eyes said so much more. Her little boy was readying for War, something she couldn't fully get her arms around. It wasn't unexpected. Charlie had been drawn to the life of a solider since he was a little shaver. Her voice quivered a little when she replied, "Yup. It's been two weeks since they left and it seems like two months", she confessed. "This is a whole lot tougher than I thought it was going to be." Wanting to change the subject Hope inquired, "now, what happened at the store?"

Rod was a little less fired up. The TV news story had brought his blood pressure down a little. But he quickly put himself back in the moment. "Well, first off, I pull into the parking lot and slide into a space", he began. I got out of the truck and I hear some little old lady say", he piped. "Sonny, I see the sticker on your bumper saying "Proud Parents of a Soldier", how can you say that?", she challenged. "My husband was in the war and he never came back. At least not alive. Buried him over 65 years ago. That was it for me", she ended. Rod continued his story with Hope. "I didn't know what to say", he fretted. "Part of me wanted to call her everything in the book and the other part wanted to reach out to her. I froze though. I couldn't think of anything to say. It's like she hit and ran, because she was gone in an instant", he explained.

After the tongue lashing Rod got he made a dash, a mad dash for the store entrance. Maybe he could grab some serenity among the fruits and vegetables. As he was checking the condition of the Grimes sweet corn display he heard a familiar voice. It was the words of Jerry Foster, a former AAU baseball coach from several years ago. Foster had been an adversary on the diamond but somewhat of a friend off. They loved to compete against each other. So had their two sons. Eddie versus Jackson. Jackson versus Eddie. That had been fun.

"Dude, how you doin?", inquired Jerry. "I heard about Charlie going to Afghanistan with the other Guard troops. Are you scared what might happen", he asked. "What do you mean?", Rod shot back. "Aren't you worried that something's going to happen to your son? I sure would be", he continued. Rod's face turned a beet red. Foster must have realized his inconsiderate question as he quickly became fidgety dangling his car keys in his right hand. "Well, not so much, I guess. That is until you put it that way" Rod drawled. At that moment, Foster realized the insensitive remarks he'd made and seemed to be looking for the nearest foxhole to jump into. Rod would have helped him to if it wasn't for Jerry's wife yelling from the deli area of the store. "Jerry, can you come here?" she beckoned. "Gotta go", said Foster.

Rod was thankful for the spousal interruption. "Good golly", he wondered. "How can people be so dense? Maybe the next time someone acts so ignorant I'll give them the undressing of their life. Yeah, that's what I'll do. That goes for you too Foster, although this time I'll make an exception."

Hope hugged Rod ever so closely. When they broke the lock their eyes met. Without uttering a word today had been a lesson for the journey ahead.

"You know babe", Rod marveled. "I read a piece the other day in the paper that I thought was pretty prophetic. Essentially it said this. "National Guard soldiers are people like you, your brothers, your neighbor, your mom or your dad. They read books, go to ballgames, care for their parents, worry about their children. They have lives, jobs and commitments that non-military people can relate to.

That is, until they're called up on federal orders to serve in places like Afghanistan." "I think we're just beginning to find out", Rod piped.

CHAPTER 15

It was well past midnight. There was one lone little light showing through the Martin bay window. Hope was sitting in her brown overstuffed Cherry Pickins chair with her favorite feline companion, Big Bubba Bruise on her lap. Hope Martin was experiencing another sleepless night. She could count on one hand the number of good night's sleep she had since her two oldest sons had left home. When it was evident it was going to be another one of those nights, she'd gotten up out of bed, sauntered down the steps, grabbed a soft blanket and reached for a shoe box beside the chair. She was thumbing through the treasure full of cards, notes and letters her boys had written to their parents over the years. One in particular caught her eye and her heart. It was from Eddie.

Dear Mom and Dad,

I'm gonna start off this letter by telling you both thanks for being there for me always through thick and thin, hard and easy, good and bad situations. I really know I don't show I appreciate it but I really do, I don't know what I would do without you two in my life..you have shown me what good parents you can be, not only now but in my past as well. I can see where the strictness and rules come into play from years past to now. I know I have not always followed the rules 100% but I am ready to be a changed person and begin staying on the

right path with all the effort I can. I will put forth everything I've got to be the leader you guys have always wanted.

Eddie's note provided Hope some peace of mind. It also took her back to a time when he needed help and correction. Eddie was sorry for some trouble he'd gotten in to and the grounding that ensued. The note was expressing his remorse. That was the thing Hope could recall about her middle boy. He might be a stinker at times, but he had that compassionate side too, she thought. Eddie's remarks were impressive when he wrote them a couple of years ago. They were equally impactful tonight.

Hope closed her eyes and tried to picture Eddie. Not from years past but in a present state. What must he be going through right now at Basic Training? Is he struggling? Is he close to a breaking point from all the yelling and screaming that might be taking place? Is he eating? Does he know how much his family loves him and misses him? What will he be like in another 7 or 8 weeks? Those are the questions mothers are good for. Much more so than fathers. Hope was reaching way down into her mother's instinct bag to get some answers. There were times when she squinted a little deeper looking for clarity but when fifteen minutes had passed and she opened her eyes, all was well. At least to her. In regards to Eddie anyway. Next was Charlie.

Charlie was a different cat. He'd never been one to go deep on any subject or situation. Several years ago she and Rod had sat with their oldest on the front porch of their Indianola acreage asking Charlie what was going on with him. "Nothing", Charlie grunted. "Look son", Rod had barked. "There has to be something going on. You're not talking at all and you don't make eye contact with anyone. You're grouchy most of the time and angry the rest. What is it?", he finished. Still nothing from Charlie. That's the way Charlie looked at life. There was the occasional silliness he could exhibit but more often he was as stiff as a board. And quiet.

Certainly "silence is golden.". At times anyway. Certainly there are times when silence pays rich dividends. Hope recalled King Solomon saying, "The one who guards his mouth preserves his life; the one who opens wide his lips comes to ruin. Let him who means to love life and see good days refrain his tongue from evil and his lips from speaking guile." There are other times, however, when silence is not "golden". It may be just plain "yellow". These are times when one should speak up because they are guilty. How many times in nearly every field of endeavor has it been true that silence could be traced to cowardice? Even in the service of the Lord this is true too many times. Charlie's parents were concerned his lack of connectivity signaled something significant going on in his life. He didn't share in that belief. So it stayed with Mom and Dad. Hope took it one step further. She took it to prayer.

This was Hope at work. Whenever she faced tough times she headed straight to the Word. That's where she found her answers. Hopefully the time she spent in talking about the Lord with her sons in their earlier years would show the importance of having a Christian walk. There were her other less conventional ways too.

A few nights before Charlie deployed Rod smelled some smoke coming from the garage. Not cigarette smoke, but some other foul odor. As he opened the door, it hit him. Cigar smoke and whole bunch of it. Peering through the swirling cloud he could make out the images of five people puffing their brains out. "For crying out loud", Rod shouted. "What the heck are you guys doin? Tryin to start a fire?" "Just having a smoke with Staci and the boys", the Mrs. answered back. "I wanted to give them a memory. Wanta join us?" Rod shook his head in disbelief as the next song on the CD began to play. An old Kenny Loggins tune appropriate for the situation.

"There've been times in my life,
I've been wonderin' why
Still, somehow I believed we'd always survive

Now, I'm not so sure
You're waiting here, one good reason to try
But, what more can I say? What's left to provide?
Are you gonna wait for a sign, your miracle?
Stand up and fight."

The five sang in unison. Not perfect harmony mind you, but they sounded pretty darn good.

"Make no mistake where you are
(This is it)
Your back's to the corner
(This is it)
Don't be a fool anymore
(This is it)

The Swisher Sweet memory began to fade almost as quickly as it started. Hope looked back down at Eddie's note wanting to soak up the remainder of the heirloom.

I mean I can't guarantee you that I will be perfect because that is nearly impossible but I can tell you this...I will put forth an effort to keep my grades C's and above in school. When I am ungrounded I can guarantee you that I will get a job, which will help me pay for my own truck. This grounding has been something that has taught me a lot and given me time to do plenty of thinking. What I just wrote to you is pretty much what I have come up with. I hope you can find forgiveness in your hearts and once again to trust me and allow me some freedom. Lastly, I want you two to know that I will always try my best to be safe and stay out of trouble no matter what I'm doing. I really don't know what else to say but....

Thanks, Your son Eddie

The note remained in Hope's left hand for another five minutes. Part of her wanted to keep it there forever. The rational part of her won out and prompted her to move on. "Okay, I'm ready", she thought. Looking up from her captain's seat she could see her youngest son Dan's light on in the upstairs bedroom. Dan was about to get a late night visitor.

CHAPTER 16

Dan Martin had a lot of Eddie in him. But if you looked at his mannerisms and his disposition he was a clone of Charlie. Dan kept his emotions in check and more often than not, if you asked him a question he'd offer very little in response.

The knock on the bedroom door startled the youngest Martin. He'd been tinkering around for several hours with his phone and had also read a couple of cycle magazines. Sleep hadn't even crossed his mind.

"Hey", said the voice from the hallway. "Can I talk to you for a minute", said Hope. "Sure, mom", came the reply. "I wanted to check in with you and see how you're doing with both your brothers being gone", she asked. "It's not easy, is it?"

Charlie, Eddie and Dan had always been close. There was less than four years between the three of them which was good and not so good. The three births in such a short period of time had been somewhat stressful for Hope and Rod. It seemed like the Martin's were in diapers forever. And formula. And car seats. But eventually those days passed. Hope never went as far as calling the boys the Three Musketeers, but they were pretty darn close. Even more so when Rod decided it was time to bring a dog into the mix. A visit to the Animal Rescue League of Iowa offered the perfect solution. A golden retriever by the name of Nala became the three rascal's permanent shadow. Everywhere they went, she went. Almost. When it came time for school, Nala, would follow them to the bus and watch while they proceeded to leave. At 4 p.m. she was sitting in the driveway and waiting their return. The boys clearly showed their love to her and she back. They were as tight as anyone could ever imagine. Several years later the golden buddy had to be put down because of cancer issues. That loss had broken a string of deep friendship. Charlie and Eddie's departure had brought another.

"Mom, I'm not sure what to think." Dan began. "I try not to think about it all that much", but my mind wanders a lot", he added. "I get it", Hope responded. "I do too. I find myself hearing them come in the back door but there's no one there. Or I think I hear their cars coming down the street, but when I look there's nothing in the driveway. It's kind of eerie", she concluded.

Some of Dan's struggles with his brother's absence was dealing with questions from friends and schoolmates. If he could have a dollar for every time someone had asked him how he was doing, he'd be a rich man. Some had the audacity to tell him they knew how he felt when they'd never had anyone with any connection to the military. It'd be like telling someone who experienced a death in the family you could relate when you'd never suffered such a loss. Experience is a teacher, but even then no two stories are the same. Sometimes he wished people would keep their thoughts to themselves.

It wasn't more than a couple of days ago Dan was at a party with some of his friends and some guy started bad mouthing the Guard troops that were headed to Afghanistan. The dude had said "anyone going there ought to have their head examined". Dan had done a burn, and not a slow burn, either. It took all the energy he could muster to avoid getting in the guy's face. A couple of his buddies could see his response and quickly got him out of the apartment before he waxed the guy. Tonight he had been on the internet and seen a story about another idiot who was voicing his disgust with all the gracious doings people were offering people because of their service. The story mentioned somebody giving up their first class seat to a uniformed soldier and how offensive that graciousness was. Sadly, the guy was a college professor who was flapping his lips. Said it bothered him so much, "he could vomit." "They don't get it. People like that just don't get it", Dan reasoned.

Actually the thing most on Dan's thoughts was whether he should join the Guard too. Eddie had joined to support Charlie's decision. Dan was feeling some pressure that he should do the same. There were days he was pretty convinced that he'd join, but then there were others that convinced him otherwise. Thankfully, he didn't need to make a decision today.

"Honey, just want you to know that if you're struggling with anything, we're here to listen, okay?, advised Hope. "Sure, mom", Dan shot back. "No, I'm serious. We're all going through this together. We're going to need each other to lean on", clarified Mrs. Martin.

Hope turned to leave the bedroom hoping she'd gotten through to her youngest. Sleepiness had finally started to overcome her. She hustled down the stairs and made it to the master bedroom. The snoring coming from her husband wouldn't be a distraction tonight. She was now bone tired.

Back upstairs, Dan took some marijuana out of his little medicine bottle, filled up his pipe and lit it. After a long draw he held his breath for about 30 seconds. As he released the smoke from his lungs, he felt a little relief. He wasn't going to think any more about anything. He was going to another land. Unfortunately there wasn't the word Disney in front of it.

CHAPTER 17

There were smiles all around. If you looked closer though, they had various degrees of authenticity. Some were genuine, others were of a nervous variety and there were some that looked glued on. The sixty or so people that were in the Johnston Middle School Auditorium were part of a town hall meeting focusing on the deployment of the National Guard troops to Afghanistan. Each person was carrying their own baggage. Hope and Rod were more of the nervous variety. They weren't sure what to expect but felt they needed to be better educated in how to deal with this "thing". Hope was dressed in a white polo shirt, faded Levi blue jeans, a pair of Sperry Top-Sider boat shoes topped off with some dangly hoop earrings. She was looking like a mother of a young elementary child rather than the nineteen year old she was representing. Rod was showing his allegiance to his country with a gray Army sweatshirt, khaki shorts and a pair of brown Nike's.

"Thanks to everyone for coming today, said Frank Lloyd, an assistant specialist with the Iowa National Guard's family services branch. "To say the least, we are in some uncharted waters with the deployment of the 2nd Brigade. This is the first deployment since World War II of this great a number of soldiers. But we've got experience on our side to draw from and to help you in your daily lives." Very matter of factly, Lloyd went down his checklist of do's and don'ts. On more than one occasion, the Martin's looked around the room to see how the message was resonating with the other families on hand. In the front row sat the father of a young private. He no doubt came from a military background himself. He was as rugged as they come. He weighed in about 220 pounds on a 6 foot 3 inch frame. With guns for arms. He exuded military. And intensity. It wouldn't have taken much imagination to visualize him sneaking on a flight and heading to Afghanistan. Idle down mister. It's your son that's deployed not you, Rod thought.

In the corner of the room behind Rod and Hope sat a mother and two younger children. She had to have been in her early forties, the kids most likely ages 9 and 10. She looked like death warmed over. Her demeanor was sad and lost and hopeless. She fought back tears most of the meeting and was using Kleenex profusely to wipe away the salt and runny nose.

Lloyd's discussion topics included soldiers' living conditions, leave time, communication with loved ones, new uniforms and body armor, rumor control, power of attorney documents and insurance, as well as support resources for families at home

"No matter where you live, there's somebody out there to help out the families of the service members," added Lloyd. "If they need to get an emergency message to the commander, I kind of guide them. If their water heater goes out on a Friday night or the car breaks down, I link them up." It was messages like these that provided some assembalance of support.

The town hall boosted David Sloan's confidence in the leadership of the brigade. He and his wife, Brenda, were also new to the process of deployment. Their son, Dick, lived in Des Moines and had been with the National Guard for six years. "They've got a tremendous job to do, but I'm glad we came because now I'm comfortable with who's going to be watching over him and taking care of him," Sloan said. "It appears, from not having had anybody deploy before, that they're really trying to make it as painless as possible. I appreciate that."

Rod and Hope were a little more relaxed now too. Not only in their feelings, but in their countenance. Lloyd had done a lot to ease some worries. Some additional words especially hit home. "You may feel scared, nervous, confused, excluded and anxious or even begin to withdraw. Keep in mind these are all very normal reactions and typical feelings of concern in this situation. More than likely, your service member is also going through the same emotions. It's during this time your family should be concentrating most on communication and preparation. Knowing each person's view and thoughts, and knowing what to expect will make the adjustments easier and make everyone feel more involved."

The town hall concluded with a representative for the family readiness groups offering another source of wisdom. "Deployments do not discriminate. Whether you are a service member, spouse, parent, significant other, child, sibling or friend, resources are available to assist you. You have the choice in making the deployment journey more understandable and an easier road to travel by developing effective communication strategies, thorough preparation, asking for help when needed, accepting support and using positive coping skills."

As the Martin's rose from their auditorium seats they were both wearing a significantly different smile than when they entered. Hope and Rod felt the night was a homerun. A tension-reliever. Now all they had to do was to put it to practice. The buzzing in Hope's purse was a call to action. When she saw the number on her cell phone was from Charlie she realized there was no time like the present. "Hi, Honey", she panned. "What up?"

CHAPTER 18

"Hey Mom", said an amped up Charlie Martin. "I wanted you to know that we're in California now at the National Training Center. "We've got several weeks of training here and then we'll deploy to Afghanistan." Charlie explained the reason for the move to California from Mississippi. Fort Irwin is a major training area for the United States Military and is a census-designated place located in the Mojave Desert in northern San Bernardino County, California. With over 1,000 square miles for maneuver and ranges, an uncluttered electromagnetic spectrum, airspace restricted to military use, and it has isolation from densely populated areas. He sounded like a tour guide for the place but nothing like being read up on the subject. This wouldn't be home for very long. Time for deployment overseas was drawing near. For the soldiers, family and friends this journey was becoming all too real. Before Charlie had placed his call to his mom, he'd been thinking of what the last six weeks had entailed. There was the send-off in Boone. He enjoyed the day and wasn't the least bit uneasy about what was taking place. This was his calling. He was certainly anxious and excited. He remembered the looks on some of the faces around him. Many were sharing in his enthusiastic thoughts but others had a much different reflection. Those soldiers had been extremely nervous and scared. "It was a little sad in not knowing when or even if you were going to come home", he'd recalled. Those thoughts didn't linger. Charlie put them in the back part of his consciousness for another time and place.

The past weeks the 2nd Brigade had been holed up at Camp Irwin in Mississippi. At this first stop, the warriors had been issued their deployment gear, received medical shots, saw slide shows on what to expect in the Eastern country and the lifestyle and culture of the area, received vehicle training, did weapons qualifications and were educated on safety procedures. A typical day consisted of waking around 5:30 a.m., doing physical training, showering and then breakfast. More PT. Lunch and more PT. Dinner and then a whole lot of down time.

Now they were getting serious. Dead serious. The California terrain was as close as you could get to a clone of Afghanistan. Big tents had become their homes. The bedding? Cots. A whole lot of them. Over 200 soldiers became tent roommates overnight. Days focused on combat related tactics and developing routines. The nights were again quiet and left a lot of time to think. Rumors were spreading non-stop. Many had heard of various companies headed to the "box".

"I wanted to let you and Dad know you might not hear from me for a while", stated Charlie. "We're going to be out on maneuvers where we don't have any communication with the outside world. I'll give you a call when we get back to our base area", he passed on. Hope had a whole bunch of questions but there wasn't time to address any of them. Charlie was in a hurry and he lovingly cut her off. "Bye mom. Tell Dad I love him and the same to you", gotta go", he finished.

The Martin's took their time on the walk back to the truck in the Johnston Middle School parking lot. There was a whole lot of information to grasp. The support group meeting had been a life-saver in many respects. Things they never thought about suddenly jumped off the page. Now with Charlie going into a "silent mode" they were going to get a trial run in dealing with their emotions and keeping a routine in place.

"I don't know about you dear, but I could use a cold beer right about now. You up for one?", Rod inquired. "That sounds perfect", Hope fired back. "How about Saints?", asked Rod. Hope's nod sealed the deal. Night was beginning to set on the Central Iowa town. The sky was a mixture of oranges and yellows something straight out of God's creation. As the Martin's made their way to the neighborhood pub each was in their own thoughts. An adult beverage was about to bring some of those restrained concerns to light.

Rod held the door for his bride as they entered the eatery. A small table near the back wall offered a great place for solitude. "And how may I help you!?", said the young blonde barmaid. "Two Blue Moons, please", Rod said. "Coming right up." As Ms. Perky turned to head to the bar a part of Rod thought why couldn't Charlie have stayed home and met some nice little thing like that. She was darn cute, had a beautiful smile and was an attentive waitress. Besides with her tall frame and long legs, she could easily pass for an up and coming fashion model. The Martin's knew a good waitress when they saw one from their days of owning their own restaurant. Not everyone was cut out to be one. But his thoughts ended there. Rod could sense someone watching him. He knew the look was coming from Hope. "Just thinking. Why couldn't Charlie have met someone like that?" Hope cocked her head with a sly smile. It was time to move on to another subject before Rod got into further trouble .

It was time for talk. Real talk. "I'm starting to get real conflicted with Charlie leaving", started Rod. "I've done some reading about what he's going to encounter and one thing that stuck with me was this. For some who had experienced combat, they never wanted to experience it again. It wasn't really a situation sane people tended to embrace. Some, who were sane, embraced it countless times because they had signed up for the job. It changes people completely and irreversibly. It could make a person a killing machine. Where you could slaughter people in ways unimaginable to most folks." He paused for a minute to let the words sink in. "At the end of the day, or for that matter any time of day when you look at the reflection in the mirror, what do you see?", asked Rod. "I know Charlie could be in for some tough situations. I know he won't come back the same as he left. But what will his return be?"

Hope stared at Rod. Words were not going to explain this question. She kept staring until a little stream of tear slid down her right cheek. That said it all.

CHAPTER 19

Eddie was thinking good thoughts. His smile was as big as ever. The only thing is you couldn't see it. No matter how close you looked you wouldn't be able to make it out. The smile was on the inside. If he gave any of his higher ups any thought at all that he was enjoying himself his days would be in ruin. So he kept that feeling in a place where only he knew. It had been eight weeks that he'd endured this thing called Basic Training. He had been through a lot. His plan is what made the difference, kept him on track and would eventually lead to the completion of the 10-week hell.

Fort Knox had been a time where boys became men and girls became women. All types had come here to set a course in their military careers. Or hoped to. Eddie had some vivid memories of people breaking literally and figuratively. He also had been surprised at those who had risen to the occasion. One fat little dude named Ozzie who came in at 5' 8" and 220 pounds had been the most impactful. Rotund, as they nicknamed him, made believers of everybody at the Fort. He'd been pegged as a wash out but he dropped some 40 pounds and was now a chiseled specimen. And meaner than could be. At least in the battle field. Off it, he was a puppy dog.

When Martin had had some down time he thought of the many who had been on these honored grounds. Some good and some bad. The Fort had been many things over the years. During the 1930s, it was an induction center for the Civilian Conservation Corps (CCC) enrollees. Train loads of young men were sent to Fort Knox from West Virginia, Indiana, Ohio and Kentucky. It served as the "Home of Cavalry and Armor" for seven decades. It had been a POW camp in the 1940's.

A number of Axis prisoners died while at Fort Knox and 18 are buried in the post cemetery. One tragic incident involved the accidental shooting of a number of prisoners in which two died, Ernst Schlotter and Frederich Wolf. Perhaps the most tragic event occurred on October 18, 1993. Arthur Hill went on a shooting rampage, killing three and wounding two before attempting suicide, shooting and severely wounding himself. The shooting occurred at Fort Knox's Training Support Center. Hill died on October 21 of his self-inflicted gunshot wound.

One of the dudes Martin befriended, was a little wiry guy from Florida by the name of Sansui. His "favorite" place had been the assault course. It was called Tokyo Ridge. The soldiers had live ammo and targets popping up as they moved forward. Sansui was along nearly every step of the way. But so was someone else.

Martin had heard voices during the many marches he and his buddies accomplished on hills with names like Agony, Misery and Heartbreak. Their names couldn't have been better worded. This is where the PLAN was most evident. Eddie had figured the wisest thing he could do to make it through Basic was to envision his brother Charlie with him. When he went through physical training, Charlie was there encouraging him. When he was alone at night and homesick, Charlie was there. The marching was the most difficult. With each step, Eddie imagined his brother in front of him going through the same hardship. One step at a time. In looking at the boots of the soldier in front of him he sensed Charlie's encouragement. He felt Charlie. He nearly became Charlie. Soldiers literally left parts of themselves on those miles of pavement. Eddie had heard the names the minute he'd reached Fort Knox. "I marched up all of them with full field gear and rifle", Eddie reflected. They made soldiers out of us with the training that was done by instructors who drilled the hell out of us." Less than two weeks remained but Martin could readily recall one other part to the hills. "I'd have to say the worst was doing it while wearing our pro-masks before going to the gas chambers. The Gas Chamber is something he'd never forget either. He'd gone in four times because his drill sergeant wanted to find out who the real men and women were. So when he went in each time the question was yelled by a superior, "who's the real ones here?" How'd he get through it all? Charlie had been the difference pure and simple.

Sleep was near for Eddie Martin. The final thoughts of the day were crystal clear though. The PLAN he'd executed to making it through Basic was nearly a success. Yet he wouldn't share it with anyone. It was going to be his secret. Only he'd know. He'd take it to the grave with him. People do that. Things they don't want anyone to know about. Not their mom or dad, wife or husband. But God did. And Eddie hoped the two of them would keep that pact in place. Thanks God for being there with me and giving me hope, Eddie thought. And with that his eyes went shut.

CHAPTER 20

People were coming and going. Coffee in and coffee out. And other things like rolls and donuts too. But that's what the gist of the morning had been at Panera Bread in Johnston. Rod Martin had holed up in a corner near the window. He had the best seat in the house. Nothing was going to get past him. It was now D-Day minus 1. The time to head to Kentucky was just about here.

Rod sat at the table throwing some words and thoughts on his Hewlett Packard laptop in hope he could factually recall the past ten weeks. His family had undergone a transformation. He wanted to remember the highs and the lows and everything in between. It's amazing what a person forgets when time passes. Things you think you'd be sure to remember are nowhere to be found in your memory bank. He'd been putzing on the project for over two hours. He'd experienced a myriad of interruptions. Some caused by loud people, some of an attractive woman or two or three and then there were his own. He couldn't get on a roll. Much of his thoughts had been on the Martin's small group meeting from the previous night.

Rod and Hope were part of a group of twelve Christians that met once a month. They'd been meeting on the first Monday night of the month since they'd met at Alpha at Cornerstone of Hope in the fall of 2009. None of the people had any connection with the military. In some respect not having any prior knowledge left each one of them clueless. In another respect, just being able to talk about the Martin's situation had provided some ideas they'd never thought about. Just being close to a situation didn't mean you had all the answers.

"I don't have any idea what you guys are going through", offered Candy Loveland. "My boys are in college and they're not putting their lives on the line. But I do know that when they first left the nest I went through some real tough times. I was depressed and felt alone." Loveland, a petite woman of 45 looked as if she'd lived life and gotten some answers along the way. Her short auburn hair made her look older than her age. Her blue eyes jumped at you when you first encountered her. You forgot everything about her age, her weight, her height. You were instantly drawn to her words. "Someone told me about a book called the Butterfly Effect. I'm not sure I took away everything hook, line and sinker but this one sentence jarred me to a reality", she continued. "When you know that everything matters-that every move counts as much as any other-you will begin living a life of permanent purpose. Maybe that will help you. Not sure but try that on for size", she said.

Rod had been trying to make that message fit all morning. He hadn't gotten there yet, but there was a certain ring to it. He looked up at the customer group in the eatery. His glance went from one table to another. Then to the front door. Behind the counter. And then into the kitchen. He was looking for a particular face. One of joy. He didn't see one. He saw a whole lot of prunes. Faces distorted and nearly lifeless. He thought, was his timing wrong? Was he catching most of these people at a wrong time? Or was fact, fact? Were these ones still looking for their purpose in life?

"Sir, sir", squeaked the dirty blonde hair waitress. "I see you've been here for some time and we're getting ready for our lunch hour. Will there be anything I can get you?", she inquired. Initially Rod was upset she'd interrupted his thoughts. But he realized he'd been there long enough and he needed to make way for other customers. "No. No thanks", he timidly offered. "Probably time to move on."

Hours later the Martin family, what was left of them, Rod, Hope and Dan hit the sack. Tomorrow they'd be heading out for Kentucky and Eddie's graduation from Basic. Sleep was going to be hard to come by. There was going to be a whole lot of tossin and turnin all night. Eventually the three nodded off. The birds would be singing all too soon. Hopefully the notes would be good ones.

Rod was the first to wake the next morning. He was anxious beyond belief. He'd been dreaming of his family's situation. Eddie was to graduate and Charlie was deploying to Afghanistan in the next few days. Words had come to him through his dream. Something he had to put down now. Right now. So he opened his HP and the fingers moved across the keyboard. God was directing the message. It wasn't Rod.

"A tear drop hit my pillow last night as I lay awake .....followed moments later by a second and a third. The last one was a long, streaming one, which I think had a more profound significance than the others. Certainly this was the one that forced me to choke back a real melt down.

It has been two and a half months since I had really let my emotions come forth. It was tough saying goodbye to my oldest son, Charlie, that day at the Boone campus. He along with some 100 other National Guardsman boarded 4 busses and headed off to Camp Shelby in Mississippi. It was a day unlike any other I had known. Families being stretched to the greatest of emotional lengths. Some said goodbye to husbands, others to wives, sons and daughters. There were young spouses no doubt left with the responsibility of trying to explain what was going on and why mommy or daddy was leaving on a bus with a whole lot of other people. Another young lady, looking to give birth within a month or so, tried to hold back

tears. She wasn't doing a very good job, but who was I to talk. Yet, looking around me, I could only think of how each of our lives would become different. Yes, our tears were real that day……..

Last night though, my tears were different. They were bigger and they came out of nowhere. And they were much different than the ones back on July 30th. And they are different again today as I try to put my feelings down with words that don't do justice. Justice for me, my family and all the other men and women and their friends and families who are experiencing their loved one deploying to Afghanistan. Today, when my son leaves, and in the following weeks more than 4,000 Iowa Guardsman will be leaving our safe shores to DEPLOY. Not train, but deploy.

What does deploy mean? I had to look it up to make sure. Google had a short definition which stated, "to move into a position of readiness or availability." Okay…that makes sense. Yet, I feel there is one important word that was left out. REAL. There will be Real bullets and a Real enemy for REAL. And it's all for Real life and Real death in a region that I'm still trying to get my mind wrapped around. Is Afghanistan all that important? Are we fighting on level terms? Those questions alone are enough to make a person tear up.

So as you can see, my tears have been different. They were a "safe" tear when I knew my son was here in our country preparing for his duty. Now, it's the furthest thing from that. Safe tears have been replaced by scared tears, followed by proud tears followed by scared tears.

It goes without saying,, that I have come to a greater appreciation for our military and our country through this whole deployment process. Men and women have taken to their responsibility and are making all Iowans proud. I won't kid you, it's going to be a long 9 months. What do my future tears hold in store for me? Will it be for someone who has a solider wounded? Or will it be for one killed in action? I can't even think of going there.

It has been said that tears are good for the soul. It's our reaction to an experience. It has an awful lot to do with living, I think. If you've seldom let your emotions or experiences take you there, then today, think about those whose lives will be challenged from every angle possible. An old sixties song, "96 Tears" sure comes to mind right now. "Cry, cry, cry...96 tears, tears for the warm hearted, 96 tears." How many tears do I have left? I don't really know, but I do know this. The shortest and sweetest verse in the Bible is.... "Jesus wept." Puts it all in perspective, don't you think?"

Rod closed the lid on the laptop. He was emotionally spent. Or so he thought.

CHAPTER 21

"Wow. What hit you?", exclaimed Hope. "I heard you up so I know you've been up for a while, but you look like you've been drug round the block. What's up?" Rod stood in the kitchen in his underwear and Chicago White Sox t-shirt. His hair was a mess. He knew he probably looked like crap. How could a person not? "I don't know", he tried to offer. "I had this dream and I woke up and started pounding out a bunch of words about Charlie's deployment". Words that weren't mine but somehow ended up on my screen. I know that doesn't make sense. One sentence led to another and then another. Here, take a look", he insisted.

Hope looked at her husband a little disconcertingly. The family needed to get on the road for Eddie's graduation. It was going to be a long day. When she had gone through her planning the night before she hadn't allotted any time to do reading. But something seemed different. First, it wasn't typical of Rod to write a letter early in the morning. And secondly, the manner in which it came to life was pretty surreal. "Ok, let me take a look", she began.

Five minutes later Hope looked up from the laptop and smiled. "This was a gift. The Lord blessed you by giving you the words of what so many soldiers, families and friends are going through. Not only yesterday, but today and then again tomorrow." Rod looked stunned. But then a little turn of his lips brought about the beginning of a smiley face as well. "What do you think I should do with this?", he asked. "If you think this might help someone, what should I do?", he urged. In her light brown terry cloth bathrobe and pink slippers Hope was frozen in thought. A myriad of possibilities existed. Thirty seconds of silence turned to a minute and then slowly her words came out. "Let's pray about it and see where God directs you", she declared.

"Father God. You have given my husband the words to put a face on what everyone is experiencing with our troops deployment. Be a director to us to put this message in the right hands to move these thoughts along. Be visible to those who are struggling and give them assurance no matter how hopeless the situations seems, you are in control", she finalized. Hope and Rod looked at each other with excitement. They both felt a tingling sensation. Surely God was at Work.

The next hour was a beehive of activity in the Martin household. Dan had joined the party and was dragging suitcases, pillows, books, snacks and the like out to the SUV. Hope was primping in the master bathroom and Rod was sitting at the laptop again. This time he looked calm and assured. He was on the website of the Des Moines Register looking at their "letter to the editor" page. He had gone over the submission part a couple of times and felt like his information met all the requirements. "Honey", he yelled. "I'm sending this to the Register's letter to the editor. Here goes." Rod looked at the send button with a tremendous amount of Hope. He pushed the little black square. It was history.

Kentucky here we come.

CHAPTER 22

"Alright, everybody", let's hit the road", shouted Rod. The Martin's were ready to make the ten-hour trek to Kentucky. Actually past ready. It seemed like this day was never going to get here. Now it had. Hope, Dan and Rod made one last look around the house and seemed satisfied they hadn't forgotten anything. That is until Rod felt the buzz of his cell phone in his pants pocket. "Yup", said Rod. "Sure. Okay. Did you try this? And still nothing", he added. "Okay. Let me see what we can do. We were just ready to walk out the door."

A peeved Rod disconnected the call and turned to look at two faces showing more disgust than his. "It seems as though the University of Iowa sports website isn't working right and I need to go in and rectify it. Sorry everybody. Hopefully this won't take long, but they're a big account and I can't leave this hanging", concluded Rod. With those final words, Rod sped out the door and Hope and Dan collapsed on the couch. Hopefully the wait wouldn't be long.

The Iowa website was a project Rod had been part of for a couple of months now. His role was to keep Marketing Director Rick Joseph happy. That in itself was a big job. It was all part of a remake of the athletic site and in essence a recruiting tool for the athletic department. Rod motored the five blocks to the McNally offices and slid into the video room. The time was now 9 a.m. Seven hours later he and Editor Brant Snodgrass came up for air. It had taken way more time than either of them had imagined. All the bugs had been ironed out and the project was back on track. Now it was time to get the family on the rails. So much for a leisurely trip to the Bluegrass State.

Rod called his wife on his way back home. "Let's get the heck out of here", he suggested. "Be ready the minute I hit the driveway." A minute later the shuffle took place as Dan took his Dad's place behind the wheel. Rod took co-pilot and Hope stretched out on the back seat. With plans completely changed by the website issues Hope charted a new course. Des Moines to Peoria, Illinois a four hour trip and a stay overnight. That would be stage one. As Dan floored the SUV entering Interstate 80 east the tunes blared from the CD. It was going to be a boring drive to the home of Bradley University, but music was certainly going to help the situation. Steely Dan, Boz Scaggs, James Taylor and Firefall blasted a walk in the memory banks. It also soothed some anxieties and offered an opportunity to think about the last 12 hours. "Alright. Everybody take a chill pill", said Dan. His words were right on. Time to chill....

About two hours into the trip Rod's cellphone phone buzzed. He took a look to make sure it wasn't work calling again. There wasn't much he could do now if there was something else wrong with the Iowa website. Fortunately it wasn't them calling. Still he didn't recognize the number on the display. "Let's see who this is", he thought. "Hello, Rod Martin", he offered. For the next several minutes all Rod did was nod his head in agreement and say an occasional "sure". As he pushed the end button he glanced into the backseat at his wife with a look of astonishment. "That was the Des Moines Register. They got my letter today and they want to run it in its entirety this coming Sunday", he exclaimed. "They said they were moved by the message and felt it was something very appropriate in its timing. So guess what?", he questioned. "Amen, thank you God", Rod stated. See I told you he'd offer direction", said Hope. "That's pretty cool." Dan looked at both his parents not fully understanding the dialogue. He knew Rod had written something about Charlie's deployment but was completely unaware of anything else in the works. As Hope caught Dan up on the whole matter, Dan replied, "you know Dad, you should take advantage of social media and blog about Eddie and Charlie's experiences." But Rod had no idea what language his youngest son was speaking. "I've heard about blogging but I wouldn't have the foggiest notion as to what to do. How hard would that be?", he inquired. "Not real. You could make a site and it would be like a website where you could write articles and post them", Dan responded. "People could read your articles and make comments."

The remaining two hours into Peoria went by quickly. The conversation centered on how to put a blog together and what name would be attached to it. There might have been a hundred possible names thrown out but none seemed to stick until...Hope offered, "My Father's Voice". "That's got a nice sound to it and it sure offers a great message with a great title." Dan looked at Rod and Rod back at Dan. "There is a time when you don't argue with a woman's intuition, son. And this is one of them." My Father's Voice it is", exclaimed a smiling Rod.

The Martin's pulled into the Super 8 lot off War Memorial Drive in Peoria. They needed to get checked in, grab some grub and see if the internet would offer direction on how to put a blog in place. It was around 9 p.m. and the night was quickly getting away from them. As the three entered the front door to the motel they could see there wasn't anyone at the front desk. There was a note posted on the counter. Ring Bell for Service. Two dings on the bell jostled someone to life inside the nearby office. Rod envisioned the look of the clerk they were about to see. A 5'7" Middle Eastern stick of a dude with jet black hair and beard with the word Assan on his name plate. He wasn't friendly. It appeared he'd been woken up from a nap. The Martin's wondered if he'd provide a room or just take their money. Somehow they got a room key.

Hope met the rolling eyes of her family members. She looked and smiled at the desk jockey. "Thanks for all you do. I'm sure we'll enjoy our stay", she let roll off her tongue. The thought went through Rod's mind, "why does it seem like everywhere you go these days, there's someone behind the hotel/motel counter from some place unknown? Okay, he reminded himself, let it go." One down, two to go. Food was next on the agenda. Cracker Barrel wasn't too far away.

CHAPTER 23

When your stomach is making all types of hungry sounds it's amazing how fast you look for resolution. The Martin's had done that. The Peoria Cracker Barrel was going to be the remedy with a little home cookin. The little itty bitty hostess could tell by the looks on the three they were starved. She sashayed through the dining room to find the right table to couple with her best waitress. "Here you go", she said with a hint of flirtation. Hope and Rod had to imagine that it was meant for Dan. Dan kept a close eye on her gait as she turned to head back to the hostess area. Beautiful blue eyes, long, long blonde hair, dazzling red lipstick and fingernails and a nice little wiggle. A bombshell package. Most likely Dan's age too.

"Hi y'all", greeted the middle-aged waitress. Her demeanor exuded personality. Hope smiled at her. Rod surmised the two would probably engage in some lengthy woman discussions. He'd seen it many times before. The Martin boys had often accused their mother of talking to almost anyone and everyone. "Hey, those are some great tunes you guys are playing. Music from the 70's are the best", suggested Hope. "I think so too", responded the waitress who most likely had been a hippie in her earlier years. She had long auburn hair pulled back into a pony tail that ran half way down her back. She had large hoop earrings and turquoise rings on three of her fingers. She put on a little shimmy at the table and rattled off three of her fav's from the time period. She let the names of the songs roll off her tongue. "Let's Stay Together", "Heart of Gold" and "Killing Me Softly." Not to be outdone Hope countered with "Best of My Love", "I'll Be There" and "I Like it."

"Okay ladies, okay", offered Rod. "Maybe you two can talk after we eat. You know I'd like something off the menu from a band from the 70's. Do you know what that is?" Rod sat admiring his line and how witty he was. They both stared at him with puzzled looks. "How about some Meatloaf", he concluded. The ladies belly laughed and for now their jig was halted. "What sides can I get with that", queried Rod. Minutes later the gal was off to the kitchen to place a hungry family order. Within ten minutes Ms. Shimmy was back at the table with a tray of delicious looking food. The Royal Gorge began.

Hope was the last one done. When she put her fork on the table it signaled a truce. By the looks of the empty plates the Martin's had been famished. Dan had chosen the Roast Beef and Hope the Chicken Fried Steak. All of the meals had hit the spot and had been prepared perfectly. But time was now fast approaching 10:30 p.m. If there was going to be any surfing of the internet tonight for blog purposes, they'd need to beat feet. After exchanging the last remnants of their chit-chat with the waitress the three headed for the door. Dan took one last look back at the young hostess. She returned his glance with a down turned lip clearly bummed of the stud's departure. Maybe Eddie wouldn't miss him if he stayed in Peoria and didn't go to Fort Knox, he thought. The old man interrupted those ideas. "Come on son", maybe we can stop on our way back", Rod chuckled. "Funny dad. Funny", snarled Dan.

When the tribe entered through the automatic sliding doors of the Super 8 they found an empty lobby. There was a small TV located behind the counter with video of CNN broadcasting headline news. The announcer was putting an end to his report as he stated, "In other technology news, the Wall Street Journal has revealed Facebook users are inadvertently providing access to their names and in some cases even their friend's names to advertising and internet tracking companies." "Wow, that's nice to know", observed Rod. "So I should go knee deep in social media with my blog, huh son? Those are reassuring thoughts. Okay. Let's get 'er done." Just then, the little Middle Eastern clerk poked his head around the corner to see who was making noise. Satisfied he wouldn't have to do any more work, he slid back into la-la land and the Martin's headed for Room 222.

"Here Dad. Take a look at this", suggested Dan. The Martin men had been on the laptop for about an hour when Dan suggested settling on blogspot.com as the site for Rod's work. Within another few minutes they checked out designs, fonts and templates to use for "My Father's Voice". Once the foundation was built, Dan showed his Dad how to put a post onto the site. Post number one came October 19, 2010. The text used was the letter to the editor that would be published in the Sunday Des Moines Register five days later.

As Rod slid into the queen size bed he grabbed a fluffy pillow from behind his wife's head. He could see the contentment she was experiencing with her much needed sleep. He was pretty certain he wouldn't be shedding any tears tonight. Sheer exhaustion would likely keep him from that. Tomorrow would be another story. One more day and they'd be seeing one son for the first time in 10 weeks. And the oldest son was days away from being deployed. Talk about overlap.

CHAPTER 24

As the Martin's walked out the lobby door they glanced around to see if their favorite clerk was still on the job. It was 8 a.m. and time for the final stage of their trip to Fort Knox. Not to their surprise, Mr. Customer Rep. could be seen rummaging around the back office. He didn't acknowledge the three. "See ya later", Dan murmured. Back on the road again.

The route of choice was I-74 to Indianapolis and then I-65 onto Louisville. It was some pretty scenic country but asphalt is asphalt. After a time no matter what the surface is it gets boring and sooner or later a pit stop was needed to refuel, both in the tank and in the stomach. Dan was doing the bulk of the driving that way he didn't have to think about the cute little number he left behind at the Cracker Barrel. Maybe another pretty face would appear down the road. Dan had stopped once before for gas and the restroom. The second pitting was in Seymour, Indiana. Dan had a distinct impression the town had some history behind it so he googled the little hamlet. Seymour a town of about 1,900 had quite a mention in Wikipedia. It's called the "Crossroads of America" because the north/south and east/west railroads intersect in downtown. The north/south line, the Jeffersonville, Madison and Indianapolis Railroad, was built in the 1840s connecting Indianapolis to the Ohio River at Jeffersonville. It ran through a family farm at the area that is now Seymour. In 1852 when the east/west railroad, the Ohio and Mississippi Railroad, was going to be built, Capt.

Meedy Shields, who was the cousin of General John Tipton persuaded the surveyor, John Seymour, into putting it through his land, in return for which he named the town Seymour. All trains had to stop at a crossroad, making Seymour a bustling community. However, what many people know about this sleepy hamlet is that it's the birthplace of John Cougar Mellencamp. Johnny Cougar rose to fame in 1982 with hits like "Jack and Diane, Hurts So Good and Lonely Nights." Mellencamp was also one of the founders of Farm Aid an organization that began in 1985 with a concert in Champaign, Illinois to raise awareness about the loss of family farms and to raise funds to keep farm families on their land. One has to wonder why he didn't choose his hometown...the "Crossroads of America" as the concert site. It could have been a Country version of Woodstock.

Hope slid behind the wheel for the balance of the trip into Louisville. Dan drifted off to sleep in the back seat. Rod was checking out the sports news on his cellphone. The headlines spoke of the Texas Rangers win over the New York Yankees in Game 5 of the American League Championship Series. The Rangers were advancing to their first World Series. Texas had won the game decisively 6-1. Their reward? They would be facing the San Francisco Giants in the best of seven games beginning next week. Fall baseball and the question of who the next Mr. October would be were beginning to be knocked around. Maybe we should say Mr. October-November by the way the calendar was playing out. The Rangers were led by pitcher Cliff Lee and outfielder Josh Hamilton. The Giants were to counter with pitcher Madison Bumgarner and catcher Buster Posey. It had all the aspects to be a very good World Series.

Rod looked up from his sports ticker. Just then he saw a billboard touting the Louisville Slugger Museum and Factory. "Hey, we have a little time to burn, how about we go to the Louisville Slugger Museum?", he suggested. It was really more of a statement than a question. Hope's expression showed her lack of interest. Dan on the other hand was mildly inquisitive.

"Sure. Count me in." "Why don't the two of you go through it then and make a memory", Hope replied. "I can find something to do in the truck." It was an order that didn't need repeating. Ten minutes later Hope pulled into the parking lot of the famous bat house. The guys exited the SUV and pulled on their team garb. Rod zipped up his Chicago White Sox jacket and Dan pulled a Colorado Rockies sweatshirt over his head. They were representing their favorite team and apparel was important.

"Oh, my Gosh, will you look at that", shouted Rod. "Look at the size of that bat." What Rod was going nuts over was the towering bat that extended some 120 feet in the air outside the museum. Come to find out, they say the bat is an exact-scale replica of the 34 inch bat Babe Ruth used to pummel Major League pitchers during his heyday. Maybe this is where the old line came from. Walk softly and carry a big stick. "This is going to be fun", exclaimed Dan. They both turned their attention to the Big Glove. A giant, prehistoric ball glove handcrafted from old Kentucky limestone. The 17-ton sculpture is entitled, "Play Ball." The two of them had a fellow ball fan take their picture next to the monster sports display. "I never would have thought about taking this in" suggested Dan. "Let's go do some exploring", fired Dad. And explore they did. If ever there was something to take your mind off of stress in the family life, this was it, Rod thought. There was a throng of people waiting for the next tour time. Luckily they got right in. "Good afternoon y'all" microphoned the little black-haired southern belle guide. "If you're here for the factory tour, come on over here", she spoke in her slow drawl. Dan looked intensely at the young thang. He might have followed her anywhere. But for now it would have to be a walk into baseball history. Ms. Peoria nice knowing you.

The tour lasted about twenty minutes. It was amazing to see each of the six steps in the bat making process. There was a sense of chaos in the production methods. Controlled chaos. Wood chips flying in the air with each cut. Machines whirring and moaning. Lathes doing their perfecting.

The smell of wood hung throughout the facility and you could imagine the sizzling of each brand as the stamp went on the piece of wood. This all began in 1884. The workers were taking the same great pride from workers past. Everything all came together by design. Assuredly this is one of the reasons why baseball is America's sport. And at the end each person received a free miniature Louisville Slugger bat. Dan and Rod also took time to appreciate The Great Wall, a display of thousands of signatures from players who signed contracts with the bat company. The same signatures burned into the bats that made them famous. Honus Wagner was the first. Thee Honus Wagner. The dude won eight batting titles, led the league in slugging six times and stolen bases five times. The man they call the "Flying Dutchman" who played from 1897-1917. The museum offered more astonishing pieces. Dan was especially enamored with Batter Up and Feel the Heat. Batter Up was a pitching simulator that gave you three pitches to try and hit. Dan's swing, while still picture perfect didn't make contact with a single pitch. Total skunk. Feel the Heat enabled visitors to feel what it would be like to face a 90 MPH fastball. Good thing it wasn't a curveball, Dan thought. Rod was most fascinated in Holding a Piece of History. A fan could hold onto a used bat from stars like Mickey Mantle, Johnny Bench and Andre Dawson. This was history like no other. If only all these pieces of wood could talk.

About 4 p.m. the two ball enthusiasts made their way back to the truck. Hope was reading a book and was in her own little world. She about jumped out of her skin as they unlocked the doors to the vehicle. "Have fun?" she finally got out when she got her breath back. In stereo came the response. "Oh yeah."

Dan drove the little distance left into Elizabethtown, a town of about 30,000. Hope's job was to find a hotel for the next two days that offered comfort and service. Her eyes searched to and fro as the Martin's navigated U.S. Route 31. Rod was in the back seat soaking in the trip to baseball lore.

One of his biggest passions was baseball. He'd been a coach to each of his three boys. Martin recalled how good a little catcher Dan had been as a youngster. He had one of the sweetest little swings any nine-year old had from the left side. "Picture perfect", one coach had said to Rod. He looked at his son driving the vehicle and a serious thought came over him. When was the last time the two of them had played catch in the backyard? Gosh, it had been ages, he thought. They needed to do it again some time. It's a memory for life. When you do something for the last time you seldom ever realize it, Rod thought again. For that fact, he couldn't recall the last time he'd thrown each of his boys in the air when they were little. One day he did and the next he didn't. Did they get big enough that it made sense to stop trying for fear of hurting himself? It wasn't that big of a thing then, but now it was. He used to read books to Dan at bedtime. When did that stop and why? There were a whole lot of when was the last time coming to him. That's why life has so many look backs. Rod needed to relish the moments more. Tomorrow was going to be a day when Rod could begin putting that to practice. It was going to be Graduation Day for Eddie. And the Martin's had arrived to soak it all in.

CHAPTER 25

There was an eerie feeling present. Like someone was aware of every move they made. It was a feeling that emerged when the Martin's had pulled into Elizabethtown. Hope was the first to voice what everyone was thinking. "Does it seem like there's some eyes on us", she challenged. "Maybe it's just me, but would Uncle Sam check every vehicle entering town", she questioned. Rod and Dan laughed. Kind of. It was the kind of laugh meant to cover up what a person truly felt. "Heck I don't know, would they?", countered Rod. "I've heard of stranger things than that. I know one thing. I'm not going to give anybody reason to think we've come here to commit a crime." "That's probably the smartest thing you've said today, Dad", said Dan. And with that they all had a good chuckle.

The reason for the Martin paranoia was the close proximity of the Fort Knox Bullion Depository where the U.S. Treasury stores most of its gold. They were about 14 miles from the fortified vault building. "I've got to google this", barked Hope. "Maybe the weird feeling will go away when I know more about Fort Knox's history." What she found out was this as she read to her men from her cellphone.

Below the fortress-like structure at Fort Knox that resides on 42 acres lies the gold vault lined with granite walls and protected by a blast-proof door weighing 20 tons. The Gold Vault was built in 1936 for a cost of $560,000. Members of the Depository staff must dial separate combinations known only to them. Beyond the main vault door, smaller compartments provide further protection. According to a Mosler Safe Company brochure: The most famous, if not the largest, vault door order came from the Federal government in 1935 for the newly constructed gold depository at Fort Knox, Kentucky. Both the vault door and emergency door were 21-inches thick and made of the latest torch- and drill-resistant material. The main vault door weighed 20 tons and the vault casing was 25-inches thick.

The facility is ringed with fences and is guarded by the United States Mint Police. The Depository premises are within the site of Fort Knox, a US Army post, allowing the Army to provide additional protection. The Depository is protected by layers of physical security, alarms, video cameras, microphones, mine fields, barbed razor wire, electric fences, heavily armed guards, and the Army units based at Fort Knox, including unmarked Apache helicopter gunships of 8/229 Aviation based at Godman Army Airfield, the 19th Engineer Battalion, formerly training battalions of the United States Army Armor School, and the 3rd Brigade Combat Team of the 1st Infantry Division, totaling 30,000 soldiers, with associated tanks, armored personnel carriers, attack helicopters, and artillery.

There is an escape tunnel from the lower level of the vault to be used by someone who has been accidentally locked in. For security reasons, no visitors are allowed inside the depository grounds. This policy has been enforced ever since the vault opened, and the only exception was an inspection by members of the United States Congress and the news media on September 23, 1974 led by then Director of the United States Mint, Mary Brooks.

The bullion depository has become a symbol of an impregnable vault, leading to phrases such as "locked up tighter than Fort Knox" or "safer than Fort Knox". Many business names in the surrounding areas are references to the bullion depository".

"Good Golly", finished Hope. "I never would have imagined anything like that. Oh, my gosh turn here", she yelled. They'd reached their home destination for the next couple of days. "Sorry guys I didn't find a place with Fort Knox on their marquee. Will that be alright? I guess Quality Inn and Suites will have to do."

No one said a word as the Martin's strolled through the front door of the Inn. All eyes centered on the clerk's desk straight ahead. No one was there. Just about the time Rod was going to say something sarcastic, a rough looking middle-aged woman stuck her head up from behind the counter. "Hi there", she roared. "Welcome to Fort Knox and to the Quality Inn and Suites". A shocked Rod looked at his wife and son. This was such a different reception than most of the places they'd stayed in recent months. Even though he'd been caught off guard, he stammered the words, "well thank you. Thank you very much." The friendly lady behind the counter was as efficient as they come. She did however look like she'd completed a recent Basic at the Fort. Her features displayed a firm tense jaw, short cropped blonde hair and the body make of a tank. A smiley thing though. Within two minutes they were checked in, had their room keys and been given direction to their short term residence. It was a good thing Rod thought, that he didn't look over the counter to see what clothes were paired with her Quality Inn polo shirt. Most likely she had on camo pants.

The group stopped at the door to their room. It was Room 222. AGAIN. They all came to the conclusion there must be some sort of theme going on since that famous room number kept popping up at their hotel stays. On entering the room, all bags were tossed into their respective corners. And a mini-collapse took place. It was good to finally get to a place and settle in. At least for a couple of days. The Martin's were a mere 14 minutes from Fort Knox. Just that close to Eddie.

A half an hour later Dan's stomach began the hungry growls. A couple of minutes later, Rod responded with a like tune. Not wanting to add three part harmony to the situation, Hope suggested the hangry guys run across the parking lot to the local pizza parlor and pick up some food. Twenty minutes later they were back in the room and the food was dispensed. While they had been gone, Hope had pulled out some letters Eddie had sent her while at Basic. She'd already begun her reading. Feeling like they'd better leave her to her own thoughts, Dan and Rod slid off to the other end of the room and pulled up a table next to the television. Rod looked at the movie guide resting near the lamp. There was one movie that caught his eye, Wild Hogs. One of his all-time favorites. Dan pushed a couple of pieces of the pepperoni and mushroom Rod's way and they were off and running. One little room and there were two different worlds within it.

About thirty minutes into the movie, Rod stole a glance at his wife. She was totally immersed in the letters. No one, no thing could distract her. There could have been a bomb go off at the Quality Inn and she'd never have known. Rod was satisfied that his wife had found something to occupy the time. He turned back to the HD set just in time for one of the funniest exchanges in the movie. Dudley, one of the four middle-aged suburban cycle dudes who was a computer programmer in real life, had tried to take on the motorcycle gang the Del Fuegos. All by himself. What it got him was a cellophane wrapping around his midsection and an offering up for ransom. The leader of the clan Jake Blade yelled to the townspeople of Madrid that he was going to take the tire iron Dudley had brought with him to fight with and use it to break his legs. Dudley yelled. The gang wanted a ransom and they wanted it quickly. "Don't worry I'm a computer programmer, I don't need my legs!" Which drew a response from the cycle leader. "In that case, I'll break your hands." Dudley quickly yelled out, "Bring the money! Now!" Rod about fell off the bed laughing. Dan just shook his head.

Hope was loving lines of her own. One letter dated October 3rd had gotten her fancy. It was simple yet poetic.

"Dear Mom. It's 3 p.m. on Sunday afternoon and it's a really cold almost winter feeling day. You can tell winter's getting close here in Kentucky. I think today is the coldest day since I've been here (almost two months). It's crazy that I've already been gone for so long. It feels like forever though. I can tell and sense that since I've been gone away from home my relationship with Dad has gotten better, somewhat strengthened. At least that's how I feel, which is a good, no great thing! When it comes to my latest card, I'm glad your feelings were hard to describe. I put a lot of thought and work into it. Are you really going to frame it? I know how you feel when you say it seems life has gone by so fast! I feel like mine has gone by really fast too, sometimes I just wish I was a kid again. But I can't be, which sometimes sucks. But I'm becoming a man now, I just have to deal with it. In your letter you wrote about when Dan texted you and told you to come downstairs and then he started crying. I could picture in my head exactly what he looked like, sitting downstairs in the chair breaking down into tears and it made me do the same thing. I cried reading most of your letter. I feel so bad for him because he has to experience both of his brothers being gone at the same time in his life. I'm sure it's really hard on him, but there's nothing I can do. He just has to look forward to October 21st to see me again. Which isn't far away. I love you so much more than you think. Miss ya lots.

Your son, Eddie".

Hope folded the letter and placed it back in the envelope. When she flipped it over she was amazed at how official the letter looked. It had the U.S. Army insignia in the upper left hand corner. The return address said Pvt. Eddie Martin, 2nd Platoon, D Co. 1-46IN, Building #6547, 3596 Wilson Road, Ft. Knox, Kentucky 46121.

There was one lone long tear streaming down her left cheek. Eddie's message had been straight forward and right on. She let the tear stream a little longer actually helping her enjoy even more satisfaction in the moment. She picked up the remainder of Eddie's letters off her lap and put them into a big baggie. Then she wiped away the tear. Closed her eyes. And whispered the following.

"Our Father, who art in heaven,
hallowed be thy Name,
thy kingdom come,
 thy will be done,
on earth as it is in heaven.

Give us this day our daily bread.
And forgive us our trespasses,
as we forgive those
who trespass against us.

And lead us not into temptation,
but deliver us from evil.

For thine is the kingdom,
and the power, and the glory,
for ever and ever. Amen."

Hope slowly opened her eyes and glanced at the boyz still enjoying their Hog movie. She was comforted in the fact everyone was ready for a big day tomorrow. She was also comforted in the words she had just uttered. The most complete and powerful prayer one can give to God. She could have ended there but felt moved to add a few more of her own. "Thank you Lord, for all your blessings and all the Hope you bring us each and every day. Be with us especially tomorrow for Eddie's graduation and the opportunity to see his smiling face once again. Amen."

The Martin's were down to hours now and the surprise of their lives. The Lord no doubt had his hand in that.

CHAPTER 26

Everyone had rolled out of bed early and hit the showers. Hope had made a journey to the hotel lobby for three coffees to wake the group. Dan was putting the finishing touches on his wardrobe as he tied his new red Nike tennies. He had on tan shorts and a white Aeropostale pullover. Across the room, sat Rod watching ESPN's Sports Center looking patriotic in a pair of blue shorts, a red pullover and white Adidas tennis shoes. He was focused on the discussion of the on-air talent regarding the upcoming game of his beloved Chicago Bears and the Washington Redskins on Sunday. Chicago entered the game with a 4-2 record. Washington was 3-3. The Redskins were led by Donovan McNabb and the Bears by Jay Cutler. Rod wasn't feeling good about the matchup. In fact the more he listened the larger the doubt was. He glanced at the small sink where Hope was completing her makeup routine. She was dressed casually exquisite in a white blouse with a denim jacket, a black pleated skirt and pair of red high top Gucci sandals.

A tune came into Rod's head as he watched her primping. He sang it to himself for a while. Then he started singing it out loud softly at first, but a little louder each time he came to the end of the verse.

> **I've got the joy, joy, joy, joy down in my heart**
> **Where?**
> **Down in my heart!**
> **Where?**

Down in my heart!
I've got the joy, joy, joy, joy down in my heart
Down in my heart to stay.

Hope looked over at her husband and froze. Then a big smile covered her face. "Do you know the next verse?", she asked. Rod shook his head back and forth with uncertainty. "Then let me teach you", she began.

And I'm so happy
So very happy
I've got the love of Jesus in my heart
Down in my heart
And I'm so happy
So very happy
I've got the love of Jesus in my heart.

"Okay!", she said. "All join in". Rod picked up on the second verse and then they went back to the beginning for a complete rendition. Along the way Dan joined in. There wasn't any three part harmony but they had to admit they'd done a pretty good job. "Not sure where that came from", offered Rod. "It just felt right for the occasion, ya know. Alright everybody, you ready to see Mr. Ed?" It was time to get serious.

Dan offered to drive his folks to the Fort Knox. He'd just as soon drive as sit in the back. Leaving the hotel parking lot and turning onto US-31W, Dan's focus was on making sure he didn't get his family lost. His Mom and Dad's thoughts were somewhere else.

Rod was 41 years younger. He was sitting in front of the television set in his dormitory room at Mankato State. Two other college friends were present. Gary Scott and Jay Underwood. They each had downed their share of beers. This could be a glorious night or an ugly night depending on the outcome. It was Lottery Night 1969. December 1st. The first time in 27 years since the United States had held a draft lottery. An estimated

850,000 young men would learn their draft futures. Every male aged 19 to 26, whose draft status had not already been resolved, had a stake in the outcome. Roger Mudd of CBS News began the telecast. A dude by the name of Congressman Alexander Pirnie, the ranking Republican on the House Armed Services Committee read off the first lucky/unlucky number. September 14th, number 1. Rod had about puked. He didn't know if he could make it through this night. All three in the room were nervous as ever. When the night was over with there were going to be a myriad of could they, would they, should they, outcomes. Canada wasn't far away they all thought if they needed to head north. Scott was the first to get his number. June 9th, number 335. Gary had about jumped through the ceiling with joy. Underwood was next. July 4th, 279. Jay clapped his hands about 15 times and shouted, "Alright." Two down and two pretty doggone happy fellas with their results. Martin was next. Lord, please give me a high number he prayed. Please, please, please. July 16th. Number 120. Rod about crapped his pants. What was that going to mean? For days, maybe even weeks Martin dealt with number 120 and what it was to mean to his future life.

Rod was remembering his feelings again of that night and how he'd thought of his friends. You lucky stiffs. If I lose my deferment, I'm gone. You on the other hand are pretty safe. Funny how you could dislike someone just because of the day they were born. It could have been worse. 120 was certainly better than Mr. September 14th.

In the end, things turned out pretty favorable for Rod Martin. He was fortunate enough to complete college and never had to serve his country. The 1970's were an era where many tried to think of anything possible to get out of a military commitment. But times were different now. Rod had sensed that when Charlie graduated from Basic in 2009. There were parts of him that were saddened that he hadn't served his country. He was beginning to have that same feeling all over again. How different would his life be today if he'd gone into the service? Would he even be alive today?

Hope was thinking a little different. She was imagining all the other mothers that they'd be seeing today. Each one would have a different story of their soldier's life to this point. Their sons and daughters were coming from all backgrounds. They were all sizes. They had different personalities. There were no two alike. Eddie had written his mother about the troubles some of the soldiers were having in making it through the 10-week course. He'd gone in detail about the ones on the verge of a breakdown in the field. Or the ones that had cried themselves to sleep. And the ones that were physically sick to their stomachs much of the time. Hope was feeling for those mothers today. In many respects, they were getting their babies back today. In what shape was a question that had to be considered. She knew her son had grown up a whole lot during this time. Still she had apprehensions as to what she'd be seeing of her Eddie.

Rod continued with his thinking. He kept seeing Major Jenkins sitting at his desk at Camp Dodge. The Major no doubt knew several of the soldiers from Camp Dodge would be graduating today. Or did he? Did he keep track of such things? Rod wished he was here so he could see firsthand how he had helped change lives. The lives of young men and women like Eddie who had sat across the desk from him scared shitless looking for an out. Rod would get ahold of the Major when they got back home. He was certain of that. There was hope today for Eddie Martin. Thanks to the Good Lord and one Major Fritz Jenkins.

The Martin's passed the U.S. Bullion Depository and pulled up to the Chaffee Gate at Fort Knox. "May I help you?", said the rough and tough looking soldier on duty. "We're here to see my brother graduate today", offered Dan proudly. The butterflies hit for mom and dad right then.

CHAPTER 27

It was a good thing the Martins had come when they did. It must have had a lot to do with the weather which was to say the least, stunning. There wasn't a cloud anywhere to be seen. The skies were the most beautiful blue imaginable. And then there was the radiance of a thousand suns. Not Hiroshima radiance but darn close. The Fort was a beehive of activity as people were coming and going everywhere. And not just military people either. Graduation day was to be a significant day in the lives of several hundred soldiers, the 21st of October, 2010. Ironically, this day had additional significance for one Edward John Martin. He was turning nineteen today his last year as a teenager. He shared this special anniversary with celebrities like actress Carrie Fisher, notable teenager Natalee Holloway who disappeared in Aruba and major league pitcher Zack Greinke. Hope, Rod and Dan Martin were here to help support and honor Eddie on this doubly special moment.

As they entered the grounds, a young lady provided a handout of the Basic itinerary the soldiers had put themselves through week by week:

"ZERO WEEK: RECEPTION
This is where your transformation for civilian life to the Army world begins—from bidding farewell to your civilian clothes, getting your Army haircut and getting ready to become physical fit.

WEEK 1: FALL IN

Once Reception Week completes, it's now time to get down to business, lots to learn in a short period of time, new rules, regulations and processes involved in being in the Army. Classroom instruction begins.

WEEK 2: DIRECTION

Your new mentor is your Drill Sergeant, leaving the classroom for the field, it's time to test your physical and mental endurance. Possible things to learn this week are map reading and first aid.

WEEK 3: ENDURANCE

During week 3 you will have to rely on your team mate and dig deep inside yourself, it is time to start the physical and mental challenges of the simulated combat scenarios.

WEEK 4: MARKSMANSHIP

The M16A2. It is the standard issue weapon of the U.S. Army. You will be taught everything there is to know about this weapon. Learning to shoot a rifle is more than pulling the trigger. Marksmanship courses will teach you not only the proper way to hold a weapon, but also how to breathe and shoot from many different positions.

WEEK 5: TRIALS

Hope you were paying attention in week 4 because you will use all that information this week to pass the Basic Rifle Marksmanship Qualification Course and the Fit to Win Obstacle Course. You will be challenged both mentally and physically.

WEEK 6: CAMARADERIE

Your platoon is only as strong as its weakest member, this week you will learn to count on your fellow trainees. Bonds are formed and confidence is gained as trust exercises are implemented.

WEEK 7: CONFIDENCE

Confidence in yourself and your platoon has been growing steadily over the past seven weeks. Hand grenade training; live fire exercises; foot marching; and overall physical fitness will all be tested in the Confidence Course.

*WEEK 8: COMBAT SKILL DEVELOPMENT

An additional week was inserted at Week 8 to provide more time for developing combat skills.

WEEK 9: VICTORY FORGE

All the miles have been marched and the obstacle left behind. It's time to put everything you've learned up to this point to the real test: a three-day field retreat to Victory Forge. This is the true and final test of your skills and spirit – your chance to prove you have what it takes to be a U.S. Army Soldier.

WEEK 10: GRADUATION

Your family and friends have made the journey to watch you graduate. All your hard work has led you to this day. This is the day you have been dreaming of, the day you become a U.S. Army Soldier."

Of course there were many items left off the information sheet which explained in depth, might have given a better idea of the difficulty of each and every week. By appearance it looked like a walk in the park. But it was far from it. Some struggled mightily but passed by the skin of their teeth. Others didn't make the grade and were headed for a do-over. Graduation was an earned privilege not a right for those who were to hear their name called.

As the Martins made their way to Sadowski Field House, Rod had an unsettling feeling. As big of a day as this was, he was certain there were going to be a number of soldiers without anyone present to share in their glory. Gosh, how sad was that?, he thought. The more he considered the situation the more it bothered him. There were a tremendous amount of happy vibes floating around but some sad ones too. "Honey", he started. "Can you imagine how tough it would be for a soldier to go through this without anyone here to share it with. Think if someone is from California and his or her parents or loved ones couldn't make the trip here like we did. That'd be a real bummer", he added. Hope's astonished look echoed Rod's sentiments. "See how important family is?", she noted. "There are no doubt all sorts of stories here. I'm just so thankful that we try to be there for the important times in our children's lives. It'll be one of the great memories they have", she said. Dan was leading the way among the rows of chairs hoping to find a location that provided the best shot of the stage. The moment of Basic completion was quickly closing in on the growing crowd. They'd soon be seeing the latest chapter of added National Treasures to the United States military.

Right on cue at 11:45 a.m., the welcome video of Fort Knox began. The virtual reality tour gave a 5-minute in-depth look at what the prospective graduates had endured. That was followed by various administrative speeches and an introduction by the Commanding General. Then came a slide presentation by the range training officer and a rundown of the graduates most notably, Private Edward John Martin. The 35 minute ceremony ended with a HOOAH video of various experiences of the soldiers during their camp stay and finally a release to parents and family. The definitions of HOOAH are various depending on who you ask. One common thought is "Heard, Understood and Acknowledged" or maybe the graduating soldiers offered a better idea, "Head Out of Ass". HOOAH. They shouted in unison one more time. HOOAH.

The word hung in the air for the longest time. Which was fine with the graduates. There was relief on more faces than you could count. Hope began searching the crowd for a sign of Eddie. As were Rod and Dan. Hope saw him first. At least she thought it was him. She couldn't be sure. He looked so much different. Then he saw her. The look back offered little of any expression on his face. Stone faced. That's what he was. And then Private Martin saw his Dad and brother. Still the reflection was stoic. Impenetrable. Hope was uncertain of his reaction? Was Eddie uncomfortable in the changes his family might see in him? Would they see the differences he felt had taken place? Was this a change symbolic of Basic when a youngster became a man or woman?", she wondered. She simply knew it would be a look she would remember as long as she lived. Dan and Rod were equally blown away. "This was not the same person who left home ten weeks ago", Rod thought. No way no how. Dan was stuck in freeze frame trying to digest the entire moment. For the longest time the four stood and looked at one another without a word being uttered. "You look so different son", Rod finally stated. It took a little while but finally the little smirk smile that had been a part of Eddie since he was a little guy slowly emerged. That was the first inkling that this rock of man in front of them was their family member. It was as if the "brainwashing" of the last ten weeks had to be slowly chiseled away.

Two brothers finally reunited....at least for the time being

In a matter of minutes Eddie became a little more conversational. And then he became a little more animated. About five minutes later as he introduced members of his unit to his parents and brother he truly began showing flashes of his former self. "Guys, this is Private Steven Wright of Georgia. He was in my platoon. I mentioned him a couple of times in my letters. And this is Private Kennedy from Florida. We went through a lot together. A whole lot. Like the gas chamber. Right dude?", offered a laughing Private Eddie. The togetherness they shared would be a bond that they would no doubt hold for a lifetime. After meeting more of his fellow soldiers the Martins finally made their way to the barracks area so Eddie could get his belongings. The graduates had been given some family time before their new orders arrived. Eddie would be shipping out to AIT in Maryland the next morning so time was of the essence. Time for some fun and catching up.

On the way to the parking lot Hope followed up on some of her first impressions seeing Eddie after the ceremony. "We're so proud of you", she exclaimed. "My gosh, look at you. Just look at you. I can't take my eyes off of our soldier." Eddie seemed a little uncomfortable with the last part of the remark, but still he took it all in. "Yeah dude", echoed Dan. "I wasn't sure you were my brother at first".

A few droplets had fallen before they found the SUV in the Fort Knox lot. The day which had begun so brightly was beginning to show an ugly turnaround. The sky was becoming darker by the minute and the wind had started to pick up. You could smell the rain in the air. That's how heavy it was. But still Rod was holding strong in the opinion that no matter how nasty the weather got, it would not spoil the day. Still the clouds got darker and the wind was now beginning to whistle. It was a wonder he'd even heard his cellphone buzzing but somehow he did. He looked down and saw it was Charlie calling. Rod surmised he was calling his brother to tell him congrats. "Hey son", yelled Rod over the elements. "How you doing?" Charlie was short and direct. He was not calling for any reason other than to deliver one particular message. "Dad, I wanted you and Mom to know I'm in Bangor, Maine", he stated. "We're refueling for our flight to Afghanistan. We're deploying. We're leaving in a few minutes."

When you least it expect it, expect it. Those were the words that kept going through Rod's noggin. He'd been blindsided. He never thought on the joyous day of one son's graduation another son would call and say he was going to war. Talk about going from a tremendous high to the shitter in one quick moment. "Oh my God", Rod finally blurted out. He couldn't say anything other than that. And frankly he was disappointed in his reaction to a situation he'd been preparing for the last few months. Rod passed the cell to his wife without telling her the nature of the call. "Oh my God!", she exclaimed as she echoed her husband's response.

CHAPTER 28

The cell phone was passed along to Charlie's two brothers. They both had about two minutes to say their goodbye to their older bro. When Dan disconnected the call there was a long silence. Not one of the Martin's had expected Charlie's departure to have taken this path. A little advance notice would have been nice. No such luck.

Rod was in total meditation mode since his short conversation with Charlie. What happened moments ago now seemed light years away. He had just come off a tremendous celebration with Eddie's Basic graduation. Up to this point, he had one take away from the day. And it was the youthful appearance of most of the graduates. They all looked so....so....baby-faced. There was no other way around it. And then Charlie. He had graduated less than a year earlier and now he was being tasked with preserving our freedom by going to war in Afghanistan. Eddie certainly wasn't ready to do that. Was Charlie any more up to the task? Who knew? When do you ever know if you're battle-tested enough to face live bullets and dodge IED's? On the other hand, the enemy you're going to be fighting will use "baby faced" in a whole different manner. Little kids, seven, eight, nine years of age were going to be your enemy.

Now that Charlie's deployment day was here Rod was having some real issues in processing the future. His gut was turning flapjacks. Was he proud of his son Charlie? No doubt. Was he scared out of his mind over what could happen? Of course. Did he have any control over any of it? No. So what was he and the rest of his family going to do for the next nine months? Not worry? Of course not. He wasn't sure where he'd heard it but he recalled a soldier being interviewed in an article about his service time. "Was God and Country the two things that kept you going?", he was asked. "Sir, it was neither. I wanted to be able to look at myself in the mirror when it was all over and done with." What a profound thought Rod had at the time. That's what he planned on carrying with him through this W. A. R. His hope was for Charlie to be able to see the reflection in the mirror and like what he saw in return. God would be there to help. And maybe Country.

Hope had a much better handle on this thing than Rod did. Or at least he thought she did. Her most important words had come the day she had told her husband that Charlie would be her son no matter what he had to do or had to see. Rod replayed that message so many times in his head he could almost see a banner blowing across his forehead saying "You'll always be my son". The words were worth replaying.

Rod envisioned what the scene in Bangor, Maine was like. Hundreds of soldiers were calling home to say their goodbyes. Emotions were no doubt choked back by most of the deployables. Somewhere there would have to be some tears shed. How could there not be? Charlie's tone had been flat. Guarded. But somewhere was laying the excitement Charlie had desired since he first thought of being a soldier. Perhaps his demeanor had much to do with helping his family make it through the day. Maybe.

Rod looked into the backseat and gave a smile to his bride. He wondered what she might be pondering. More than likely her thoughts were much different than his. Mothers have a way of doing that. Putting moments into a proper perspective. Hope's return grin helped Rod at least momentarily. Eddie on the other hand was struggling with Charlie's news. Eddie had been motivated to get through Basic primarily because of Charlie.

Now his brother was going halfway across the world. The small tear that was streaming down the left side of his face spoke volumes. Not only for his feelings for Charlie but for the state most of the Martin's found themselves in right now. Dan was still trying to process the moment since he was the last one to talk. His goodbye, "Love you bro", was all he could force himself to utter. He quickly put the phone down as if it was a hot potato.

Hope interrupted the moment. "Guys we need to say a prayer for your brother," she offered. "I'll start and if you have anything to add, feel free. Ten minutes later the Martin's finished their private time. They'd asked God for protection, safety, and wisdom in their son and brother that was now going to fight in Afghanistan. Each had their own take on what was to lie ahead. What they all hoped for in a final outcome was the same. A safe return for Charlie.

CHAPTER 29

"We need to get our mind off things", said Dan. "Let's go get a bite to eat and figure out what we're going to do with the rest of the day." Hope was grateful for her youngest showing the way. The comment was well received because ten minutes later the clan pulled into the parking lot of Mark's Feed Store in Elizabethtown. The minute they hit the doorway it was apparent they'd made the right decision. The smell of barbecue was hanging in the air. It was going to be a tough decision. Brisket. Baby Back Ribs. Wings or Sliders. Or maybe even Sweet Corn on the Cob or Baked Apples. As the four made their way to the counter they were greeted by a rather short, rotund woman. Her name tag said Tina. "Afternoon. What can I get you today?", she asked. Ms. Tina was a perfect fit as a greeter and order taker. Her smiley face and mound of curly black hair gave her a doll-like appearance. The more Tina explained the menu the more it was apparent she could likely hold her own not only at work but perhaps at a side job. One had to wonder if she moonlighted as a bouncer at a local bar. She gave the meal commands on each order to the kitchen with colorful language. Not in sailor talk but darn close. Dan and Rod ordered the Bone Baby Backed Ribs. Eddie and Hope did the Brisket Basket. Everybody stayed away from any alcohol which was probably a good thing considering the time of day. The grub hit the spot. At least for now the hunger pangs subsided. Eddie was the first to speak as he wiped the sauce off his lips. "Thanks you guys for coming down for graduation", he began. "It sure is good seeing you again. It seems like I've been gone a lot longer than ten weeks." They all shook their head in agreement. "There were times I wasn't sure if I was going to make it", he continued.

As Private Martin was relaying some of the stories of Basic to Rod and Dan, Hope was trying to figure out a way to get the focus back on Eddie for the day. After all, this was to be a day of celebration. And not a wake for Charlie. It was the young man's 19th birthday. "We didn't bring you a present", mentioned Hope. "We knew there might be a need that you have as you head to AIT. Is there something you'd like"? A big smile came to Eddie's face. "Oh, yeah", he said looking at the beat up phone in front of him. "My cell is a piece of crap. I need a new one. I'd like to go to the T-Mobile store and see what they have."

An hour later Eddie was signing his name to the purchase of a new HTC HD2 cellphone. It had all the new bells and whistles. Probably more than he'd ever need. But he got what he wanted. And it was his day. The minute they hit the truck Eddie was fast at work in the back seat figuring out his new toy. Brother Dan was equally thrilled with the purchase. More than likely he just added that to his short term bucket list. As the Martins headed back to the hotel for a little relaxation, Rod turned on the radio. It was the top of the hour and the Big Cat 105.5 FM was providing some of the top news of the day. One item in particular got everybody's attention as the announcer read from his script, "The New York Times reports the Obama administration plans to ask Congress next year to approve legislation that requires phone and broadband carriers to ensure that their networks can be wiretapped by the government." "Oh, no", everybody yelled in unison.

The day had turned into one for recalculating. The Martins had planned one course of action for the day and seen their plans changed. It was like the GPS lady was at work. First was Charlie's call of his quick departure. Then finding out cellphones might have some potential new regulations. Recalculating. It would be the life the Martins would be experiencing first-hand in the coming months. No one set plan was a certainty. There had to be a back-up plan and a back-up to that back-up to be safe.

A half an hour later the mentally worn out group flopped on the two beds and the couch in the hotel room. It would have been heaven for them to have taken a nap, but there was way too much emotion to wind down for that luxury. The conversation continued concerning Eddie's last ten weeks and what he came away with. "Dad, I heard something this past week that really helped me put things into perspective", Eddie prompted. "One of my sergeant's said, the two most important days of your life, are the day you were born and the day you found out why. He said it was an old Mark Twain quote. I've thought a lot about that statement. Finding out my "why" is going to be my focus." "Son, that's awesome", Rod suggested. "There are too many adults who are still trying to figure that out. "You'll be light years ahead of them if you do."

Rod stole a glance at his wife who was resting on the sunken queen-sized bed. She'd fluffed the pillows all around her head providing as much comfort as possible. For the moment she was at peace. Rod returned his attention to his sons who were doing some more bantering. There was a considerable amount of "are you kidding" going on. "Or, I don't believe that." Eddie had seen a lot. While Rod was appreciating their conversation it struck him how much Eddie truly had changed. He seemed so much more confident and assured. "Dad, remember the day we were sitting in Major Jenkins office?", asked Eddie. "And me trying to decide if I wanted to do this army thing. I can't believe I actually went through with this. But I did. The Major spent a whole lot of time with me that day. I'll never be able to repay him." Rod slowly nodded in agreement. Somewhere in the back of Rod's mind he could see a smiling Major Fritz Jenkins. "Oh, I'm sure he knows son", fired Rod. "I'm sure you weren't the first soldier that had cold feet. And I'm equally sure you won't be the last. That's just the way life is."

Eddie looked at brother Dan and turned serious. "Dude, I thought about our growing up laying on my bunk at night. Like some of the stupid things we did", he uttered. "More than once I replayed the day you ran through the burn pit. I should never have let you try to run through the coals before I did. I can't believe how mean that was. I want you to know how sorry I am I told you it was alright. You were too young to know any better." What the two were yakking about was the morning accident that had taken place several years ago after a big bonfire in the Martin's back yard the night before. It had rained the previous night and the two youngins were up to their usual shenanigans. The burn pit was the choice of the day. Eddie ran through the area with his shoes on and Dan followed. There was no problem. So Eddie suggested they take off their shoes and run back the other way....Dan going first. Being the obedient little brother he agreed. The second he hit the coals there came a blood curdling scream. Dan's little feet felt the brunt of the mistake. Even though a rain had soaked the area the coals were still hot underneath the gray covering. Eddie could still hear the shrieking noise from twelve years ago. It had been imbedded in his head ever since. Eddie could also recall the days in the hospital Dan had to undergo treatment for second and third degree burns. The scraping of skin off the bottoms of his little wheels also didn't come without pain and suffering. Time did heal all wounds in this case. But had there been an apology handed out? Not really. So the grown up Eddie was asking for forgiveness. "Bro", said Dan. "Don't worry about it. If I was you I would have done the same thing", laughed Dan. The morale of the story. Don't listen to your brother.

During the next hour, Eddie and Dan continued their catching up. Dan said something Eddie disagreed with so he returned the favor with a whipping move with his right hand. The action had been defined by older brother Charlie several years ago. Charlie would shake his hand back and forth with his fingers slapping against themselves. It was a nasty response and one the other two boyz had picked up on. After all, a person had to defend themselves. The boyz had many battles over the past couple of years and "whipping" was always a part of it. "Doggone it", fired Dan. "I wasn't expecting that. Now you're going to get some of your own medicine." The two went at it for a couple of minutes. Until they woke their mother.

Hope opened her eyes and caught a moment or two between her two sons. Even though it was horseplay, it was a great bonding moment. It was a Candid Camera moment for sure. Sadly, they didn't have a camera with them. Just a darn expensive cell phone. And that was on the charger. Hope stirred on the bed and Eddie and Dan shot a look. All it took was one glance from mom and order was restored. Mothers have a way of righting a ship gone off course. Rod smirked and followed up. "Okay, guys. Time to hit the road", he suggested. "Let's do some sightseeing."

But before they began their exploring, Hope had something up her sleeve. When they reached the truck, she grabbed a pair of combat boots and an 8 X 10 of a soldier out of the back seat. Not a picture of any soldier. Her son. If Charlie couldn't be there in the flesh than he could in another way, she thought. Hope arranged the boots near the glossy and asked her young men to take some pictures of the image. And what a lasting impression it was. In many ways it put a capper on the military day.

When the Martins left the hotel area Dan was behind the wheel. Rod was shot gun and Eddie and Hope were in the back seat talking away. Dan was focused on navigating his way for the 40 minute trip to the American Cave Museum and Hidden River Cave in Horse Cave. The group was anxious to see what the website had said was "the greatest cave restoration success story in the United Sates". Rod was staring off to the clouds. Deep in thought. He suddenly glanced to his right and saw and old couple making their way down the sidewalk. The man was in a red motorized wheel chair with an American flag on the back and the hunched over woman was bringing up the rear some fifteen feet behind. The image was so sad Rod thought. Who knows where they were headed? The old guy wasn't tremendously considerate of his mate that's for sure. She seemed resigned to the fact of playing catch up. Where was their Hope?, Rod thought. Rod continued with his thinking. Do they have any Hope? They must have. Wouldn't they?? Age doesn't have any limits on hoping. There was that word again. Hope. It was a four letter word Rod had been thinking a lot about lately. He glanced one more time at the couple to make sure they weren't lost. Appearances can be misleading Rod surmised, but they at least looked like they had a route down and were on the return part of their excursion. Rod's face showed more concentration as he returned his thoughts to that word. He was in a hoping world right now. He hoped Charlie would be safe in Afghanistan. He hoped Eddie would complete his AIT and be home shortly after the first of the year. He hoped Hope and Dan and he could make it through the next months without any major issues. The longer he thought about it he came to the conclusion that he was hoping for a lot. Maybe more than he had a right to. On the other hand who's to say how much hope a person should or could have? No one. He was going to use hope. Let anyone or anything try and take that away from him.

Charlie's boots in down time

CHAPTER 30

The day had flown by. It was time to get Eddie back to the Fort. There had been an ultimatum from his sergeant when they'd left in the afternoon that Private Martin had to be back by 8 p.m. or else. Eddie didn't want to find out what "or else" meant. The goodbyes weren't as difficult as they were ten weeks previous. In a little over a month, Eddie would be home for Thanksgiving. Still it was hard for the four to part ways. Especially for the soldier. Eddie had always been a deep hearted individual who had anxiety issues when goodbyes were involved. There were individual embraces and one final group hug. As Private Martin walked through the gate he reentered military life where he would have to have a change of mind. Things were expected of him. No excuses. In about seven hours he would be on his way to AIT with some 50 other soldiers on a Greyhound bus. Their destination was the Aberdeen Proving Ground in Maryland.

As Dan, Hope and Rod were headed back to the hotel they drove by the eerie looking United States Bullion Depository. It was nightfall and the lights shining on the fortified building gave the distinct impression of a Federal Prison. Rod had a single thought. One most likely everyone had driving by the building. If he could have just a sliver of what's in that place he'd be rich and not have a worry in the world. Rod asked Dan to slow down as they were just about in line with the building. He wanted to take a long look. Maybe the last time he'd ever see the place again. He wanted to go deep in his thoughts and the additional time would no doubt assist his thinking. "With a little help maybe I could break into that fortress", Rod surmised. "Yeah and if I ever got in, I'd never get back out". He chuckled to himself. He must be nuts. Why would he ever think about such a risk? What would be the odds he could pull off such a stunt? Then again, he thought, what were the odds he'd have a son graduate from Basic on a particular day while the other one was flying across the United States and deploying to Afghanistan. Hell, he might have better luck winning the lottery. The only problem with that was, he didn't play. So that wasn't going to happen.

As Dan continued on the road to the hotel, Rod thought about the drive down from Iowa. He'd been fascinated by the number of horse farms they'd seen when they hit the Kentucky line on Wednesday. He reckoned it no doubt took a whole bundle of money to stay in the horse business. The countryside was carpeted in green. Field after field was rich with a splendor color green he had never seen before. The old saying, the grass is always greener on the other side of the fence sure applied here. People had to be rich to be a part of the horse industry. He'd never be that wealthy. The longer he dwelled on that thought he came to a bigger revelation. Sure, he might not ever be financially secure but he had riches in other areas. He had a beautiful wife. Three pretty awesome sons. And a relationship that was growing with the Lord. He let his body sink into the leather seat of the SUV and listened to the hum of the 403 horsepower engine. After listening to that melodic tune for a couple of minutes he swore he could hear the words. Dad I love you. And then a second time. The noise sent shivers up and down his spine.

CHAPTER 31

Rod had heard the darn sounds for the last ten minutes. He'd tried every-thing to shut the noises out. He folded the pillow over his head, tried bury-ing his noggin under the covers and then he performed a maneuver he hoped would end it all. He shut the window. He looked at the clock. It returned a dirty glance with the time. 4:10 a.m. "Frickin birds" he mut-tered. "Why can't you go bother someone else? "Didn't either one of you guys hear that?" His question fell on deaf ears. Hope was deep into a REM sleep with an ever so slight snore. She was clueless as to what was going on. When he looked over at the other queen bed, Dan was fast asleep as well.

Rod had enjoyed a fairly restful sleep. That is until Birdland came to life. It wasn't just one bird either. He'd heard a whistle, a twitter, a tweet and a shriek. Those were the sounds of the morning. If he'd had a gun he might have taken matters into his own hands. It's not that he didn't like birds. He did. Just not at 4 a.m. He learned minutes later when he googled "birds" what their singing meant. He found out that the cacophony of birdsong in the morning is typical. It's called dawn chorus. And the reason they're at work so early in the morning is that sounds were much clearer and concise in the morning hours. And it's thought that the better you can sing during the most challenging time of the day, the better mate and more challenging competitor you will be. Lastly, birds seem to like to be up before the crack of dawn. Maybe the early bird does get the worm.

Now that he was wide awake what was he going to do? If he went to the hotel lobby at 4:30 in the morning the clerk would most likely think he was some kind of pervert. He could do without that. He looked over at his Bible which hadn't been opened the past two days. It was resting near the TV. It would have been easier and not have required as much brain power to turn on the tube and vegetate. A little voice convicted him that he needed to get into the Word instead. There had been a whole lot taking place in the past days.

Rod hunkered down in the corner of the hotel room. The bronze armed floor lamp put out a direct shot of light on his lap. He was reading in 1st Samuel trying to get a better understanding of David and his relationship with God. One verse in particular struck a note. It was Verse 6 in Chapter 30. "David was now in great danger because all his men were very bitter about losing their sons and daughters, and they began to talk of stoning him. But David found strength in the LORD his God". "Wow", Rod said to himself. "How personal and powerful is that?" But what exactly did that mean? Rod grabbed his laptop and pounded out the verse on his keyboard. The information he got by digging deeper provided him with a very thorough understanding. First off, finding strength in the Lord is what we all need in both good times and bad. David knew the answers to any of his questions were readily available. All he had to do was seek God's voice. Rod stopped his search on the internet to ponder his situation. He raised the ballpoint pen to his mouth and struck a pensive pose. He was in deep thought. The longer he sat there the clearer things became. Most importantly, he realized the time he spent with God was fundamental to his life. Over the years he had had difficulty in finding time with the Lord daily. There was always time for something else. Sports, movies, reading a book. Just about anything else other than reading the Word. That might be the biggest negative most of the Christians in this world have. Finding time for God.

The time was fast approaching 6 a.m. The noise outside from Rod's birdies had subsided. He was going to take a little more time to reflect on the family situation as he hit the shower. Eddie was already on the road to Maryland on the Greyhound bus. Charlie. Gosh who knew where he was. He might have made it to Bulgaria or Germany by now. Eddie was going to be safe, Charlie was about to go into the Theatre of War. That wasn't going to be safe. Far from it. He knew Charlie would be careful. One thing Charlie was, was careful. He was pretty good at sizing up a situation and knowing how to react if things got out of hand. But there was always the unexpected. In fact, nowadays, Rod started to size up situations when he went out in public. He never had his back to the front door. He knew where the exits were when he was in a building. And he was much more observant of those around him. The times were much different than when he was growing up. There were a lot of nuts in the world. And Charlie was going to be with some of the nuttiest.

Rod got out of the shower and began toweling off. As he peered into the mirror running full length across the countertop he let his eyes come to a stop. He was looking at a 58-year old face. At least that's what his driver's license said. But he looked nowhere near that. How old did he look? Heck, he didn't know. He just knew that most people he ran across had a hard time believing his age. And that was fine. This next year might very well change his entire appearance.

There was some noise on the other side of the bathroom door. He figured someone had to be thinking of getting up. The Martins had a long drive back to Iowa and the earlier they hit the road the better. When he came out of the bathroom he was shocked to see both Dan and Hope sitting on their respective beds. Their look said everything that needed to be said. That and the tear streams down the sides of both of their cheeks. "Gonna be a hard time Dad", said Hope. Rod slowly shook his head in agreement. "And to think some people would try and go through this without God.

I saw you did some reading in the Bible early this morning. I need to do the same. I think once we hit the road I'm going to find some quiet time", she offered.

Dan wiped off the moisture from his face and rolled out of bed and headed to the bathroom. He figured the day wouldn't get any easier the longer they sat and talked. Pretty good observation from the youngster. In the next half an hour they were all showered, packed and Hope was putting on the finishing touches of her makeup. Rod had been motoring back and forth to the truck dropping off papers, food, books, clothes and bags. The truck was nearly loaded down. Hope put on a final dab of lipstick and turned to face her men. "Okay", she said. "Let's get a move on."

As the three left the hotel lobby they had grabbed some coffee, muffins and a couple of apples. The eight and a half hour drive back to Des Moines was going to be a long one. They figured an arrival time of about 5 p.m. It was amazing to think about the travels of the Martin family in the last 24 hours. First, Charlie flies across the United States from California to Maine. Refuels and then heads to the either Europe or the Middle East. Eddie was at Fort Knox this morning and now he was on his way to Maryland. And the final three….In Kentucky, on their way to Iowa. The great thing nowadays is the ability to keep in touch with someone. If it wasn't via cellphone, you could text, Facebook or Skype. Technology was going be used a whole bunch. It was going to be the Martin's lifeline.

Rod looked at his youngest son behind the steering wheel. He was growing up all too quick. And he was going to be doing even more of it without any of his brothers around. Again. Dan knew Eddie would be home for Thanksgiving in a couple of weeks but Charlie was a different story. "Home, James", he stated. "Oops. Sorry. Home son."

CHAPTER 32

It was an interesting ride back from Kentucky to Des Moines. An old college friend of Rod's, Jay Townsend, had put together a couple of CD's of great tunes from the 70's and 80's. Listening to the oldies made the trip seem to go quicker. There had been one hit after another from bands like Crosby, Stills and Nash, Alan Parsons Project and Cat Stevens. Hope and Rod were on a virtual musical tour. Dan was able to appreciate some music he'd never heard before. He came away impressed. Maybe his parents weren't so dumb after all. At least when it came to the music thing. Other things he would have to think a little harder about. Parents are parents for a reason, he thought.

The truck finally came to a rest in the driveway of the Martin's Johnston home. After all the luggage had been unloaded things were tidied up inside the vehicle and everybody went their own way. Dan went to his bedroom and collapsed on the unmade bed. Hope was in the kitchen doing some putzing. Dinner time was just around the corner and everybody no doubt was hungry. Rod took his laptop out of the case and set it up on the dining room table. He had every intention of checking his email and Facebook to see if he had any messages. First though, he needed to go pick up Mason from his foster mother, Elaine Powers. Powers loved Mason and was more than gracious in taking care of her favorite foster dog while the Martins were gone. She'd told Hope more than once she wished she had been able to keep Mace when he lived with her. He was one of a kind, she said. Everybody in the Martin family would have agreed to that line of thinking. In 2007, Hope and Rod had both seen the big dog's picture on the Iowa Golden Retriever Rescue Group website. Strange enough, they saw him on the same day. Maybe the same hour. There had been a fun-loving argument as to who actually saw him first. Rod had been in northwest Iowa on business and Hope was at home. They both agreed he was way too good looking of a Golden to pass up. So it wasn't a hard decision for them to reach. They'd put down their first Golden, Nala just two months previous due to cancer. They had told each other it was going to take a while to get over Nala. So much for planning. Hope made a call to Ms. Powers and the ball was in motion. All agreed to having Mason do a sleep-over at the Martins to see how he could handle the clan. He never went home. He was their Valentine's Day present in 2007….the best kind of gift. Even despite tripping Hope three months later and breaking her ankle he was a welcome addition. Somehow, someway the big lug overcame the ankle incident with Hope and won her over. He had several names but Mace, Macey and Moose seemed to stick. When Rod rolled up to Elaine's house, Mason was staring out the window…. more than ready to go home. Not that he didn't enjoy his time with his former foster mother but he had a cat or two to pester. And seeing his family again certainly would have its rewards. They had a bunch of making up to do and he was going to take full advantage of it. Dog's life ya know. Minutes later after saying thank you, Rod and his buddy jumped in the truck to head home. When they hit the doorway at the house Mace was in pure form. He played it as cool as a cucumber. Kind of like, hey great to see you, but where's my treat. Spoil me would you.

The Golden Jet…..Mason

Rod settled in at the table which was full of notes from the trip. Some were ideas for the new blog and others were from things and places on the recent trip. He lifted the lid on his laptop and punched in Facebook. He was startled to see a message from Charlie. "Guys, guys come here quick", Rod yelled. "I got a message from Charlie on Facebook." You'd never seen two people move so quickly as they joined Rod at the laptop screen. They read in unison.

> **"Hey dadpo and family!!!! i just got to manas airforce base which is just outside of Afghanistan. we will be here for the next few days until we get a military plane to take us to afghanistan and right now this is all i have for communication. anyways we stopped in sofia, bulgaria after Maine and that place is pretty crappy and the whole trip took 23 hrs! anyways its 2am here and im pretty tired but id figure id let you guys kno im ok and ill periodically be checking my Facebook for messages and what not. anyways i love all you guys!!! -charlie"**

The message had been short and to the point. Sentence structure and spelling was something an English teacher would cringe at. But the words were received loud and clear. Charlie made it across the ocean and he was safe. At least for now. They couldn't have asked for much more. God that felt good, they all agreed.

So, for now, it was back to the three of them. After a pretty hearty chili dinner Dan headed out to hook up with some friends. Rod snuck down in the basement to watch the World Series game between the Texas Rangers and San Francisco Giants. Hope was on the first floor motoring back and forth between the kitchen and living room. Finally she settled in the overstuffed chair with a soothing cup of hot tea. She hadn't been able to relax like this for several days. She swept the several blonde locks that had fallen across her eyes. She focused on the Facebook message from Charlie. She read it. And then read it a second and a third time. This would be the first of many communications they would have with their oldest son, she hoped. Would the next message be his last? You never knew. Hope was holding onto hope as big as she could praying that wouldn't be the case. Now was not a time to focus on that though. She had a song running through her mind she couldn't shake. It was by Mercy Me. Hope was having trouble remembering all the words but as she sang the song slowly they fell in line.

> **"I can only imagine what it will be like**
> **When I walk, by your side**
> **I can only imagine what my eyes will see**
> **When your face is before me**
> **I can only imagine**
> **I can only imagine**
> **Surrounded by your glory**
> **What will my heart feel**
> **Will I dance for you Jesus**
> **Or in awe of You be still**
> **Will I stand in your presence**
> **Or to my knees will I fall**

CHAPTER 33

The Martin's spent the next two days trying to refuel their engines. The mid-week excursion had taken a lot out of all three of them. Church had been a saving grace on Sunday. It had been good to get back among a group of believers. Rod's letter to the Editor appeared in the Sunday Des Moines Register. He'd already gotten numerous phone calls from people who were moved by the message of the letter. So, what was next?

Rod was sitting at the dining room table staring at the HP laptop. Okay. You've got a forum now big guy, he thought. Start writing something. He looked at the blank page of his site, my-fathersvoice.blogspot.com. Somehow he needed to fill up the space. Wax poetically. There was already his letter to the editor on the site and a post of what the site was all about. It was time for real context. The official number one post came to look like this. The story recapped many of the Martin's experiences in recent days but this time it was for an audience.

JUST HOW LONG IS THE ROAD AHEAD FOR THE SOLDIERS AND FAMILIES AND FRIENDS OF THE IOWA DEPLOYED?

Well, that's a great question. With no easy answer. How could there be? You can't take 4,000 Soldiers, representing the largest Iowa troop deployment since World War II.....assign them to various different regions of Afghanistan and expect the experiences to be the same. And then there is our diversity. So many of those affected are from different walks of life. I don't even have to go into the many ways that we're different. We just are. Yet through this, we are all part of a team, much like our soldiers came to realize back in Basic Training days.

Let me go back to last week if I may. My wife, Hope, and youngest son, Dan, and I traveled to Fort Knox, Kentucky to attend Basic graduation of our middle son, Eddie. It was a glorious day to see Eddie complete his training. The day was full of irony both in celebration and sadness. Coupled with this great, great day for one son, was also a completely different feeling for another. At the very time Eddie was receiving his "soldierization", our oldest son, Charlie was aloft in the jet streams. His destination was a refueling stop in the States, followed by departure for somewhere near Afghanistan.. The entire family knew the door was quickly closing. Charlie's last phone call to us was a signal that he'd be .....Gone. Just like that. And more than likely headed for some lengthy blackout time (a time when there is no contact from a soldier to family or friends). Where was he headed? "Really no idea, dad", he said. He mentioned some mid-point stops, but those were all just guesses. The day had come for Charlie to leave. This after a slew of texts, emails, phone calls and Facebook posts in the preceding weeks. The general nature of those contacts were love, pride, staying safe and keeping God close. And they weren't always in that order. When the last call came from Charlie to say that the plane was refueled and they were just about to take off we were driving around Fort Knox seeing where Eddie had his 10-week Basic experience. So Charlie is on the phone talking departure and Eddie is giving directions to where to go next at the Fort. Can you picture the scene? Four people in a truck and everyone is trying to talk. Somehow we muddled through each one of us took our turn to say a final goodbye. At the other end of the cell-phone, was a young man taking the biggest step of his young life down the biggest road imaginable.

I'm sure we didn't do the setting justice. Way too many interferences. Which is pretty common for most of us anymore. I wonder what Charlie thought as he boarded that plane. Did he feel that emotionally we let him down? I know we didn't hit a homerun that day. We didn't drive the ball out of the park with one specific comment that he'd take with him. However, I think if you were to ask any of us in the truck that day...we hit alot of singles in the previous weeks. We told him we loved him, over, and over and over again. We might have even discovered some new way to say it without saying it.

Later on that day, Eddie took us to a set of hills used by his company for training purposes. Here recruits "honed" their marching and endurance skills. To hear him tell of the hill climbs with nearly 100 pounds of pack, body armor, rifle, helmet, boots and uniform affixed to their body was jaw-dropping. 100 pounds! Imagine two lines of 120 members of Delta Company trudging up aptly named hills in single file. It was truly a test, one they made on a 95 degree August day. "Left, left, left, right, left, here we go again. Same old stuff again", they shouted. Over and over again up that mile long incline. Each of the hills had their uniqueness, not only in name, but in their difficulty. The first was named Agony. There echoed the voices of thousands of wannabe soldiers who had marched that road. You could sense what had taken place here. You could visualize the sweat, the anger, the disappointment and the longing for a day when this hill was in the past. I'm sure there was every type of motivation used to endure this physical torture. Eddie told us he used to look at the boots ahead of him and visualize his older brother setting the pace for him. One step at a time...up the hill and to the top. That got him through it all.

The next day on our trip back to Johnston, Iowa I was looking at my Bible for something that God could teach me that would put much of this Kentucky experience into perspective. And here is what jumped out at me. "Agony is waiting". I know it's in Ecclesiastes as I write this, but I can't find where. I just know it's there. "Agony is waiting." I'm sure many soldiers can relate to that as they think back to Fort Knox or the various other Forts around the country that serve as Training Centers. These hills serve a purpose. It's where the transformation takes place from civilian to solider, irresponsible to responsible, lacking in respect to respect and so on. At the same time, every soldier came to realize that "waiting is agony", too. Waiting and counting the days until they'd be done with Basic. 45. 44. 32. 22 and right down the line to the day they'd graduate and say, good riddance to Basic. I think back to the three hills on the Kentucky base and the significance they have. You've already met Agony. Then there is Misery. Like in Misery is waiting...... and Waiting is Misery. And then the biggest of all, Heartbreak. Heartbreak is waiting....and in waiting there is Heartbreak.

So have I answered the question of what lies ahead? Somewhat. We all want to see what's at the top of the hill or around the bend. We want to be able to see what the future holds. We don't want any agony, misery or heartbreak. Joy, peace and love sounds so much better. For the 4,000 plus spouses, the 5,000 Iowa school children and the countless number of families and friends who are affected by this Guard Deployment, the next nine months will be chalk full of uncertainties. But in the waiting and the Agony.....the Misery....and Heartbreak there is also HOPE. Yes, at the hilltop and around the bend, is Hope. A little four letter word that can move mountains...and hills and roads, even the LONG ROADS. And it won't end there.

YGG,

Rod

CHAPTER 34

It had been days since Rod had posted his first official blog entry. It wasn't that he didn't have another story to tell. He simply wanted to ponder the past weeks and reaffirm why he decided to become a blogger in the first place. As he reflected on the past he came away with one big realization. A regret. Isn't it something, he thought, how we humans are wired? If something doesn't go according to form we say, that was interesting, or amazing, maybe sad or unfortunate. None of those words actually tell the whole truth. The empty feeling Rod was now experiencing had to do with his relationship with Charlie. It wasn't where it needed to be. Weeks before Charlie deployed there had been an argument in the Martin's garage. Charlie had blown his dad off regarding some responsibilities he felt he needed to attend to. It was apparent Charlie wasn't listening. That had upset Rod. Charlie continued with his indifference and the pot boiled over. The two got into a wrestling match where Rod surprised his son with a leg trip which took them both to the garage floor. If Dan and Eddie hadn't been present who knows if any punches would have been landed. Anyway, Rod was embarrassed the incident had happened. It had put a wedge between the two of them. And to make matters worse, it was never resolved before deployment. Sorry seems to be the hardest word to say and neither one had. Thus the dilemma. Now with thousands of miles between them how can fences be mended? Rod was going to have to think further on the issue but one thing he knew for certain. He would tell Charlie each and every time he talked to him that he loved him. He wouldn't regret saying that. That's for sure.

Why are our lives so full of regrets?, Rod wondered. He could think of a whole heck of a lot more in his life. But to him family was important. The most important. Rod had seen a recent study on the matter that revealed the top six regrets fell into the following areas: education, career, romance, parenting, self-improvement and leisure. "I wonder if Adam had any regrets", he thought. How much different would this world be if he hadn't eaten that darn fruit? But then again, without that taking place would we have free will? Of course not. God gives us all choices and we all have fallen short.

Rod glanced up from his laptop and noticed Mason laying in front of the television. He was no doubt in dream mode chasing a rabbit or squirrel because his back legs were kicking up a storm. Poor Dog, Rod thought with a smile on his face. What a life! The smile continued as he thought of the real reason he had decided to jump into blog world. First off, there were going to be a lot of stories during the nine month deployment. Some heroic and others tragic. Rod had surmised he could pass along some of those events to help support a cause or to educate people who had no idea of how deep deployment affected friends and family. There would be off beat stories to tell too. Rod looked back down at Mason who had now settled his race fortunes. Either he caught his prey or they got away. Mason would most likely never tell. Then, bam. Mr. Golden sprang to attention and stared at the world box. A little wiener dog was doing some tricks on the NBA station and Mason was totally immersed. What he was watching was a walk back in time of Tiny BB, the mascot of the Washington Bullets back in the mid 1970's. Rod had never seen his pooch so intent on something on the TV screen. Clearly, the little one had grabbed Mason's attention. The announcer went in-depth on the history of the little bullet who had become a star during the 1975 season. During timeouts he would chase balls around the court wearing a little game suit. Tiny BB was listed in the Bullets media guide as follows: "Name: Tiny BB Height: 7 inches Length: 20 inches Weight: 20 pounds College: DePaw. The descriptor read: "I am a basketball star. I've been on national TV many times. I get lots of fan mail from all over the country. Like all basketball stars, I have a routine on game days. I have my pre-game meal at 2 p.m. Then I jog a little bit. When I get to the stadium, I work out some more. Tiny B-B traveled with the Bullets to Seattle for the 1978 NBA Finals and accompanied Washington's championship team to the White House, where he was the first to greet the president. Poor dog....

Mason continued to stare at the screen for a few more minutes after the piece aired. Like he wanted more. Little did he know, there would be more stories coming regarding war dogs, those four-legged heroes in our military. The Tiny BB vignette only served as an appetizer. Rod got up and went over to his buddy. He patted his head and informed Mason he should keep watching and waiting.

Bottom-line Rod decided the blogging thing was a means to educate the masses. And himself. There would be good things he'd come across. As well as some that would most likely leave him shaking his head. Still he would feel a need to report it. So, yes. Timing is everything. And now was the time for Rod to step up and be a mouthpiece. And he embraced that idea.

Several of the Martins friends had suggested to Rod that he write a book about the Martins experiences. "Good, golly, no to that", he'd say. "I can write a whole bunch of articles, but I've never aspired to write a book. That seems like a whole lot of work and I'm not sure I'd have the endurance to run that race." What Rod was most moved to do in his writing was to take the situations he encountered and tell them as truthfully and as factually as he could. There would be no need to report Fake News. Not in his blog anyway. Someone else could do that. So with that in mind, here was Rod's next blog post.

A SEED PLANTER

I have a new job, one that excites the stuffing out of me. It doesn't come with an office, doesn't have any big title and the money is lousy. But that's alright. You see, I'm the new Seed Planter in town.

I've been so many other things over the years. Doing this to get that. But always in ways that could benefit me, my family or our future. And that's come with mixed results. I've done some neat things (taken each of my children to a professional sporting event and gotten them on the sidelines)...... met some interesting people (Paul Harvey, Gerald Ford, Shawn Johnson, Mike Ditka and Ed Thomas).....and traveled to some nice places (Jamaica and Soviet Union). In every instance, it was about me. Soaking up the moment, somewhat prideful me. But I've changed. I've changed because it's time to.

Let me tell you a story. About a little boy named Jake. That's what he's remembered by, Jake. No last name is needed. Jake contracted encephalitis and died several years ago, tragically . He started feeling punky one day, lethargic, then began running a fever. No one knew what was happening. Doctors were stumped. His parents became frantic. He got sicker and sicker...until he passed away in his mother's arms. In a span of 72 hours, Jake went from a healthy, bouncing, fun-loving boy....to the end of life.

His mother, wrote a letter several days after he passed and thanked everyone for their support. The letter was written so eloquently. It described so much in a short amount of space, but it hit home. It told of their family's knowledge that Jake was their "gift" and that even though they selfishly wanted him longer, they knew God had a plan. I'm sure Jake's mother had help in writing that letter. How could she not? And I don't mean the help came from anyone here on earth. I couldn't imagine losing a child, let alone putting my thoughts down on paper so soon after burying him.

I tell you about Jake because his name lives on. Each Holy Spirit Retreat at Hope's Alpha class in West Des Moines, Iowa, this story is told. That's the effect little Jake has. Yes, his name lives on, and on, and on. He is impacting lives because of his death.

Several months ago, over 4,000 Iowa soldiers began their deployment to Afghanistan. The send-offs were magnificent. They captured the essence of the day. The pride, the dedication and the duty. Every location defined patriotism. It was a feel good moment, at least up until the time the busses left the parking lot. Then the worries set in. The next nine months are going to be difficult times. Where will the strength come from to endure? How will family and friends cope?

Yes, this important time dictates some important measures. I certainly feel that prayer is at the head of that list. Anything else comes in a distant second. We need to pray for these 4,000. Pray anything you can for them. For their families, their strength....and foremost, their safety. Pray, pray, pray. Our state could use some direction and prayer too. Perhaps the way we support our troops and conduct ourselves will be a carbon copy other states adopt. A road sign on the outskirts of Des Moines says it all. "Prayer Changes Everything."

If, and I said, if,...... not when, one of the 4,000 Iowa Soldiers is killed in action, how will they be remembered? Will it be through a series of features on the TV or radio......an article in the newspaper? How will that person, the one fighting for your "freedom" be recollected?

I am not underscoring all of the memorials that honor our troops who have served before. They say A LOT. Their mere presence renders strong men speechless, who become caught in the moment of their days of service. What am I suggesting?

I just think something in addition to those tributes is called for. Any person that lays down their life needs to be remembered just like little Jake. We have a duty and a responsibility in prolonging the legacy of those that serve. I DO know that if one soldier from our state is killed in action that I will be at their funeral. I have to. Will you? Then what next? I'm praying for an answer. I keep seeing BOLD, BE BOLD. Some of you will be able to see more to this story. Read it again, and again, if you must. You'll see much more....and that will prompt you to do more. Here is a prayer taken from Daily Guideposts, "the Daily Inspiration for Our Military Families" for November 1st. It says BOLD. "Faithful Lord, send me a Saint today to shine your light on my path. And let me be a Saint where another needs it."

I hope this moves you to think about our Soldiers, especially with Veterans Day coming upon us. I hope it hits you upside the head. Yes, I'm seed planting here. That's my new job and I love it. God help it grow.

YGG,

Rod

As Rod put the finishing touches on the article he had no regrets as to what he'd said. He wanted to say it loud and clear. Our troops needed support and they were going to need it each and every day they were in Afghanistan. He couldn't help but recall an old TV show, "The Naked City", which had a simple but unique way of ending their broadcast. "There are 8 million stories in the naked city. This has been one of them". Rod closed the laptop and breathed a long, long sigh. The story he'd told was the first real one he'd passed along. As he reflected further, he closed his eyes and realized there would be a whole lot more. It had only been one of them.

CHAPTER 35

Eddie Martin was sitting in his room alone reflecting on the past ten weeks of Basic and a little over one week at AIT in Maryland. His eyes went back and forth across the stark surroundings. The setting was not one you'd see in Good Housekeeping he thought. No color. About as blasé as you could imagine. Still it didn't keep him from his thoughts.

He recalled his letter to his dad back in mid-September where he'd shared his impressions of Basic. "It has been going good, some of the things that I've been doing lately are shooting every day. Two days ago we had a 9K road march carrying our weapons with 70 pounds on our back and our body armor on! It was pretty tough and a lot of kids didn't finish but I pushed through the pain and made the five miles. It took us about 2 1/2 hours! I've definitely started to get the hang of things here. A lot of stuff is already muscle memory. I'm also making a lot of good friends. I have a lot of things to tell you about this place good and bad. So make sure you always have your phone on you because I could call any day at any time! So be ready for a weird prepaid phone number to call your phone. If it does, it's me. I also hear you've been sleeping in my room a lot lately. What's up with that?", he'd said.

Little did Eddie know but his bedroom was where Rod did some of his best work. It had been the scene for the letter to the editor that started the whole blog thing. Still it was a funny question coming from a young whippersnapper. The days at the Aberdeen Proving Grounds were indeed different than those at Fort Knox. What was most enjoyable was the freedom Eddie and his fellow soldiers had. On the weekend they were able to leave the post and go into town for a little enjoyment. There wasn't as much yelling and there was more of a strain on the mental rather than the physical. Eddie was receiving his training as a light wheeled vehicle mechanic. Classes by night and physical training during the day. In truth, Private Martin was counting the days. He had a little over three weeks to wait until he went home for Thanksgiving. That would be sweet. As he sat there in a hypnotic state he wondered out loud what his older brother might be doing right now. "I can't even imagine what you must be going through", he muttered. If it hadn't been for the short conversation in Kentucky while Charlie was refueling in Maine it would have been three months since they'd been able to banter back and forth. It was kind of like when Charlie had gone to Basic. He hadn't been able to talk to him for a long time there either. Silence sucks, he thought. He shook his head back and forth as if to knock some cobwebs out. What he really was shooting to do was put himself in another frame of mind. Was he depressed? Gosh, he hoped not. Eddie thought of the home front and what his Mom, Dad and younger brother must be going through. Maybe they were all feeling signs of depression. It'd be easy to think so anyway. There was a couple of sentences he remembered writing in one of his first letters home. "It's not as easy as I thought it'd be, but I'm pushing through every minute of it. I'm living one day at a time. Seems to be the easiest thing to do." It kind of felt like that all over again Eddie concluded. Hope Mom, Dad and Dan are doing the same thing.

Miles away, Charlie was facing different demons. Since he arrived in the arm pit of the Middle East he had been in full catch up mode. His group was replacing a unit, the 101st Airborne, from Kentucky whose last minute responsibilities included showing their back fills how things were done and local people they needed to communicate with. What did Charlie do?

Here was an early sample: "We took RPG (Rocket Propelled Grenade) fire that skipped past our convoy. It happened near combat outpost Najil on the west side of the river. We were heading north towards the outpost and were ambushed with machine gun fire and RPG's from across the river. We stopped and returned fire and called in mortar rounds and dropped a few 2000lb JDAM bombs from F16 fighter jets." Charlie was more than getting his feet wet. He was knee deep in the Afghanistan War. But it wasn't always apparent you were in such a state. The enemy had an unusual way of going about their assaults. Hit here, hit there. Little rhyme or reason. All part of the big game. Welcome to the theatre Charlie Martin.

Charlie had little free time to himself these days. What few moments he did get he tried to catch up on sleep. So much for that. There were times where he wondered what his family was up to. If only he knew what Eddie was planning on doing? Middle Martin as he was sometimes called had definite ideas as to what he would soon be doing when he was on leave for Thanksgiving. In the last year, Charlie had gotten a couple of tattoos. One on his left shoulder had the words "death before dishonor" and had dog tags and a cross on it. Charlie had also gotten one on his right forearm with the saying, "yea, though I walk through the valley of death I shall fear no evil." How prophetic considering his situation. Eddie was going to join the tat club while back in Des Moines. He'd made arrangements with a local parlor to have some praying hands etched on his right shoulder. Brothers in life, and brothers with tattoos. Eddie could envision his mom and dad when he told them he'd gotten the "thing" done. Rod had been critical of all the people who were now part of the craze. "After I retire", Rod had said. "I think I will open a tattoo removal parlor. By then people who thought it was so cool to have some ink on their body are going to be looking for ways to have it removed."

Rod was sitting in the Johnston Panera Bread enjoying a cup of coffee with a good church friend, Jim Hankins. They'd beaten the bushes on about anything and everything life had to offer. Jim was a character that had little in his life outside of his work as a customer service representative. He poured himself into his work. Rod was trying to convince him there were other things in life. "You know, Jim", started Rod, "you need to find something to believe in other than your work. Because when you leave this life, you leave work behind. If that's all you have, you have nothing. And eternity is a long time for nothing."

A few minutes later, the two walked out to the Panera parking lot and Rod hopped into his SUV. He sat for a minute before bringing the engine to life. He'd hoped he hadn't been too hard on Jim with his comments. But friends should be able to tell friends just about anything, right? A smile came over his face as he finished those thoughts. "Maybe I should get a tattoo", he smirked. One that says, "Eternity is a long time for nothing." On second thought. Nah. Not going there. The truck came to life with the cranking of the motor. It was 5 p.m. in Des Moines. And roughly ten hours later in Afghanistan. One's day was ending and another's was about to start. Only the Good Lord knew the outcome.

CHAPTER 36

The days had flown by. There hadn't been a whole lot of news from either Eddie or Charlie. And that was good and bad. After Charlie's early interaction with the RPG's his duties had consisted of performing missions each and every day. For now, the region was quiet. The question was....for how long. Eddie was mentally fast tracking his return home for Thanksgiving. The day was Sunday. Leaving eighteen days before he flew back to Des Moines.

Hope and Rod were in the sanctuary at the mega-church. As usual, the place was packed for the 9:15 a.m. service. One of four on the day. Some 2,500 had come to celebrate and offer praise. Some came to see the production. Whatever the reason, the numbers attending were raising each and every week. One of the young pastors on staff, Jeremy Anderson, was preaching today. Rod liked him a lot. He wasn't the main guy. But he was down to earth and was a thinking man's pastor. One piece of information Rod felt was extremely well offered was Pastor Anderson's thoughts on thankfulness for the day.

"God wants His children to thank Him and show gratitude for everything that happens in their lives. We are to thank God when we are full and when we are empty. We are to continuously show appreciation for the many things we normally take for granted. Our willingness to thank God should not be based on our mood, i.e. whether we are happy or not. It should not be based only on the things we receive and recognize as gifts and blessings; we should also thank God for the miracle of sleeping and waking up, for the gift of life, for the salvation of our souls and for divine health. Thank God for the ability to use every part of your body; that you can eat, drink, see, walk, speak, learn and interact with people. Thank God because no matter what you are going through, he sees it all, he knows your name, it is his breath in your lungs."

"Wow", Rod said under his breath. "Did he nail it or what? He was going to have to talk further with Hope about her interpretation of the sermon. Right time and right message for him, at least. Rod looked over at Hope. Her face showed a little wear considering all the stress the Martins had been under for the last several months. Her new hairdo swept her blonde locks across her forehead. It was evident to Rod that Hope was following the conclusion of the pastor's message intently as if not wanting to miss any one word.

"Thanksgiving to God can be expressed in several different ways. However, offering thanksgiving to God in an acceptable manner guarantees an immediate response from God. Solomon chose to give a thousand burnt offerings (2 Chronicles 1:6), one of the lepers in the Bible fell down and glorified God with a loud voice (Luke 17:15-16), while David showed gratitude in song and with dancing (2 Samuel 6:14). God responded to Solomon by giving him a blank check to ask for anything he wanted. The leper had a partial healing at first, but Jesus made him completely whole after he offered thanks. God was pleased with David and He established his throne forever. Each of these three received a blessing from God that was irreversible. I pray therefore that as you praise and thank the Lord for His goodness and mercy over your life, you will receive irreversible blessings from Him in Jesus' Name."

The pastor concluded his message and the band followed with a perfect encore, "How Great thou Art". Minutes later the throng flocked to the atrium doors and into the parking lot. For some, the message was already gone. They were on to life. When the Martin's hopped into the SUV they talked about what they'd just heard. For them, the message had a whole bunch of implications. Hope went deep on her impressions.

"You know, as I continue on the journey this side of Heaven, I can see clearer and clearer all the time. Just this morning I read in the book Jeremiah recorded, 'I will give them a heart to know me for I am the Lord; and they will be my people and I will be their God, for they will return to me with their whole heart'-Jeremiah 24:7. And again he recorded for us, 'the eyes of the Lord move to and fro throughout the earth that He may strongly support those whose heart is completely His'-2nd Chronicles 16:9. Do you know what a comfort that is to me that God strongly supports me? To be truly thankful don't you think it is so much more real when you know God versus us merely believing in Him? I mean, I can thank Him for life, for all my possessions, for the ability to see, think, speak, hear, etc. But that seems so shallow in a way. I guess because I feel like that kind of thanks is all focused on me, like "whew, I'm glad I have all these things. But dear, how is that about Him, where is the heart and love for Him in that kind of thanks? When I have really seen myself as God sees me, now that's where real thanks bursts at the seams. Jesus calls us, who seek for Him with all our heart, His betrothed. Ever think about that? Remember when we were engaged to each other?" Rod shook his head in agreement. "I lived in Lincoln, Nebraska and you were in Des Moines. Remember the longing to be together and how you could hardly wait? I mean, I wanted to be with you. And not for stuff you could or would provide for me. But because I knew you and loved you....think about it. Jesus is our betrothed. He calls us His bride. Oh how I long to finally be with Him. That's where real thanks bubbles up from. It really is His breath in our lungs. He breathed life into us. Our very life is not our own, but His. What does that mean, Rod? Shouldn't people wonder why they are really here, I mean it's really about

Him and His reasons to create us right? Like Jeremiah wrote-"I will give them a heart to know me for I am the Lord; I will be their God and they will be my people, my bride. So many people in our churches are missing so much. They believe in God, but they don't really know Him. It's that long 12 inches from the head to the heart, ya know?"

"Well said dear", Rod offered. "So much is about truth. Do people even want the truth, the real truth? It seems the general consensus is, why waste time discovering the truth when you can so easily create it. Hope replied, "Ain't that the truth."

CHAPTER 37

Charlie was making some thankful notes of his own. His day in Mehtar Lam had started rather early. Like around 4 a.m. He had been a part of a mission that had run to the village of Qarghai early that morning. It had been rather quiet. Almost too quiet, Charlie thought. Still he was glad there had been no enemy encounters.

Home for now was FOB Mehtar Lam, near the town of the same name. From Wikipedia, "it is the only large urban settlement in the province. The town is situated in the valley formed by the Alishing and Alingar Rivers Northwest of the city of Jalalabad. There is a paved road between the cities that takes approximately one hour to travel by car. The tomb of Lamech, father of Noah is believed to be in the area, discovered by Mahmud of Ghazni."

It was now around 11:30 a.m. and the same outfit was now enroute to Alishang for a meeting with some of the tribal leaders. Alishang is a fairly important facet in the region. About five years ago, a new micro-hydro electrical power plant opened, built at a cost of US $32,000 by the Mehtar Lam Provincial Reconstruction Team. The plant provides power to some 300 homes in the area. The people inhabiting the village are stated to be cantankerous. During the war against the Soviets, Mujahideen forces who had taken shelter in the village were attacked. After initial set back and death of several soldiers and the local Mujahideen leader of Alishang,

Mujahideen forces managed to defend the village. Outsiders were outsiders. Charlie was in #3 of 5 MRAP (Mine Resistant Ambush Protected) vehicles in the traveling party. It was a rather warm day for November in the Laghman Province. It was already 75 degrees headed towards 83. The sun burned brightly. Not a cloud in the sky. It was somewhat uncomfortable for the six soldiers in full gear in Charlie's MRAP. There was the general bantering back and forth among the guys on board. E5 Clayton Thomas playfully attacked Charlie on the box of underwear and chocolate bars he'd recently received from home. "Hey, Martin", he fired. "When you gonna share some of that candy, dude?" Martin blew off his superior with a head shake. He figured not saying anything was better than giving into his E5. Gunner E2 Spencer Jensen put in his two cents by taking the subject a step further. "Hey Martin", he yelled over the sound of the MRAP. "We don't see many Big Turks in these woods. If you don't share we might have to have a night mission and raid your belongings." Again, Charlie shook his head in a not in your life posture. His Turks were his Turks sent from a mother who knew how to spoil her son. The five vehicles continued their short drive to Alishang. A little over 8 miles but not on the best of roads. The MRAP's made their way cautiously down the Alishang River Valley. Although not IED proof they had proved to be resistant to much of what the enemy threw their way. The big beast stood nine feet high and weighed roughly 15 ton. They were known for their lack of mobility off main roads and over bridges. Still there were over 12,000 of them in Afghanistan and Iraq at a simple cost of between $500,000 and a cool million. A piece.

Suddenly the convoy stopped. The lead MRAP had gotten sight of some movement in the valley. The type of motion that certainly could signal trouble. Everyone's invisible antenna came to life. The conversation over the headsets from the 5 vehicles indicated everyone was poised for a skirmish. Every gunner on board was scanning the hillside looking for anything out of the ordinary.

What the soldiers couldn't see but knew might be out there was a small band of Taliban. Four insurgents had been hard at work for several hours anticipating troop advance into the area. Their timing couldn't have been better in their eyes. The leader, a scraggly haired dude about 5 foot 9 inches and stick thin made a quick sweeping hand movement. 500 pounds of HME (homemade explosives) went to work. Seconds later MRAP #3 was blown to bits.

CHAPTER 38

"Oh my God, NO!", yelled Rod as he sprang forward to a sitting position on the bed. "NO, NO, NO". Almost as quickly as the words had come out of his mouth, Hope had reacted. "Honey, hey, honey", you're having a bad dream", she tried reasoning. "Settle down. Everything is alright. Take a couple of deep breaths. You scared the crap out of me." Rod had been in the theatre of Afghanistan. And what he'd seen was snippets of one of Charlie's missions. The only thing is, as dreams sometimes do, they fool us. Things that seem real are nowhere what the mind has told us.

Rod continued shaking his head back and forth as if to get all the images out of his head. "It was so life like, dear", he reiterated. It was in full color. There was all the dramatics of a Taliban ambush. And then the explosion of the MRAP was so doggone life-like. I won't feel good about any of this until I talk to Charlie and know he's alright." It was 5:30 in the morning so any thought of going back to sleep for Rod Martin was over and done with. After a couple of hand pats from the Hopester he rolled off the bed and into the bathroom.

The lights around the mirror did little to hide Rod's facial expression. Clearly, worry was worn all over it. He was certain he wasn't the only one in the 4,000 families affected by the deployment that was going through this dream weaver feeling. Maybe a good cup of coffee would help. A strong one at that. He quietly headed down the carpeted steps and into the galley kitchen. Opening the cupboard door he found the right grounds for the day. If that didn't solve the problem there was a shot of Bailey's he could throw in for some ample help. In fact the longer he thought about it the better the Bailey's sounded. A couple of minutes later with a cup of brew and additive in hand, Rod settled into the recliner. Now, perhaps he would have a little time to think straight and make some sense of his dream.

Rod snatched his laptop off the floor next to the chair. He fired up the HP and looked at the most recent connection he'd had with Charlie. It was a journal he'd written for his dad's blog dated November 14th.

Hey Dadpo:

Well we had another mission today. It wasn't as exciting as yesterday's but it wasn't too bad! Before every mission we go out to these hills and test fire our weapons. On our way there the ANA (Afghan National Army) that's working with us on joint patrol's vehicle caught on fire. So we had to wait on that and then escort them back to the FOB and wait for them to get another vehicle then finally we left. I was gunner today on our patrol!!! Nothing exciting happened though... we just drove on a road and did route recon.

Yesterday's mission was way better granted we weren't supposed to break a vehicle and get stuck in a village for 3 hours but it was really neat seeing all the people and all the little kids and trying to communicate with them. It's really hard because they don't understand us and we don't understand them but it was still really cool. The kids wanted pens and water, that's words they seem to know in English.

I'm trying to take a lot of pictures so I can show you guys when I come home on leave. I'm not sure when that'll be yet, but hopefully in December! Love you all!

- Your Son

Rod re-read it a second time and once more to boot. He didn't see anything that could have caused his dream to go that haywire. But it did. Okay, he thought, let's move on from this. Hopefully there won't be a repeat of that cinema in his head. Still it was a cause of concern no matter how you tried to phrase it. Danger was danger. Charlie was in the zone so to speak so it came with the territory.

Around 7 a.m. Hope made her way down the steps and into the living room. It was obvious to her Rod was still troubled. She lifted the laptop off her husband's lap and sat down in the adjoining stuffed chair. She flipped open the lid and started moving her fingers in a quick, efficient manner. She had no doubt been awake putting these ideas to action with a return Facebook message to her son and everyone else that was reading.

"I'm sure I speak for all Moms when I say that there is no way that pen and paper can hold what's in her heart. It's hard to even find a place to start when it comes to trying to put into words what she carries with her every second of every day. When it comes to our soldiers we walk tall and proud to be their Mom, but we may crumble at any moment. Our hearts are so full that the slightest movement in there causes it to spill over.

I miss my son like the desert misses rain. Even to pen that starts my tears. And with my tears right behind them are my fears. Our sons and daughters will never be the same after being at War, that is the one thing for sure. Even they fear how it will change them. I'm sure their thoughts go to, "what might I have to see for the rest of my life in my mind's eye?" The thought of how my soldier might be changed when he returns home is too much to bear.......so my advice to myself is, "don't go there, just stay in today".

Our soldiers try and do the same. They are there to do their job so every day they get up and go to work. I'm sure that thought helps to keep the lid on a soul that's full to the brim. But again, the slightest movement can cause it to spillover. And what about when they come home? When their soul could be so filled that there's no way to stop it from pouring out. How will they numb that pain?

Well, so much for staying in today with my thoughts.....I love you son. My heart is right there with you every minute of every day. Time to put the lid back on it and go to work."

Love, Mom

Hope had fired her shot.

CHAPTER 39

Another week had flown by. Rod and Hope constantly had to remind themselves…..stay the course and do the routine things. That had been the message of the support group information they'd heard. Dan was another story. His studies were beginning to suffer at school. And quite frankly he was depressed. Mom and Dad had not done a real good job of watching for the signs. Does one ever? But the grades were a signal. Dan had never been a bad student so anything less than his normal production should have been an indicator.

The Three Martins were back in the church sanctuary listening to Pastor Anderson's message. Rod looked down the row at his youngest son. It was apparent Dan was not into the sermon. He was fiddling with his cellphone and in practical terms, he was checked out. Rod tried to get Dan's attention without making a scene but when that didn't materialize, he nudged Hope to help him refocus his attention to the front of the room. Rod probably needed some nudging of his own. Try as he had, he was having a hard time locking onto the pastor's sermon. Much of that had to do with the row directly in front of him.

Pretty as a picture they were. Two little young ladies. One probably seven and the other maybe a year younger. Number 7 had on a light blue shift dress and a pair of little girls white dress shoes set off by some long blonde locks and dimples to boot. Her sis was fashioned in a dark blue heart print swing dress with the same white shoe style and a short cropped brunette haircut. A few freckles were adorning her face as well. Not only were they adorable they were seemingly mature beyond their ages. When the music portion of the day played out earlier in the service both had followed the words on the big screen. They followed it to a T. Rod couldn't get over their appearances. Maybe someday they'd trade in those beautiful dresses for some camo gear. There had been quite a few women deploy with the 4,000. So considering that possibility was not far-fetched. He had wondered so many times how different the Martin's lives would have been if one of their boys had been a girl. Things would have been different. Even more considering Hope had been a sales consultant for a number of fragrance and cosmetic lines in an earlier life. It would have been a world of bows/hair clips and brushes....oh, and lipstick. The certainty was Rod and Hope would never have a daughter. But you always wonder, don't you, Rod had questioned. Regardless the girls had grabbed Rod's attention. He let his mind wander. He was thinking back to the days his three sons were those ages. How much different life had been then. There were worries, but the worries are much bigger now. Worries. Rod recalled a friend of Dan's, Jimmy Sutton who was a worrier. He worried about this and about that. His mother had taken him to a number of doctors and psychologists to help with his problem. After more than 10 visits to the specialists with no hope of a solution she decided to buy Jimmy a worry stone. That had seemed to do the job. The worry stone is one of many folk practices that can function as a psychologically healthy self-soothing exercise. Using the worry stone can help displace any familiar but destructive coping methods like nail-biting, scratching, lip-biting, Rod had found out when googling the subject one day. He also came across information that it was a help in short term treatment of PTSD. Rod banked the information for the future. Somehow he couldn't see Charlie with a worry stone. Just didn't fit the mold.

Church let out a little early this day. Some of the parishioners were no doubt thankful about that. Thanksgiving was now just days away. As the Martins climbed into the SUV Rod harkened back to earlier in the week when an Iowan was recognized for his heroism. "My guess is", Rod stated. "There was a family doing a heck of a lot of worrying about their son several years ago. Somehow they made it through. We can too." Rod suggested Hope bring up his blog post from earlier in the week on her phone and read it on the ride home.

On Tuesday, November 16th, Staff Sergeant Salvatore Giunta became the first living person since the Vietnam War to receive the United State's highest military decoration for valor, the Medal of Honor. He was honored for saving members of his squad during the War in Afghanistan in October of 2007. As an American, I was proud to see him receive such an award. As an Iowan, it took the feeling one step deeper in appreciation for what he did that day. His actions were heroic.

I'll have to admit right up front I don't know Staff Sgt. Salvatore Giunta. I hope to meet him someday because I have a ton of questions I'd like to ask him. You probably would too. But here is where we might differ. Perhaps you might ask those famous 4 W's and H. Who, When, Where, Why and How. I'm sure there are some great questions you could ask. On the other hand, I'm more intrigued by "Now Where?"

In the days leading up to his honor there were numerous sound bytes and newspaper articles detailing Salvatore Giunta's life. There was one from his mother, Rosemary, that I found most insightful. Mrs. Giunta explained that when Sal decided to join the military he told her that he wanted to make a difference. He had this overwhelming feeling to do something for his country and he wanted to do it, right. Let me say that one more time, he wanted to do it R....I....G....H....T

Giunta himself is uneasy with all the accolades being thrown his way. "I'm not at peace with that at all," Giunta said. "In this job, I am only mediocre. I'm average....And coming and talking about it and people wanting to shake my hand because of it, it hurts me, because it's not what I want. And to be with so many people doing so much stuff and then to be singled out—and put forward. I mean, everyone did something."

The definition of hero has several interpretations. The meaning that led to his being recognized with the Medal of Honor most likely falls in the area of "a person, who, in the opinion of others, has heroic qualities or has performed a heroic act and is regarded as a model or ideal". If you look at that definition it's not hard to understand where Giunta's conflct bubbles to the surface. He doesn't feel that he has heroic qualities....he says he is "mediocre...I'm average". He did though perform a heroic act. No doubt. He did it right.

I'm reminded of the HBO miniseries, "The Pacific" and a certain Sgt. John Basilone who received the Medal of Honor for his actions at the Battle of Guadalcanal during World War II. He was the only enlisted Marine in World War II to receive both the Medal of Honor and the Navy Cross. After receiving the Medal of Honor Sgt. Basilone stayed stateside and promoted war bonds for his country. But that wasn't enough, it wasn't fulfilling, even for a Hero. What Sgt. Basilone found most rewarding was being with a company of men working toward a goal. After several requests, Sgt. Basilone was granted a return to action. Seven months later while serving as a machine gun section leader with Charlie Company, Sgt. Basilone was killed in action at Iwo Jima.

I've been trying for several days now to understand Staff Sgt. Giunta and Sgt. Basilone and what makes them unique. Maybe a word that really describes them best. Actually, I'm going to borrow the "word" from a friend of mine who made me see it in a different light and enabled me to see its significance. The word is.....dauntless.

To be dauntless is to be incapable of being intimidated or discouraged, fearless. DAUNTLESS. Dauntless to serve, dauntless in country and dauntless in life. So, now where Staff Sgt. Giunta? Once the wild ride ebbs and your life returns to some sort of normalcy, then, now where? I have no problem visualizing you taking on the next task put in front of you and doing it right. It's that type of "right" that we should all strive to achieve in our lives. I wish you the best, Staff Sgt. Giunta. Continue to be DAUNTLESS in all that you do. Because that's what you are to me.

Hope tipped down her phone and looked at Rod. Neither one said a word.

CHAPTER 40

Dauntless is also the word Rod had in mind for his oldest son Charlie. He was in a fairly active province in Afghanistan. Laghman was proving to be grounds the Taliban wanted control of again. So there was a lot at stake. In October there had been 60 U.S. deaths in Afghanistan. November was on par for another high number of U.S. casualties. Did Rod have a sense of noteworthiness with his desire for Charlie's welfare? For sure. Charlie didn't seemed fazed by a need for fearlessness though. A new email spelled out what was going on in his world.

> **Hey dad...**
>
> I figured I'd write you another journal entry since i have some time on my hands tonight seeing as how I'm working in the TOC until 630a.m. which kinda blows cause I've been awake all day also... Nothing new has really happened in the last few days besides me getting moved back in with some old buddies and going back to HHC from A Co. It looks like I'll be working in the TOC AND going out on missions so I'll have to juggle both of those somehow and I'm really also hoping i get to go to JFO school in Germany.
>
> I found out I probably won't be getting leave until May sometime because they weren't tracking me and that i was even here. They thought i got here like a week ago and I've been here almost a month now. This is just another reason

why I wish I never would have gotten switched out of C Co and going to Kalagush. I don't have the guys with me that I've known since day 1 of the deployment anymore and I really don't have any chain of command telling me what I need to do which really sucks. I have to find everything out on my own and do everything myself. There still might be a chance that I get switched back to Kalagush and I hope I do. There's still 8 months left of the deployment and who knows what could happen in that time or even what could happen tomorrow for that matter.. The scenery here is getting really old really quick.. I look out at the same city, the same mountains, the same everything every day. And each day is about the same any-more. I wake up, shave, shower, put on a clean uniform, and go about my day like usual. The same routine over and over again.. Man I can't wait to come home and change things up and go back to a normal life. It's not that bad here it just gets old really quickly. Every day is just another day at least it goes by pretty fast. I hope things back in Iowa are good as they can be. I pray you all are doing well!

-Charlie

"Okay", Rod said under his breath. "He seems to be alright. He wasn't talking danger. He was more frustrated by goings on from the higher-ups. Get used to that son. Logic does not always prevail." Charlie was safe for now, Rod thought. And that was the important thing. At that moment, Charlie was in the chow line getting ready to have some breakfast. Thousands of miles away his family was readying for something much different.

"Come on Mom", Dan shouted. As if she could hear him. Hope was in the master bathroom and Dan was in the back seat of the SUV want-ing to get a move on. Rod was semi-patiently waiting in the driver's seat. It was late afternoon on Wednesday the 24th. Eddie was enroute to Des Moines from his leave in Maryland. "Dad, why do females take so long to get ready?", Dan questioned. "Son, I have an answer for that, but probably not the right one", Rod somehow got out between his laughs. "That's been a question for nearly all-mankind. It might be best that we men keep those thoughts to ourselves, son. Unless you want your life shortened."

A few minutes later the woman of description came out the garage door. Her extended time to primp had been well rewarded. Hope was dressed in a nice pair of Lady Levi's, a light blue V-neck sweater and a pair of blue Nike Zooms. 'Wow", said her husband. "You sure look like a million bucks", Rod offered as he looked in the mirror and winked at Dan. "Eddie probably won't even recognize you."

A half hour later Eddie came strolling down the ramp at the Des Moines International Airport. He was dressed in his Class A military uniform. Dressed to the hilt. He looked like a model for the U.S. Army. Alongside he carried his green duffel bag stuffed with clothes and presents. Thanksgiving was tomorrow but Eddie had a few treats for his family members. The hugs from his Dad and brother and the kiss from Mom was a great welcome home. The four turned and headed out of the terminal to the parking lot. Four-fifths of the family was back together. That was sure something to be thankful for.

CHAPTER 41

Minutes after the bags were dropped in the mud room of the Martin's foyer, Eddie and brother Dan scooted out the door. Their destination was anywhere they could have some fun. It had been almost four months since Eddie had an opportunity to let his hair down. Time could wait no longer. Mom and Dad had figured this would most likely be the move on the young mens part so they weren't upset by their immediate departures. Still it would have been nice to sit around and catch up. But that would have to wait until later in the Thanksgiving holiday.

"I'm not sure I'd have blown out of the house and left my parents hanging when I was their age", suggested Rod. "I know times are different. I guess it's no different than when your kids choose to be with their girlfriend or boyfriend rather than mom or dad". Hope looked at her husband with a reassuring smile. "Get used to it dear", she chuckled. "It's only going to get worse. Mom and Dad will always be there. And gosh, they might miss out on something if they sat at home". With his wife's wisdom at heart, Rod recalled reading something about this exact thing a few weeks ago. For the life of him, he couldn't remember where he came across it, but it went something like, "people have to be able to live their lives. You can't deny challenges and experiences that will shape them". That's a hard thing to do sometimes, Rod thought. "As a parent you want your kids to do things the right way. And you want them to do the right thing, right now. Not years from now. But it doesn't work that way".

"Okay, maw", let's figure out some good table talk for tomorrow, shall we", inquired Rod. "Let's see, we could discuss how Speaker of the House Nancy Pelosi got re-elected by her fellow Democrats to lead her party in the next Congress. And that she will lose her position as House Speaker, since the Republican Party will be the majority party beginning in 2011. Or maybe....Former House Majority Leader Tom Delay of Texas being convicted of money laundering and conspiracy to commit money laundering involving corporate campaign contributions and that he faces up to 99 years in prison. Or how about...the Pentagon announcing that repealing the "Don't Ask, Don't Tell," law, which forbids gay and lesbian service members from serving openly in the military, will not affect the military's strength. Surveys showed 70 percent believed repealing the law would impact their units in a positive, mixed, or neutral way". The look on Hope's face was one of bewilderment. Had her husband gone nuts?, she wondered. You have to be kidding. Right? That would be a great dinner killer if I've ever seen one. Can't you stick to sports or something light hearted?

Rod's table talk rundown had been a failed stab at humor from his wife's perspective. Sometimes he did stuff like this to see if Hope was paying attention. She sure had been today. "Alright, then", he snapped back. "I'll stick to the 3 NFL games being played tomorrow. Three dog games. New England at Detroit, followed by New Orleans at Dallas or the night game Cincinnati at the N.Y. Jets. Will that do?", he asked. Hope nodded her head in agreement. "I think that might go a little further", she shot back.

Rod's mind was elsewhere while Hope was mentioning the problem scenario with his dinner conversation. He was recalling a recent small group gathering. The members of the Martin's Alpha group had been talking about issues they face each and every day. Rod threw out a line he often used concerning problems. Either you are going into one, in the middle of one, or coming out of one, he'd said. One of the ladies of the group offered a resistance to the statement. "I don't see it that way at all. I just don't", she had countered. Her remark had been quick and cut to the bone and had presented some uncomfortableness to the group. It might have been the first time any of them had heard the phrase. On the other hand, the quick fire rebuttal by his fellow small grouper had left Rod rather smitten. He'd known how he'd reacted when he first heard the statement. It took him several days to rationalize the remark. "It made sense", Rod thought. Weeks later at another meeting the lady had changed her tune and had done a complete one-eighty. Inside Rod felt a little victory but he let dogs lie where they were and figured a higher power had provided some wisdom to her. Yes, the Lord works in mysterious ways, Rod concluded.

In truth, the Martin's were living out the statement Rod had laid out. Charlie's deployment along with Eddie's military commitments had pulled the family in a myriad of directions. Mentally and physically. Eddie would be done with his AIT some time in February. Charlie on the other hand, was a long way from seeing the finish line. The Martin's were "in" the moment. In some respects they'd done a good job of managing the situation. In other ways, they'd come up short. The one area they could do a better job in was taking care of their own needs. Strange as it sounds, that often gets forgotten.

That was one side of the story. Rod recollected a recent Facebook post from a mother who had deployed to Afghanistan. Rod had asked her how deploying had affected her and her family. "It hit me the day before I left. I felt it hit me that I was leaving and would be gone for a whole year and was scared to think what would happen when I wasn't there. It still does hit me every once in a while to realize I am here and they are at home going on as best they can with their everyday tasks. When I get a letter or a box from them or friends and family it brings me such joy to know that they thought of me in all the hustle of their everyday lives. The girls have all grown up so fast. I can't believe those little ladies I see sometimes on Skype are really mine. My husband has adjusted to being the sole person to run the house. Although I know that he gets frustrated with it sometimes. I know that my family's faith has grown a lot during this time as mine has too. I know that my oldest (bless her heart) has grown up too fast because of how she feels about being the "mom of the house." I wish I were there to take that feeling away from her but I can't. She is so strong willed and will always feel that way until I come home and tell her to be a kid again. I know that all three of the girls have had to grow up and be more responsible because of this deployment but I also believe it has helped them to be such wonderful girls. I have been imagining seeing my girls since the day I left!!!! I can't wait until I can hold them and see their beautiful faces again. I know I won't be able to get on my knees in front of them because they have grown so much! But to actually touch them and stand next to them will be such an awesome feeling it brings me joy inside!!!

That's a perfect example. Going into a problem. In a problem. And how you can come out of the problem.

Rod was now sitting in the old recliner. He could hear the pattering of rain drops on the roof. He was thankful the moisture was rain and not snow. He could hear the small snores from Mason beneath his feet. The big Golden was fast asleep. Bubba Bruise was as comfortable as one could be on the back of the chair slowly batting his tail back and forth across the back of Rod's head. In a few hours there would be smells of turkey and dressing and a whole lot more present in the Martin household. Rod lifted the lid on the HP and looked at Charlie's most recent message. He reread the final paragraph a couple of times.

> **The scenery here is getting old really quick.. I look out at the same city, the same mountains, the same everything every day. And each day is about the same anymore. I wake up, shave, shower, put on a clean uniform, and go about my day**

like usual. The same routine over and over again.. Man I can't wait to come home and change things up, back to normal life. It's not that bad here it just gets old really quick. Every day is just another day.... at least it goes by pretty fast. I hope things back home are good as they can be.

"Amen, to that son" Rod spoke ever so slowly. "Amen". His message had been similar to one several days earlier. Apparently, Charlie was sticking to the same story.

CHAPTER 42

The smells were just as Rod imagined. Not only was turkey delight hanging in the air, but the scent of roasted sweet potato casserole with praline, an old family recipe for Sage and Onion Stuffing, potato au gratin and green beans with bacon were right alongside. Waiting in the wings was a delicious pumpkin pie and some chilling Cool Whip. Hope had outdone herself. Sparks weren't flying off utensils at the dinner table but everyone had done a great job loading up their plate for a Thanksgiving onslaught. Initially conversation was limited to a few grunts and groans of ecstasy. Eventually, the table talk began as Rod updated Eddie on some recent happenings.

"I wanted you to know Ed that Dan and I made a short jaunt to the Iowa State Capital this week for Staff Sgt. Salvatore Giunta Day. Tremendous day....hundreds of people showed up to hear Governor Chet Culver offer the proclamation for the Medal of Honor recipient" reported Rod. "You remember hearing about him, right? Afterwards, I asked Dan to venture over so we could introduce ourselves to his parents, Steve and Rosemary. Dan, of course asked why. "What do you want to do that for", he'd said. "Just never mind", I replied. "Come on". So we strolled over to the area where his parents were receiving well-wishers and I offered a handshake to his mother. "Congratulations", I said. "You must be very proud. We have two sons in the military, one just deployed to Afghanistan". "That's awesome", Rose responded. "I'm a strong believer in prayer and so is Sal.

We'll pray for them". I can't tell you how shocked I was. I'm not sure what expression crossed my face, but words escaped me, I will tell you that. This wasn't what I expected...yet I had felt there was some inexplicable reason that I needed to speak further with the Giuntas, and Rose in particular. Needless to say, the comment about her faith "opened" the door for further conversation. I'm hoping to write a blog about it." "Wow, you guys did that", replied Eddie. "That must have been neat to have met them. And you got to shake Sgt. Guinta's hand and got a picture too?", he asked.

By now the Martin's were beginning to feel the effects of the meal beginning to take shape. Eddie and Dan headed downstairs to check in on the NFL games. Rod was sitting in the recliner nodding off and on. Hope was in the kitchen putting away a few of the holiday dishes. A short time later, Rod came to life and ejected himself from the chair. He slowly made his way to the kitchen. When he reached the doorway, he began to talk. "Dear, you did a great job on the dinner. You really did", he began. "There would be only one thing that could have made it better. And that would be if Charlie was here. There's a hole. A big hole in the day. I know he was at Basic last year, but at least he was in the States. This year is so much different."

"I agree with that", shot back Hope. "I've tried to keep busy and not think so much about it, but it's hard not to. Let's hope Charlie checks in today", she said. Rod and Hope met in the middle of the room and gave each other a reassuring hug. "I think I'm going over to mom and dad's", stated Hope. "Things might have quieted down from the rest of the family being there. Hopefully the house full is beginning to head their own ways. Anyway, it will be good to see them". A smile came to Rod's face and he replied, "go right ahead. I think I'm going to listen to some music and relax a little. And wait to see if Charlie reaches out to us".

This time Rod settled on the couch sinking deep into the cushions. He tuned into Direct TV's music platform and hits from the 60's. They were doing a countdown when he tuned in they were at number 5 which was "I Want To Hold Your Hand" by the Beatles. To number 4, "Tossin and Turnin", by Bobby Lewis. Number 3 was a "Theme from Summer Place", by Percy Faith and his Orchestra. Number 2 checked in with "Hey Jude", by the Beatles and topping the list was "The Twist", by Chubby Checker. Each song had taken Rod on various musical journeys from his past. But it was a song that played right after the countdown that really changed things. "My gosh", Rod exclaimed out loud. "I'd forgotten all about the song and the group", he recalled. "How could I ever have done that? They were awesome to listen to. The group was Vanilla Fudge.

The band has been cited as "one of the few American links between psychedelia and what soon became heavy metal. Vanilla Fudge also was known to have influenced other major bands such as The Nice, Deep Purple, Yes, Styx, and Led Zeppelin. Their claim to fame was "You Keep me Hangin On". It had been a song he'd loved. And he'd played the heck out of it growing up. The tune struck another chord as well. "Isn't it funny", he thought. "I kind of feel the same thing with us waiting to hear from our son. It's like we're hanging on."

Hearing the old hit once wasn't enough. Rod googled the band name and came across the song. He hit the arrow and settled back for some deep seated memories. He didn't want to misremember any of them. Life had been a whole lot simpler then. A whole lot.

CHAPTER 43

Thanksgiving Day had come to a quick halt and it was now time to move on to other things. Eddie spent the next couple of days enjoying some quality time with old friends and a little bit with his Mom and Dad. Then it was off in the big bird for a return to AIT in Maryland. Christmas would be here before you knew it and he'd be back for a much longer R and R.

The past week had been a blur. Every year it seems like the time between Thanksgiving and Christmas is getting shorter. It must have something to do with age, Rod thought. Rod was seated at a table near the west windows of the Johnston Panera. He'd been there for over an hour jotting some ideas down for a story to put on the blog. He'd given an occasional glance outside to the gloomy day that was taking place. There had been a trace of snow during the previous night signally Old Man Winter was about ready to start in. He'd also done a fair amount of people watching. A young 20ish blonde haired gal had caught Rod's attention several tables down the line. She'd been working her cellphone for some time now texting away. Rod was amazed at the speed of her navigational skills. Her thumbs were going a hundred miles an hour as she put her thoughts on the screen. The longer he watched her, the nastier he felt. "Alright Ms. Thumbelina, you think you're so doggone fast", Rod said under his breath. "I'd take you on to a challenge of your texting ability and my typing ability. Then, we'd see just how fast you are." Rod had been a 90 word a minute typist in high school so he felt he could hold his own. Just then the young lady's phone rang. Looking a little peeved, she stopped her movements on the keypad and clicked on her phone symbol. "Hah", Rod verbalized. "Let's see how you do talking to someone just like we used to do in the old days". Her conversation was short and sweet. Within seconds she was back into her texting mode. So much for real communication.

A ding on Rod's phone signaled another type of transmission. His Facebook account showed he had a message from Charlie. As Rod began to read the message everything around him became irrelevant. His focus was completely on the message he was trying to comprehend.

> **"Dad-That mission i went on two days ago that turned into an overnight mission.. we got ambushed and took rpg, ak47, and pkm fire from all around us. I called in 27 mortar rounds on the Taliban that were in a village, in a valley, and on a ridge. I took gunfire and rpg fire 3 different times and we had fighter jets on site to drop bombs on those guys. It ended up being a 7 hour long gun fight and we ended up staying the night out there and I got no sleep what so ever but I am fine. This is the first time I've been able to tell you guys but I thought I'd let you know".**

This time Rod was dealing with reality. Much different than the dream he'd conjured up several weeks ago. His eyes moved to and fro around the dining facility. There was a young man dressed in blue jeans and an Iowa sweatshirt with shoulder length brown hair buried deep in thought in the morning paper. A much older plump woman dressed in black sweatpants and a green polo shirt was fixed on the front door no doubt expecting a friend for some coffee talk. Behind the counter was a pretty young Syrian gal with a dark blue Hijab on her head readying for the lunch onslaught Panera was going to experience soon. None of these individuals had a remote idea of Rod's mindset right now. They were deep into their own situations. Could any of these people be of help in making the message make sense? No. Rod needed to vent his feelings quickly. This was serious, right? He knew Hope was at work but this couldn't wait. So he made the call not to her cellphone but to her business line. Luckily, Hope answered the phone and he didn't have to try to communicate with someone other than his wife. "Dear, I need you to come down to Panera as soon as you can", Rod sputtered. "It's not anything where Charlie has been injured or shot, but you've got to come right away". The click at the other end of the line showed the return mindset of urgency. In minutes Hope was sitting in front of her husband reading Charlie's message.

As Rod patiently waited for Hope to finish her evaluation of Charlie's message he heard a train whistle eerily blowing in the distance. That was rather strange he thought, because to his recollection, there weren't any railroad tracks close to their location. Had he mis-heard the noise? Or was this some sort of danger signal to be alerted to. Hope interrupted his thinking. "It appears Charlie is fine", she said. "Pretty weird that he could go through something like the firefight he mentioned and then end his message with something so abstract by saying...." **also Colby said just make the price $5500 for my motorcycle cause he couldn't get the other light to work so he's just putting the regular one in so I'll pay $5500 for it. I love you guys". - Charlie.**

"Maybe that's how soldiers channel things", she continued. "His words were so matter of fact. Even if he looks at things that way, we need to send this down a prayer chain for him and his fellow soldier's protection". Rod sat across from his wife moving his head up and down in agreement. He reached across the table and twirled the laptop back in front of him. A few minutes later he twirled it back to Hope for her approval of the message. "Perfect", she responded. "Perfect". "Hit send then", Rod replied

All:

Got a Facebook post from Charlie today. One that I had a feeling was in the works...you know you just feel like something is telling you to be on the alert, that danger might be lurking.

Anyway...Charlie and his buddies were on a mission Sunday and got ambushed by the Taliban. They took fire from RPG's, AK 47's and Soviet machine guns. The battle lasted for some 7 hours....Charlie was responsible for calling in 27 different mortar strikes to the town, valley and hillside where the insurgents were located. No one in his unit was hurt....he didn't care to share the casualties on the other side. In the end, Charlie's captain congratulated him for a job well done.

If you would, please say a prayer for him and his fellow soldier's safety through this and for their continued coverage by God!!!!

With Love,

Rod and Hope

The lunch crowd was beginning to descend on Panera. The conversation noise had gone to another level, one the Martin's could no longer tolerate. Hope needed to get back to work and Rod had a phone call within the hour with a local radio host concerning an upcoming interview on the Guard's deployment. As they headed to their vehicles, Hope looked over at her husband and mouthed the words, "love you". His mouth formed the same type of message, 'love you too'.

Rod climbed into the SUV and he sat there for a few moments. He had a big question forming. "Charlie, is this all you want from life? Is this what you feel like you're here to do is fight for our country and protect us and nothing more?", he questioned.

As soon as that idea had spewed forth he recalled Rose Giunta's words in how she dealt with her son's time in the Army. "Don't ask questions", she'd offered. "Just be there and listen. They'll tell you what you need to know and if you need to know". The words took Rod back to the movie, "A Few Good Men". And the dialogue between lawyer (Tom Cruise) and officer (Jack Nicholson). Cruise is trying to get Nicholson to crack on the witness stand and shouts to him. " I want the truth". To which Nicholson responds, "you can't handle the truth".

Most of us can't. Just the same, be safe son.

CHAPTER 44

Danger, uncertainty and fear had seeped into the Martin's world more than ever now that Charlie had been involved with his first battlefield incident. One word stuck out to him in particular. Rod had read the words in a recent article on the military, "Fear is necessary in a war, if you're the one fighting it. Nonsense. Fear makes one weak. A solider who feels is not a real soldier". Interesting comment Rod thought. He wasn't certain if he agreed with it. Where he stood, his hankering told him a little fear is a good thing. Kind of like the butterfly syndrome athletes and actors have before a performance. All he knew is he and his wife and youngest son would be looking at the deployment thing in a much different manner, now. This was no longer a skirmish, an incident or a kerfuffle. Scooby Doo probably verbalized the situation better than anyone could with his famous line, "Rut Row".

Later that night the Martin's received a phone call from Charlie. "Everything is fine", he told his folks. And as expected, he tried to skirt the issue and focus on other things to talk about. As hard as it was, Rod heard Mrs. Guinta's voice loud and clear. One thing was for certain. Charlie was not injured and he'd all but forgotten the incident and was ready to move onto his next mission. After the conversation with Charlie ended, Rod turned to Hope and shrugged his shoulders. "This is going to play out a whole lot different than I would have thought", suggested Rod. "I get not asking questions, but it's almost acting like it never happened if you approach things that way. I hope beyond hope that we find a way to make sense of all this. We need hope. There is hope. There is genuine hope that can bring joy back. We haven't used the word Hope a lot as we've discussed this journey, have we?", Rod questioned his wife. "But it's there at every corner we turn. Hope is essential for surviving. Every farmer hopes that it will rain and he will have a good yield. Every businessman purchases goods hoping that he can sell them and make a profit. Even the beggars live on hope that someone will give them food and or money for survival. Nearly everyone survives on a hope that tomorrow will be better than today. We have to hold onto those thoughts". Hope nodded approvingly. "I couldn't have said it any better", she related. "I think my parents were onto something when they named me. At least I hope they were", she said laughingly. "Alright, dear", let's not get carried away", Rod postured.

The Hope game continued on into the night at the Martins. Hope had more than enough fodder to throw at her husband regarding the word. It's like she'd been saving all these little nuggets for the right time and place. As the two headed for bed they'd firmly established a word that would be front in center throughout the remainder of their son's deployment. A four letter word of the best kind. HOPE.

The next morning Rod's feet hit the bedroom floor as soon as the sun showed first light. Today was going to be a big day. It was Friday, December 10th and he and James Drake, a local talk show host on WHO Radio in Des Moines, were going to talk about the deployment of the Iowa National Guard on his afternoon show. Rod's emotions were somewhat raw considering the timing of Charlie's firefight, but still he was looking forward to the opportunity to let the listeners in on the inner workings when a solider leaves home. He threw on a pair of blue jeans, a dark blue polo shirt and a pair of his favorite NIKE runners. He wanted to be relaxed and casual in the studio for the 2 and 1/2 hour time commitment. A little after 9 a.m.

Rod received an email from Jill Frost, a fill-in host at the station. James had gotten sick and she was going to be filling in. "This could be interesting", he told Hope as she stood in the kitchen with a hot cup of coffee cupped in both hands. "Who knows, it might be better that Jill is going to be asking the questions. Sometimes it's better to have a woman's perspective". "God will lead you today, dear", said Mrs. Martin. "I have no doubt you will do a good job. And having Rose Giunta on with you at the back part of the show will be awesome."

The next thing Rod remembered was sitting outside the studio preparing with Ms. Frost for their air time. Rod could sense she was having concerns her guest might become emotional in discussing some of the questions she might ask. On the surface, Rod might have looked in shock, but deep down, he was calm. He'd been on the radio many times. He often showed some pre-interview uneasiness, but once the red light came on, he was ready. Today, would be no different, he thought.

WHO Radio has a reputation as the blow torch of the Midwest. Its signal is as strong as they come. The Iowa market would be saturated with their midday interview. There would be a good audience. And time flew by. There had been great conversation between the two of them and a fair amount of call-ins. A number of the callers asked to talk to Rod off air so they could keep in contact throughout the Guard's deployment. Ms. Guinta was the icing on the cake. She put a mother's imprint on not only what she went through but also what her son had endured while he was in Iraq and Afghanistan. There had been only one issue to work around. The weather was rearing its ugly head and there had been several "break ins" throughout the interview. Despite that, Rod felt like he'd found a new friend in Ms. Frost. Days later he fired her the following message.

Jill-

In all seriousness....there was a reason you were hosting Friday. I have reached out to Rose to have her "lead" the process of placing a wreath in the front yard of deployed families. Not only did the families take a great amount of pride in being recognized, it let the community know who was facing some difficult struggles in the holiday season. I think her comment spoke loud and clear how Sal's deployment impacted her family. Think what it could do for all!! I think God is moving for something more than the message we started. -Rod

But it wasn't the interview as much as it was impact. One email Rod received spoke volumes. It came from a friend of theirs who'd lost their son in a car accident shortly after marrying his high school sweetheart.

Rod-

We heard you on WHO last night. You did a fine job of visiting with Jill. Your point about not asking about the activities over there and talking about back home was very timely for listeners. Also enjoyed the caller that mentioned the 91st Psalm. Went back and reread as a lot of that Psalm has been quoted. I can relate to the fear that Hope and you experience, as that is like what we went through after losing Scott. It was always that deep fear that we would lose another child or grandchild. But over time, our Christian faith helped lessen the fear (but it's still always there) and we just put our faith in God that he will protect us from all harm and danger. That is also our prayer for Charlie and all of you. God Bless, Dick and Gwen.

Christmas was 12 days away. Rod couldn't remember if the Drummers were Drumming or the Partridge was in a Pear Tree. What he did know was that Charlie would be in another part of the world this year. That was a certainty. And in a place where you had to look close to see God's presence. Rod hoped that would be revealed to his oldest son this Holiday season. He couldn't think of a better gift.

CHAPTER 45

The next morning Hope was in front of the bathroom mirror prepping for the day. As she put on the finishing touches to her makeup work she was deep in thought regarding the safety of her son, Charlie, in Afghanistan. She recalled her husband's mention of fear. What was it like for Charlie?, she wondered. Did his first encounter with the enemy instill an uneasiness within his soul? How would he react if there was a next time? Just then, her thoughts were interrupted by a loud crash from the kitchen on the lower level. A few loud words of disgust followed. "What happened?", yelled Hope. "Are you alright"? "Yeah, yeah", Rod tossed back. "I dropped a bowl of cereal on the floor. There's Raisin Bran and milk all over the place".

Moments later Hope was in the doorway of the kitchen surveying Mason taking full advantage of Rod's misfortune. His tongue was lapping up the mess. Rod looked at his wife and shrugged his shoulders. "I thought this was the best way to have the place cleaned up. Pretty creative on my part, huh", he said. Hope looked back down at Mason who was in thorough enjoyment mode. "Sure, I guess. We can do a second going over after he cleans up the first stage", she suggested as a smirk emerged on her face. "Thanks, hon", he shot back. "This day isn't starting out like I had in mind. I've got a whole muddle going on in this head of mine". To which she replied, "what's up?"

Rod motioned Hope to the living room couch. "This might take a while, so you'd best have a seat", he started. "Maybe I'm finally getting a chance to catch up with myself now that the radio interview is over with and I can think more about the firefight Charlie was involved in. I'm going to say some of these things to you that I'd probably not repeat outside our house. But I'm disgusted with a bunch of things. The more I talk to people who have had a family member or friend deploy the angrier I become." "Why so?', she questioned. Rod took a long look at his wife. What he was about to say was something they'd never talked about even though it was a big Elephant in the room each and every day. "Well", he started despite the emotion rising in his voice. "I know this is what Charlie wanted to do since he was an eight year old. I get that. But I'm not ready to give up my son for what I'm beginning to believe is a hopeless situation he's involved with. Are you ready for a knock on the door to have someone tell us Charlie has lost his life? Cause I'm not. It would kill me to get that knock. It kills me every time I hear that knock and it's someone who has come to visit. I'd never know the difference until I answered the door. I.....I couldn't handle that". Rod stopped moving his lips. At the moment, silence was the best thing imaginable. He stood and shuffled across the room to the front door. He turned and looked at Hope. "Are you?", he gulped with a knot in his throat. She didn't say anything. She didn't have to. Rod knew what her answer would be. Almost on cue, Hope's cellphone rang. The interruption had come at a good time. "I need to get this, it's my mom", she pronounced. "She went to the doctor today and I want to see how she's doing."

As Hope left the room Rod began settling into his own little world. What was he feeling right now? Was he suffering from depression or were the family issues simply beginning to pile up? Last Friday had been a high. A big high. The interview time on WHO Radio had provided an opportunity to educate listeners on the Guard's deployment and the effects on family and friends. It was an adrenaline rush. Now, he felt low. Really low. It was hard to explain his true feelings even to his wife. In a sense, he looked to his left for help and there was no one there. And then he looked to his right and no one on that side understood either. He was in a quandary. He felt alone. And what does one do when they feel alone?, he thought. They isolate themselves. And when you isolate yourself, all sorts of ideas can emerge. But most of those are not the proper solution to a problem.

All Rod knew was, he was becoming angry. Angry at the Army for taking his son into battle. Angry at an enemy that he wasn't sure we had any true reason to fight against. Disgusted with people and their lack of compassion and common sense when it came to having a loved one placed in the theatre of War. And maybe even at himself. Couldn't he have been a better influence on Charlie at a young age so his skills were in a laboratory, courtroom or even on the athletic field. Not some shit hole in Afghanistan. "Were these valid thoughts?", he wondered.

Hope re-entered the living room and could tell from the look on her husband's face he was still in the same mind set she'd left him in minutes ago. "Dear, you and I look at things from a much different perspective", exclaimed Rod. "I'm trying to keep a good outlook on things, but today it came to a screeching halt. You, on the other hand think good thoughts. I can't always do that. As much as I hate to say this, I have a real gut fear this year might be the worst of our lives. Somehow, some way I need to find a way to navigate this. And right now, I don't have an answer". Hope stood motionless in front of her husband of 21 years. For the second time in the last ten minutes, Hope didn't have answer. The knock at front door broke the silence helped along by Rod's question. "Do you want to answer that, or should I".

CHAPTER 46

Hope was on a path to the front door when Rod raised his stop sign hand in the air. "I got it", he exclaimed. His attitude suggested he was ready for anything on the other side of the casing. Bring it on, he thought. I'm ready for anything. Or so he thought. But as he found out, he wasn't ready for this. He imagined he'd be focusing on something at eye level as he swung the door out. However, in this case it was much lower. There at his feet was a little guy dressed in a red Old Navy parka with a white muffler wound around his head and a pair of black North Face snow boots completing his fashion look. He was dwarfed by a beautiful Gaia wreath. Standing off to the side was a proud papa who Rod didn't recognize. "Mr. Martin", the little elf began. "My family wants to thank you and your family for all you do to keep us safe. Merry Christmas". Not only was Rod speechless, he was expressionless. He slowly began to digest the situation. A smile formed on his face and just kept getting bigger. "Aah, Hmmmm", Rod spit out. "Gosh, you are so welcome", he said as the young man thrust the wreath into his arms. "Thank you. That hardly is enough. But that's all I can think to say". "No problem", said Papa Elf. "We heard your interview on WHO Radio last week. Our family decided we had to bring you a wreath to show you our love and support". Rod bent down on a knee squarely in front of the little bearer of gifts. "Young man. I want you to know how much this means", Rod choked out. "I also want you to remember this day for the rest of your life. What you and your family did was priceless." "There's also a poem that we put in the wreath", the little one offered. "Read it after we leave and pass it on". With those words, the two gift givers left the Martin doorstep and headed down the driveway. When they got to the street they both yelled back, "Merry Christmas". And just like that they vanished.

Rod's eyes searched the neighborhood. He was looking for a camera. This felt all too weird to be happening to him. He thought of the old TV show, "Candid Camera". The show involved concealing cameras filming ordinary people being confronted with unusual situations and when the joke was revealed the victim would be told the show's catchphrase. "Smile, you're on Candid Camera." This had to be one of those moments. He couldn't figure out any other reason. But after a few moments it became apparent there weren't any cameras and he wouldn't need to work bringing his smile back to life. The only people to have experienced the exchange were Rod, the little elf and the little guy's dad. Hope's voice beckoned, "what's going on, dear?".

Rod was going to explain but thought otherwise. "Here, take this", he said offering his wife the wreath. "There's a poem in it that we need to read first. Then I'll try to tell you what just happened." Hope located the poem on the back side of the ring and began reading out loud.

> **"IT'WAS THE NIGHT BEFORE CHRISTMAS,**
> **HE LIVED ALL ALONE,**
> **IN A ONE BEDROOM HOUSE,**
> **MADE OF PLASTER AND STONE.**
> **I HAD COME DOWN THE CHIMNEY,**
> **WITH PRESENTS TO GIVE,**
> **AND TO SEE JUST WHO,**
> **IN THIS HOME, DID LIVE.**
> **I LOOKED ALL ABOUT**
> **A STRANGE SIGHT I DID SEE,**

NO TINSEL, NO PRESENTS,
NOT EVEN A TREE.
NO STOCKING BY MANTLE,
JUST BOOTS FILLED WITH SAND,
ON THE WALL HUNG PICTURES,
OF FAR DISTANT LANDS.
WITH MEDALS AND BADGES,
AWARDS OF ALL KINDS,
A SOBER THOUGHT,
CAME THROUGH MY MIND.
FOR THIS HOUSE WAS DIFFERENT,
IT WAS DARK AND DREARY,
I FOUND THE HOME OF A SOLDIER,
ONCE I COULD SEE CLEARLY.
THE SOLDIER LAY SLEEPING,
SILENT, ALONE,
CURLED UP ON THE FLOOR,
IN THIS ONE BEDROOM HOME.
THE FACE WAS SO GENTLE,
THE ROOM IN DISORDER,
NOT HOW I PICTURED,
A TRUE AMERICAN SOLDIER.
WAS THIS THE HERO,
OF WHOM I'D JUST READ?
CURLED UP ON A PONCHO,
THE FLOOR FOR A BED?
I REALIZED THE FAMILIES,
THAT I SAW THIS NIGHT,
OWED THEIR LIVES TO THESE SOLDIERS,
WHO WERE WILLING TO FIGHT.
SOON ROUND THE WORLD,
THE CHILDREN WOULD PLAY,
AND GROWNUPS WOULD CELEBRATE,
A BRIGHT CHRISTMAS DAY.

THEY ALL ENJOYED FREEDOM,
EACH MONTH OF THE YEAR,
BECAUSE OF THE SOLDIERS,
LIKE THE ONE LYING HERE.
I COULDN'T HELP WONDER,
HOW MANY LAY ALONE,
ON A COLD CHRISTMAS EVE,
IN A LAND FAR FROM HOME.
THE VERY THOUGHT BROUGHT,
A TEAR TO MY EYE,
I DROPPED TO MY KNEES,
AND STARTED TO CRY.
THE SOLDIER AWAKENED,
AND I HEARD A ROUGH VOICE,
"SANTA DON'T CRY,
THIS LIFE IS MY CHOICE;
I FIGHT FOR FREEDOM,
I DON'T ASK FOR MORE,
MY LIFE IS MY GOD,
MY COUNTRY, MY CORPS..."
THE SOLDIER ROLLED OVER,
AND DRIFTED TO SLEEP,
I COULDN'T CONTROL IT,
I CONTINUED TO WEEP.
I KEPT WATCH FOR HOURS,
SO SILENT AND STILL,
AND WE BOTH SHIVERED,
FROM THE COLD NIGHT'S CHILL.
I DID NOT WANT TO LEAVE,
ON THAT COLD, DARK, NIGHT,
THIS GUARDIAN OF HONOR,
SO WILLING TO FIGHT.
THEN THE SOLDIER ROLLED OVER,
WITH A VOICE SOFT AND PURE,

WHISPERED, "CARRY ON SANTA,

IT'S CHRISTMAS DAY, ALL IS SECURE."

ONE LOOK AT MY WATCH,

AND I KNEW HE WAS RIGHT.

"MERRY CHRISTMAS MY FRIEND,

AND TO ALL A GOOD NIGHT."

-This poem was written by a Peacekeeping soldier stationed overseas. The following is his request. Would you do me the kind favour of sending this to as many people as you can? Christmas will be coming soon and some credit is due to all of the service men and women for our being able to celebrate these festivities. Let's try in this small way to pay a tiny bit of what we owe. Make people stop and think of our heroes, living and dead, who sacrificed themselves for us. Please, do your small part to plant this small seed.

"Wow, it looks like your interview made an impression on a number of people", Hope suggested. "You never know where your message will end up and who it will affect, do you? Rod spent the next ten minutes filling in his wife on the encounter with the Christmas wreath twosome. She didn't say much but simply nodded her head in agreement. Hope had a way in doing that. "Well it looks like we need to pass it on, if that's what the message suggested", Hope said.

Several hours later, some 7,000 miles away, a half-awake soldier made his way to the MWR tent in Mehtar Lam, Afghanistan. The green vinyl maintenance enclosure provided a communications center for soldiers on the base. MWR stood for Morale, Welfare and Recreation. No doubt, a lot of that went on there. Charlie's day was about to begin but first he wanted to check and see if he had any communication from home. He pulled up the email from his mother and began to read the story of the Christmas wreath delivery and the accompanying poem. When he finished he shut down the laptop and looked at his surroundings. There had to be some 20 other soldiers communicating with their loved ones either via email, Facebook or Skype. He wondered if any of them felt alone like the soldier in the poem. Not everyone was cut out to be a soldier. And if they weren't. Who would? Charlie looked down at his cellphone and saw it was almost time for another mission. Once the trucks rolled he'd have to leave his thinking of the Holidays at the base. What he wouldn't give to be headed home. Oh, the cost of freedom. "Martin. Come on. We're headed out", yelled the sergeant in charge. Charlie grabbed his backpack, weapon and munitions all the while muttering under his breath, "Merry Christmas to you too, Sarge".

CHAPTER 47

Charlie was sitting in Humvee #2 of a group of 5. They were en route to Dawlat Shah roughly 45 miles from their home base. There were four other soldiers on board including the churlish E5 who'd told him to get a move on 15 minutes earlier. Charlie had a few names to call the dude other than churlish. Butthead would have been a good one. There was enough to worry about regarding a mission without a superior showing disrespect to everyone around him. Charlie decided to let the antics of his boss go. What good would it do to complain anyway? He sat back and thought how his day had begun and where he found himself now.

How did the day start for Charlie? He'd rolled out of the sack around 5 a.m. (0500 in military speak) did a few knee bends and toe touches, threw on his camo's and stepped outside into a blustery winter morning. He hustled down to the gym in total darkness and spent 30 minutes tossing some weights skyward. He spent another 15 minutes on the rowing machine before heading down to the mess area to grab a few bites of egg, sausage and toast and a hot, cup of tar.....errr, coffee. Next he made his way to MWR and communicated with a few buddies and his mom and dad. Then the sergeant came on the scene.

Charlie wasn't certain what his mental state was. Every mission was that way. Should he be angry? Cordial? Guarded?. Or all 3?, he pondered. It would perhaps be easiest to be angry. Especially when you think about the despicable enemy he was fighting. Or the Afghan people who made fools out of the Americans in the things they took and took and took. All of which usually signaled no loyalty in return on their behalf. Dawlat Shah is known as a place with poor communications and only one main road that runs into the center of the village. The majority of the population suffer from poverty. Also known is the fact that due to lack of work most young men are without occupations and many are armed and become involved in criminal activities. Not what you'd call a recipe for a mission success. Today they were going to meet with some of the leaders of the village and talk about the horrific water conditions they suffer from.

Could he have told his dad about today's work and what it entailed? Probably. But he was never real good about sharing stuff like that. Maybe he should be a little more open about what he does, he reasoned. Last week, he'd read a story called, " A Mission in Afghanistan", by Jeremie Lucia, which gave a pretty good indication of what a mission looked like. He'd cut the copy out of the magazine and had it folded in the right front pocket of his uniform. He shifted in his seat to take a view of the bouncy pavement ahead. Seeing all was well, he grabbed the article and began re-reading.

"Anytime you leave the wire on a mission a monkey leaps on your back, clutching on to your body armor with fantastic resolve. Only upon a safe return to base does the monkey release its hold; it then goes to lie in wait for the next person to torment. I don't necessarily want to label this apparition as fear, though it certainly can conjure it. There are better words for this feeling ... Unease. Disquiet. Trepidation. As service members, we know the feeling and what it means to us – it pretty much keeps us alive! Attempting to explain the sensation to a civilian is impossible. People of science might call the stir a "fight or flight" reaction brought on by stress, but to put it in such black

and white terms, completely stripped of emotion and meaning, diminishes the reality."

On this particular day the other members of my team were all away conducting critical tasks, leaving me to hold down the fort as the sole Civil Affairs contact on the F.O.B. Petty Officer Duke's mission was to carry out an assessment for providing solar lights to a local bazaar. It was time to get the project moving forward with a site visit.

One important function of Civil Affairs is to create a framework for a stronger economy with help from the local government. Providing these solar lights would allow the local bazaar to maintain longer hours of operation, thereby adding a little more fuel to the economic fire. The merchants benefit by selling more, patrons benefit by getting products they need, the government benefits by establishing more legitimacy, and coalition forces benefit by earning a more positive reception from the locals – something desperately needed in this particular area of Afghanistan.

Three Humvees make up a scant convoy traveling along one of the few paved roads in the area. The omnipresent mountain ranges paint the horizon against the clear, blue sky overhead. A plain white car dots the road, coming ever closer to the convoy. Inside, a militant conspires to explode himself and the vehicle next to the American procession, hoping to take lives of brave service members with skulking monkeys on their backs.

BOOM!

The second Humvee is his target. In a brilliant flash and a deafening blast the suicide bomber successfully carries out his mission, sacrificing his life for a terrorist cause. The detonation sends the armored truck off the road as it drives into a neighboring ditch.

"Is everyone alright?! Anyone hurt...?! Sound off!" Stunned and shaking off the effects of shock, each soldier

speaks up one by one to the tactical commander in the Humvee, who then radios their condition back to home base.

Time had seemed to stop while my heart succumbed to the bubble inflating in the back of my mind and the vortex spinning in my gut. "Everyone is fine. No one got hurt." My heart rises back up to its rightful place in my chest. "Good ... thank God," is all I can muster as the void dissipates.

"Yup", that pretty much says it", thought Charlie. "Maybe that will help the family deal with our day. Just a little sense of understanding". As the five military vehicles drew closer to Dawlat Shah they passed a number of women and girls carrying water back to their homes. Not one man was among them. When they pulled up to the building where the meeting was to take place it was apparent where they all were. Charlie had some sense that something wasn't right. He just knew it. But then he remembered. TIA. This Is Afghanistan. The place was overrun with Afghani men. Four hours later, the soldiers climbed back into their Humvees. There had been much conversation about improving water conditions with no apparent solution. There would have to be a follow up. Two hours later Mehtar Lam came into view. There was a collective sigh from some 25 soldiers when they reached the wire.

That night as Charlie sat on the edge of his bed he said a little prayer. Not one that anyone could hear. It was simply between him and the Lord. "Thank you for keeping me safe today, God". He pillowed up with all sorts of buzzing going on in his head. Tomorrow was not promised to him. Who knows what it would bring?

CHAPTER 48

As Charlie finished his short talk with God and laid back he began staring at the ceiling of the little wooden shack he shared with E2 Johnnie Perry. Martin was examining his life during his 20 years on this earth. He'd seen a whole bunch but nothing like he was experiencing in this Graveyard of Empires. Charlie had done a little history lesson on the subject and found out that three powers in the world had tried their hand at dusting off Afghanistan. None were successful. First there was Alexander the Great who conquered Persia in six months and then spent nearly three years attempting to subdue Afghanistan. Heavy losses of life and resistance were contributors to the eventual fall of his empire. Then came the British who partook in three Anglo-Afghan wars in the 19th and 20th centuries. They failed. Then, the Soviets tried to capture the country by spreading capitalism. Many tribal forces resisted and the Soviets struggle with the Mujahideen, which many believe, led to the end of the "Union". And lastly, came the United States. Same old story, different country trying to change the world.

A bevy of images came to Charlie. It was the occasional encounter with a jinglytruck that caught his fancy. The brightly colored Afghan trucks often decorated with chains and bells that make them jingle as they drive along were a hoot, he thought. The farmerbarma was the nickname for guides who escort a patrol through a village for their knowledge of local IED placements. They had been life savers. And then the depravity he'd seen. A U.S. military surveillance helicopter surveying a village in Afghanistan captured infrared camera footage of Afghan men sodomizing a poor goat. The world was full of good and bad, Charlie realized. And he was seeing the worst.

Back home in Iowa, Rod was sitting in front of his laptop dressed in a Hawkeye sweatshirt and plaid pajama bottoms. A real fashion statement. He was doodling some thoughts on paper. He used those ideas to pen his next blog post.

> **We're about five months into the deployment of the 4,000 Iowa National Guardsmen to Afghanistan which is a great time to assess what has taken place from a personal view and from feedback from other deployed military families and you the reader. Not necessarily a good and bad, but a time to vent and a time to reflect. Let's hit on the vent part first, followed by reflection.**
>
> **VENTING.....**
>
> **Why do some people/companies/and churches get it when it comes to support of deployed families, while others stand on the sideline?......Where oh where are our community leaders/media when it comes to heightening awareness of our deployed troops and needs of the families, not the soldiers, the families.....Family readiness groups are available for every deployed family, how many families truly understand the role of the FRG and use them?.......One person "can" make a difference, but how much more effective would they be if others came alongside?.....When was the last time you called a deployed family friend to check up on him/her?......Did you check on the family next to you that might need help with snow shoveling this winter, or some other need they might have?......Did you reach out to help the husband who has a wife deployed and has three daughters that he is trying to**

navigate life with? ......Got all your Christmas plans in line or how about doing something different and adopting a military family? In fact, why not adopt that family for the remainder of the deployment period?. Where were you when the Christmas lights went out?..........The Taliban is 3-0 versus Superpowers, did we not learn anything from the Soviets? Remind me why we are in Afghanistan again, would you?....Our troops are the best equipped and trained military in the world, why are we fighting from a defensive mode?..... A lot of people think crying is a sign of weakness, how could it be, when it shows you care passionately about something?.....When was the last time you prayed for our troops and what they sacrifice?....How many people know who Staff Sgt. Salvatore Giunta is?............I wonder if people think military families take care of each other, do you?.....I wonder how many more times our family will have to go through a deployment......Why are some people so ignorant when it comes to feelings?......Why do some people want to do things with their own agendas, rather than letting God offer the direction?........I wonder if War is_____? You fill in the blank on that one, okay?

REFLECTIONS....

We are a proud family of two young military men and another who watches with curiosity........I'm in awe of the courage and sacrifice of our troops each and every day....Support can come in so many different ways, not always money, maybe time, maybe prayer, maybe love, maybe ears to listen, maybe just being a friend.....We all say we need more time, find it!!! ....The Christmas lights never go out at our house.... Compassion is a trait that can help change the world...... Prioritize your day, but be ready to juggle things up when called upon......Faith is the foundation of our family's hope, our dreams and our existence......I can't wait to place a Christmas wreath in the front yard of a military family I know.....I'm looking forward to going to the Des Moines Skywalk on Christmas Eve and helping clothe the homeless, might just be a Vet there that needs some love.....I'm going to keep moving forward in drawing attention to our troops deployment and their families...... There is always another door if one gets shut.....Thank God I live in the United States of America.....I was bowled over in some support that I've gotten recently, thank you, thank you, thank you.....The writing of this blog has been inspiring, but the people I've met and the stories I've heard, have been even more inspirational.......When you least expect it, expect it......It is better to give than receive, trust me. .....Merry Christmas, yes Merry Christmas! I hope you're not offended by me saying that, because if you are, then I'm offended that you're offended..... and most importantly, thank you for being an Awesome God!!

YGG, Rod

CHAPTER 49

In some respects Christmas had come early for the several hundred soldiers of Forward Operating Base Mehtar Lam, made up mostly from the 2nd Infantry Brigade Combat Team "Red Bull" Division. The FOB had taken a big step of being "built up" on the 20th of December with their own postal exchange. Charlie was enjoying some of the shopping he could now do with the ability to feel a little more like he was at home, to go out and buy something like a cold drink, a sweet tea, or an energy drink.

"One of the biggest things the post exchange brought was a morale builder for the soldiers," Army Capt. Shane Hunter, of Grundy Center, Iowa, HHC, 1st Bn., 133rd Inf. Regt. commander, said. When Charlie's group had first hit Mehtar Lam in November it was most evident this was needed. Now the FOB had a few of the nuances some of their bigger counterparts enjoyed. Martin had gone into the exchange and made some mental notes of things he liked and hoped to buy in the future. Tonight he only had one purchase in mind. Minutes later he was sitting cross legged on the ground near the Technical Operations Center sucking down a Monster drink before he entered the building for his twelve hour shift. He was all by himself. As he stared off in the distance the only things being contemplated were some recent Afghan experiences. It was a cold crisp night, there was a dusting of new snow on the ground and the moon was providing an ample light of the surrounding land. He let out a little sigh.

Maybe it was the amp he got from the drink. Or maybe it was simply that he had more time on his hands. Having a little more of an opportunity to ponder things provided deeper thought with much more take away. First, he'd gotten some strange feedback from home from his girl, Staci. It wasn't anything she'd said but more of what she didn't say. In truth, their relationship had hit a low. She was a senior in high school with all the temptations that go with youth. Maybe it was a good thing, he considered, I wonder how many guys break up with their girlfriends when they deploy? Charlie had no interest in finding out the percentages. But he bet it was high. Would he and Staci remain an item until he came home on R and R? He couldn't be certain.

Somehow, someway, thoughts of Grandma and Grandpa Taylor entered his thought pattern. He was sure missing them. A tear formed near the corner of his right eye. Charlie looked around hoping no one had seen the little release of emotion he'd let spring forth. He could hear voices of his supervisors saying something like, "Get over it and move on". "Whatever", mumbled Charlie. Back to the thoughts of the Taylor's. They were super grandparents. When the Martins came visiting, Grandpa T loved to take the young Martin boyz to some farm property outside the Des Moines area. There in all their splendor were a couple of horses the three kids had come to adore. Grandpa named the big stallions, Camel and Jack. No one ever knew for sure how he came up with those iconic choices. But it stuck forever. Grandma was a spoiler. She served her role exquisitely. The three little rascals always felt their love when they went to the Taylor household. Holidays were the best and that's where Charlie's heart was at the moment. He'd love to be there this year, that's for sure. He took a long swig from his drink savoring the taste. Then off in the distance he heard a couple of gun shots. The sounds were far enough away to not cause an immediate concern. With the interruption, Martin's thinking took another direction.

He was now immersed in the happenings of the recent firefight he'd been in on December 6th. The 7-hour standoff had been his first. The effects were lingering. It was the first time he'd taken enemy fire. That in itself was an eye opener. But in his terms, it was doggone exciting. After months of preparation, he was finally getting an opportunity to put things to work. No matter how you train for something until you see it or feel it for the first time there is nothing to compare it to. The adrenaline rush was beyond anything he'd ever imagined. He'd been told he'd feel a great sense of strength when it hit him. He probably wouldn't feel any pain, his senses would be at an all-time high and his breathing and heart rate would jump off the charts. Every one of those descriptions fit.

The Taliban were an unusual opponent. They'd laid in waiting in a lush green valley for the five vehicle group to make its way into their crosshairs. Their ambush took place along the Alishing River separating the Americans from the village of Sagin. The tranquil morning was rudely interrupted by the sounds of what Charlie and most of his buddies thought were rocks hitting their vehicles. One after another pounded on the metal all the while increasing in their intensity. It became a virtual rain effect. The noises, however, weren't rocks but ammunition from AK 47's and PKM machine guns. Then the RPG's started. Realizing they were now under attack, Charlie's chief duty was to radio the coordinates to a mortar group. In order to do that, he needed to jump from the Humvee yet make sure the vehicle provided ample cover. Gunners on each of the trucks returned fire. After determining their location through the use of binoculars and using the direction they were traveling, Martin made the call. Five minutes later a response came in the form of some heavy explosions from his military group. Even with mortar support the Taliban were a dogged foe. Thinking back a number of years, Charlie recalled a movie he'd watched with his dad called, "Butch Cassidy and the Sundance Kid". It was a flick about a couple of bank robbers who were trying to outrun the law and no matter how hard they rode or obstacles they tried to put in place, the posse maintained pursuit. There was one line Cassidy tossed to his partner that showed his frustration in shaking the law. "Who are those guys?" That's a little what Charlie had felt with this enemy. Shoot one and two more appear. Did the Taliban aim straight? Charlie wasn't sure. He'd heard they were fairly poor shots. All he knew, the Taliban quit firing and the fighting ended.

Martin let out a longer sigh. What he'd just lived through was not something out of dad's old "Combat" TV show. It was as real as it gets. Maybe even surreal. The good thing? No one was killed or wounded from his group. Charlie coughed a little and shook his head thinking of what E5 Halverson had told him hours later. Several Taliban were found dead. Nothing would be the same in his world ever again. Nothing. He was seeing War in all its ugliness. Death had a way of doing that.

As military time 2100 approached, Charlie picked himself off the ground, brushed the snow off his camo pants and headed for the TOC. As he was walking the short distance to the building he felt something strange. It was common in this evil place to experience oddities. They were all around. But this was something else, something he'd felt a lot lately. Maybe always would from now on. He sensed someone watching him. TIA. Yes, somebody was always watching. Always.

CHAPTER 50

The 4 Martins were leaving the Hope parking lot. Eddie had flown in from Maryland for his leave and he was sitting in the back seat of the SUV with brother, Dan. Mom and Dad were in the front of the vehicle after having just seen another tremendous Christmas production. They all agreed, the church staff sure knew how to throw a good theatrical piece together each and every year. 2010 was no different.

"Isn't it awesome guys what we saw tonight", Hope announced. "I'm amazed at all the things God did for us, does for us and will do for us. I think of 2nd Chronicles 16:9; 'For the eyes of the LORD move to and fro throughout the earth looking for whose heart is completely His that He may strongly support them."

Hope's words were in stark contrast to what Charlie had felt a short time ago in Afghanistan. Her mention was from God, Charlie's was from a satanic empire. Much of what this war was came from that perspective. Good vs evil. Why did the U.S. get into this war anyway? It wasn't because of oil. The Caspian Sea region has potentially the world's largest oil reserves, likely making Central Asia the next Middle East. Maybe our government is trying to liberate the people of Afghanistan from Taliban tyranny. Hardly. A whole slew of countries have tried that. And there need not be an argument that we're trying to win the war on terrorism. Terrorism is a tactic not a political or social force. Anyone can use it. There isn't just one face.

So Charlie was quite right in the "feeling" he'd had recently. There are eyes virtually everywhere you turn. And most are of the haughty variety. If anything, E2 Charlie Martin was growing up fast. Life's lessons were having an effect on him. Rod hoped he'd someday be able to sit down with his oldest son and discuss his observations and assessments of war. He was certain he wasn't going to be supplied with any intimate details of Charlie's deployment. Nonetheless, he could put some real definitives on the subject.

Part of that maturation included realizing how important family was and is. In the past Charlie had been fairly selfish. His next move signified a change. It was approaching 4 a.m. in Mehtar Lam. As Charlie sat in front of the keyboard to his computer he typed in Hy-Vee, a Midwestern grocery store chain. Once on their website he maneuvered into their floral area and looked for a good gift for his mother. After a five minute search, he settled on a beautiful flower arrangement. As he processed his request he wondered if they'd ever had an order from Afghanistan before. Could be a first, he thought. With his job complete he moved onto his Facebook page and fired off the following message. It quickly turned into a string of thoughts.

Friday, December 24, 2010 at 5:13pm CST Merry Christmas to you guys!!!!! I love and miss you all!!!! I'll be calling you guys tomorrow and you should be receiving something from a delivery service sometime soon!

The only thing was, Charlie didn't say what day the surprise would come. The arrangement was dropped off on Christmas Eve while the Martins were at church. The delivery people left the package underneath a bench on the front porch and no one saw it. It wasn't until Dan opened the front door on Christmas morning for Mason to do his duties, that the arrangement was found. Hope fired back a message of her own.

Saturday, December 25, 2010 at 8:47am CST Hi My Uhgz!!! (nickname for her beloved first born) I got the flowers you had

sent. Oh my gosh I have never had such a beautiful arrangement. But the love that comes with it means so much. I miss you so much. They sang a PEACE ON EARTH song at church last night. I cried through the whole thing just thinking about you and the shame that war is. I love you Charlie.

Saturday, December 25, 2010 at 8:56am CST Hey Mompo. All the technology here is being stupid and the line for the phones is years long cause everyone wants to call home but I'm gonna call you guys in a few hours after it dies down. I'll be able to leave the TOC and call you guys. But I'm glad you liked it Mompo. Tell dad, dub, and pub (more nicknames) that I'll get them something later when I come home on leave to make up for it. I miss you too Mompo and I love you guys.

Saturday, December 25, 2010 at 8:57am CST on our way to Gma's. You can call us anytime!!

Saturday December 25, 2010 at 9:01am CST I will Mompo. It will be a few hours but I'll call as soon as I can. Sorry I couldn't call when I told you I was going to. I tried and it wasn't working too well. I'll talk to you soon tho! Have a safe drive! And tell everyone i love and miss them!

Hope had actually told a little white lie. She wasn't on the road to Grandma's house. Heck she wasn't even in the sleigh. She was sitting on the couch with a hot cup of steaming coffee between her hands. Hope's blonde hair was swept back behind her ears which gave greater evidence to the remainder of her garb…a purple UNI sweatshirt and little red Santa shorts. The festive lower part of her wardrobe was something she'd fashioned for a number of years. It was quite a sight. Hopefully, Charlie would be able to see next year's rendition.

CHAPTER 51

The FM radio was blasting out the old standby Christmas song, "Here Comes Santa Claus", as the Martin's made their way eastward on I-80 to the town of Montezuma. It had been a slow moving morning but Rod had finally got everyone in motion. His mother, Janice, and his older sister and brother-in-law, Raeanne and Frank Kuster, lived there in a quaint ranch home on Lake Ponderosa. Grandma Martin was the consummate food maker. Years of owning your own restaurant does that. The Kuster's had built the lake home back in 1996. The initial plan called for Grandma to live in her quarters and care take the homestead while the homeowners continued with their careers in Omaha, Nebraska enjoying their investment whenever they could. That quickly changed once the house was fully completed. Plans changed rather quickly. Raeanne and Frank quit their jobs and made it their full-time residence in 1998. Rod had been closest to his sister growing up as there was only two years difference between them. They both shared the same brother, Ray, who was the oldest and somewhat of the family head. Ray had assumed that distinction 22 years ago when their father, Randy, had passed away from a sudden heart attack.

Rod and Hope were manning the front seat of the vehicle. Eddie and Dan were holding down things in the back. "Can you turn that crap down?", yelled Dan. "We have to hear that stuff all month long. It gets kind of old". Eddie laughed at his little bro, but added, "I'll second that." "Okay you big sticks in the mud", yelled Rod. "But expect something very similar when we get to Grandma's", he said with a big loud hoot.

It was an ugly overcast morning. Temps were in the high teens and wind chills were hovering around 5 degrees. There'd been a trace of snow overnight to coat the six inches of stuff already on the ground. Those who wanted a white Christmas got their wish. The sixty minute drive to Grandmother's house always seemed longer than it was. Winter made it even more so. The route was speckled with a number of hills and valleys. Trucks seemed to make I-80 their favorite course as they used the beejeebers out of it. However, the traffic at 10 o'clock in the morning was few and far between. Most holiday travelers had already arrived at their expected destinations for the glorious day. Rod and Hope were discussing family matters on next year's holiday plans. Christmas Day would most likely be spent at the Taylors. One year, one family, the next year, the other.

Dan was using some colorful descriptors as he launched on his brother about a multitude of things he was going through. Every other sentence he punctuated with "I Don't Care". And clearly he didn't. It had been that way for a couple of months now ever since he and his folks returned home from Eddie's graduation from Basic in late October. Dan had hit a wall of discontent and withdrawal. "Dude, the days drag on with you and Charlie both gone", he offered. "I try to stay away from home as much as I can so I don't have to be around mom and dad and their talking about this deployment stuff 24-7. I just get tired of hearing about it all the time. I don't really care. I Don't Care."

To add fuel to his fire, Dan was reliving the accident he and Eddie had been in after church the night before. For some unknown reason, or more appropriate some stupid reason, the two had ventured over to the east side of Des Moines. Not the best of places. Supposedly on their way back home, Dan pulled onto University Avenue and was T-boned by a Hispanic young hottie. The 1992 BMW once owned by Rod was one of his favorites. He'd gifted the black classic to Dan on his 16th birthday. Now it was smashed metal. Well, actually totaled. Both drivers exchanged names. One had insurance. The other did not. Miss Costa Rica knowing she was completely in the wrong offered to pay for the damages. "Alright, move along", the man in blue suggested firmly. He clearly was not wanting this incident to turn into a police matter. The car was at least drivable so the boyz headed home. As they were making their journey, lo and behold a Polk County Sherriff cruiser pulled Dan over to the side of the road to question the damage to the vehicle. More crap ensued. Once Dan explained the crushed car the officer was somewhat accepting but proclaimed, "Sir, the damage I can believe, but the dark tint on your windows, I can't accept". So the less than friendly peace officer wrote Dan up for a $75 dollar ticket. "Wow, and Merry Christmas to you too", Dan had shouted as he pulled back onto the roadway. More than likely there was another word or two thrown in. "See Eddie, I can't catch a break", Dan continued. "And that's why I don't care".

Eddie tried to soothe the situation by giving Dan some brotherly advice. What Dan was experiencing was not all that unusual. Most teen-agers go through a myriad of emotional issues like this, the Martin's had heard when they attended a workshop on deployment offered by a local Military support group. All kids were different and each react differently. Some of the things they mentioned the Martin's paid "red flag" attention to was any high level of aggression or violence toward people, pets or prop-erty. And especially any mention of suicide or harming oneself and total withdrawal from the family or running away. And lastly, considerable and prolonged drop in grades or considerable and continued changes in mood, eating or sleeping patterns. Did Rod and Hope see any of their youngest in these mentions? Of course. Mainly grades, mood and withdrawal. When Eddie returned to Maryland after the Holidays, Mom and Dad realized they'd need to be more connected. One thing that was going to help was that Eddie would be coming home for good in February upon his completion of AIT.

About fifty minutes into the journey, Rod swerved off the Interstate onto Highway 146 and headed south to the little town of Searsboro. Population 148. Truly it was a speck in the road. It was one of those towns. Look right, look left and you've seen virtually everything. No traffic lights. But it did have one claim to fame. Former National Football League offensive lineman, Jeff Criswell hailed from these woods. Criswell played 171 NFL games with the Indianapolis Colts, New York Jets and Kansas City Chiefs from 1987-1998. Goes to show anyone can rise to fame despite how little or big their surroundings are.

Rod navigated a series of curves and hills as the crew maneuvered the final 5 minutes to their destination. Moments later when the presents and luggage were safely inside the lake house the holiday party began. Lake Ponderosa was a man-made lake with 500 full or part-time residences. It was really a little jewel. Tucked in a valley, there were several different fingers to the lake. It was just about the right size. Not too big and not too small. The old TV show, "Bonzana", that ran from 1959-73 and focused on a piece of land the Cartwright's owned called, the Ponderosa, brought back a multitude of character memories. However, there would not be any Little Joe, Hoss, Ben, Adam or Hop Sing present. Although, Rod and the family did have in mind the "bonanza" they'd soon be salivating over. Turkey, ham balls and a whole host of salads would be on or near the table. Snicker salad was the hands down favorite. Although, Dutch Apple pie with Cinnamon ice cream was a close second.

Once the feast was devoured the men headed to the TV area to catch the NFL Dallas Cowboys battle against the Arizona Cardinals. Nobody was a Cowboy's fan. A big contrast to the notion they were "America's Team". At least in these whereabouts. It was a weird game. The Cardinals won on a field goal with 5 seconds left to play after the Cowboys had gone ahead

26-24 late in the game. Dallas missed the extra point opening the door for the Arizona win. Talk about a Christmas gift. Final score. Cardinals 27 Dallas 26. There had been sufficient joking around during the contest among the men. The ladies had stayed busy in the kitchen. Everyone had tried to maintain status quo. And not one person had the sarcasm to say, "Sorry, Charlie".

CHAPTER 52

The next day, Rod was back in front of his laptop. It was time for another blog post but he was a little uncertain what to write about. Christmas was now a memory, one he hoped he didn't have to see in the same manner again. Not having Charlie with the rest of the family was awkward to say the least. It was like someone had passed. Thankfully that wasn't the case.

Earlier, Eddie told his mom and dad a little of what Dan was going through. While it was difficult for him to share some things the most important takeaway was Dan was not thinking suicide. Now, the in-tune connection to Dan needed to take place. Hope and Rod would need to do it without making it seem forced or fake. Kids have a much better antenna than adults give them credit for. Bingo. That's the story he needed to share. So, for the next 30 minutes he pounded the keypad and came up with the following.

> **How far back can you remember? Think about that for a minute and conjure up a memory of your age at the time. Were you 2, maybe 3 or perhaps even a little bit older?**
>
> **My memory banks take me back to an age of about 4 years old. I can recall some wallpaper in our house in Goldfield, Iowa with cowboys and horses and ropes, a real good Western theme. There's not a whole lot more I remember about the house or life in the town while we lived there. I can remember**

some of the people, but mostly because my folks kept in contact with some of them. We moved to the big city of Clarion just before I started kindergarten.

So again, I ask you. How far can you go back in your memory? Was it some traumatic experience that you recall, some miracle happening or just a run of the mill remembrance? Isn't it amazing how our minds work? Some things seem like they happened yesterday and others are completely wiped from our thoughts. What's up with that?

Anyway, the reason I bring this subject up is that I think a lot about how children are affected by the deployment of our 4,000 troops. I think of the army husband who watched his wife deploy and who is left with three teenage daughters to raise. Gosh, that must be difficult, trying to be a mother and a father at the same time and having to deal with his children's emotions and everyday struggles. I think of the father who has gone and left a young son in the care of his mother...knowing that he missed some important part of his youngsters growing years. I wonder how these children channel their emotions and feelings knowing they have a big security blanket gone

I attended a seminar this past summer that spoke to the resources available for families and educators. I was amazed to find out, that the military can't let the school systems know who deploys from their communities. I guess it makes sense, but I was still surprised. So, in many cases, children go undetected within their schools....and guidance counselors often find out when a student's grades suffer or they become a behavioral problem. I do know in one case where the parent went and met with the guidance counselor up front to let them know a deployment would be happening in their family. Kudos to them for taking the initiative to think ahead.

It's not that parents are unconcerned about the welfare of their children. Most are not even thinking that far down the road until issues begin to appear. If you know of someone that is struggling with family concerns, let them know that help is available. There is a DVD titled, "Military Youth Coping with Seperation...When Family Members Deploy". It's a great support in walking through recipes of help. You can find this and other resources at the Military Youth Deployment Support Website.

Most of all, remember the memories you help make during a deployment period will be important to your child's growth. Make the hugs and kisses when their soldier returns home the focal point when they look back on this period in their life. Make a memory.....a lasting one...a healthy one...... and a happy one!!!

YGG,

Rod

There was only one more day left in the year 2010. Hope, Rod, Charlie, Eddie and Dan....had endured a full five months of deployment. Somehow. Someway. The good news? There had not been one casualty in the 4,000 Guardsmen that left back in July and August. That in itself was a miracle. Rod had a feeling that fortune might not continue. Hope wasn't even thinking along those lines. Rod was sitting in the oversized recliner leafing through some little booklets his wife had gotten. He wasn't figuring on something hitting him between the eyes. But it did. In fact, he read the article and sat the book down and rubbed his eyes real fast at first. Then ever so slowly as if the words might look different when he regained his focus. He slid his glasses back down his nose and looked at the booklet on his lap. He needed an inspirational lift. And did he ever get one. Joni Eareckson Tada provided the text.

"Sometimes hope is hard to come by. Like the other week when I visited my friend Gracie Sutherlin in the hospital. Gracie has been volunteering at our Joni and Friends Family Retreats for many years, and despite her age of sixty-one, she's always been energetic and active with the disabled children at our camps. All that changed a month ago when she broke her neck in a tragic accident.

Gracie has always been happy and buoyant, but when I wheeled into the intensive care unit to visit her, I did not even recognize the woman lying in the hospital bed. With tubes running in and out of her, a ventilator shoved down her throat, and Crutchfield tongs screwed into her skull, Gracie looked completely helpless. She couldn't even breathe on her own. All she could do was open and close her eyes.

I sat there by Gracie's hospital bed. I read Scriptures to her. I sang to her: "Be still my soul, the Lord is on thy side." I leaned as far forward as I could and whispered, "Oh, Gracie, Gracie, remember. Hope is a good thing, maybe the best of things. And no good thing ever dies." She blinked at that point, and I knew she recognized the phrase. It's a line from the movie The Shawshank Redemption".

Eareckson Tada knows how the woman feels. On July 30, 1967, she dove into Chesapeake Bay after misjudging the shallowness of the water. She suffered a fracture between the fourth and fifth cervical levels and became a quadriplegic, paralyzed from the shoulders down. She concluded with these thoughts.

"Tomorrow morning I will wake up, and I guarantee you I'm going to be tired, my neck is going to hurt, my back is going to ache, and I'm going to say, "O Lord God, I just cannot fly all the way across the ocean. O Lord, sixteen hours on a plane. I cannot do that. Jesus, I can't do that." But I will do it because suffering produces endurance, and endurance produces character, and character produces hope, and hope never, ever, ever disappoints us". -Romans 5:3-4

Rod let the message seep deeply into his mind and soul. From now on, the word, Hope, was going into his tool belt. It was quickly becoming his all-time favorite four letter word. Not because it was the same spelling as his wife's name, but because of what it stood for.

CHAPTER 53

Eddie woke from a deep sleep. Completely disoriented. He had no idea what state or bed he was in. It took him a couple of minutes to realize he was in his own surroundings. At home. He'd been in so many beds in recent months it was hard to keep 'em all straight. He looked around the room and saw snippets from his childhood. A black t-bird model race car in one corner, a signed baseball from one of his AAU baseball teams on the nightstand and a bulletin board full of athletic game tickets and decals. On the largest wall in the bedroom was the picture of some babe dressed in a bikini and a tool belt. He had no idea of her name. It really wasn't important. Air brush did a fantastic job he chuckled as he took a long gander at her smile. The lady was a fairy tale for sure. Mr. Mason, the golden extraordinaire, was lying next to him in the sack. Seeing Eddie come to life signaled his movement as well. He stretched his long dog legs out. Just a little at first. And then seemingly enjoying the feeling, he stretched further and further. Then he flipped over onto his back. Eddie squinted at the vibrant sunlight entering his bedroom just as an image of Charlie came into his head. Is he scared to death of the country he's in? When was Charlie to get leave to come home? They were terrific questions. But there weren't answers. A now wide-awake Eddie visualized his brother beginning to wind down from his day in Taliban Country. He was probably listening to some tunes.

Something he liked to do a lot. It was getting to the point where Charlie could check another day off the deployment calendar.

Thousands of miles away there was a rustling in the shack on the Mehtar Lam base. A lone figure was watching the sun go down out the open door. The reds and oranges of the sky provided a picture worth a thousand words. An artist would have been enviable of the beauty that was present. In about five hours, Charlie would see his red Sonic Alert Bunker Bomb Extra Loud Vibrating clock move past 12 o'clock. The big numbered contraption was closing in on the signal to end 2010 and hopes for the next year, 2011. Martin was sitting on his bed dressed in a white tank top and a pair of black gym shorts mulling what most people do on New Year's Eve. Usually, people think of all the bad from the year gone by and make bold statements of how they'll change. It was New Year's Resolutions time. Before Charlie could begin deep contemplation on his list his thoughts were interrupted by a tune on the headphones strapped around his head. A new release by Bruno Mars, "Just the Way You Are", came across the waves. For several minutes Charlie was distracted by the lyrics. Funny, he thought, the Mars song said a lot about remembering a lady. But it could easily have been about him, the unforgettable person he was. But maybe more to the fact, that he was "just the way he was". But......

Martin had a couple ideas to consider with the New Year coming. One thing he could be, was a better communicator. Like telling people how much they meant to him. For his twenty some years on planet earth he'd done a pretty good job of keeping to himself. So much in fact that his parents, in particular, wondered what he was thinking most of the time. He was for all practical purposes, locked up in his thoughts and emotions. Another great consideration was to learn how to save money. He'd always been a spend first, think second, kind of guy. Good thing he had a couple of more hours to contemplate because he wasn't married to those two resolutions. But he had to think, they wouldn't be half bad ideas.

Nine and a half hours back to the west Eddie had a few New Year's Resolutions of his own to consider. Let's see, he could do this.....ah, forget that. Or maybe be this. Gosh, that would take far too much work. Maybe he could procrastinate less. That's it. He could do that. Or could he? He'd have to think about it some more. Eddie wasn't alone in his lack of commitment. Over 80% of people who make a New Year's Resolution forget them by February 1st. And only 8% carry them out long term. "I'll have to think about this", he muttered. "Maybe later. Not now." There were other things to think about. Like where to party tonight. After all, it was New Year's Eve. Maybe Dan could help him decide where to go. Two heads were always better than one. In most cases. In this case, maybe not.

Charlie was still inside the dust filled shack. He was now staring out the window with a different perspective. Being in Afghanistan, or maybe in a war zone, was something he'd wanted to do for as long as he could remember. He'd laid in his bed at night more times than he could remember thinking about how he'd react under fire. He'd had dreams about that. Tons of them. He was chomping down a stick of Wrigley's Spearmint gum as if his life depended on it. And in some respects it did. He remembered one of his elementary teachers, a Ms. Bryant that had tried to discourage his interests in being a solider. "You don't want to do that, Charlie", she cautioned. "No one wants to go get themselves killed. And that's what you'd do. For no real reason." That pissed Charlie off. Even at the young age of 11. He thought dreams were something you wanted to do and you just did it. Little did he know there would be those who wanted to rob you of those thoughts. "And she was supposed to be a molder of men and women", he said disgustedly out loud. He threw up his middle finger at the window for anyone who was watching. Maybe someone would see his anger, he hoped. As he brought the digit back into a fist, his mind questioned how long the "bird" had been around. His curiosity led him to Wikipedia for his answer. "The gesture dates back to Ancient Greece or Rome. It was meant to be a sign of disrespect". How fitting, Charlie concluded. If they can make sense of it in those times and countries, then everyone should be able to make sense of his displeasure. He raised both his hands with the middle fingers upraised. "Here's to y'all", Charlie yelled. That should get notice. Someone had to be watching. Double the pleasure. Double the fun. He'd heard that somewhere before.

2010 had been quite a year for Charlie Martin. He'd experienced one heck of a lot. And he was glad he did. He enjoyed what he was doing. It all came to light a number of years ago when he watched the movie, "McArthur". Gregory Peck, who played the role of the military giant, Douglas MacArthur, so eloquently spoke these words to a group of West Point grads. It could just as well been addressed to any soldier in the field. It was this quote that he would always remember. "Duty. Honor. Country. Those three hallowed words reverently dictate what you want to be, what you can be and what you will be". Want. Can. Will. It might not be a New Year's Resolution. But in Charlie's world, it would stick around a whole lot longer.

CHAPTER 54

The New Year was off and running. Dan was back in school. Bored, but trying to act otherwise. Eddie was in Maryland at AIT hoping his remaining weeks would fly by. Rod and Hope were.....well......hopeful. Hopeful that 2011 would be better. For everyone.

The world was hopeful too. Surveys suggested the biggest problems being faced in 2011 were some of the same old ones. Leading the list was Poverty. In second was Climate Change. Followed by Economics, International Terrorism and Availability of Energy. Down the Top 10 list was Armed Conflict and Proliferation of Nuclear Weapons. One had to wonder if the list had changed at all in the last 10 years. And then there was Charlie.

E2 Martin stepped out of the door to his Afghan home. The snoring of his shack mate was enough to drive him nuts. So rather than go down that road further, he cupped his hands as he lit the cigarette dangling from his lips. The sun was beginning to rise over the mountain range bringing a day he was never promised, yet was glad to see. Charlie let the moment sink in, soothe him from his core right out to where the dawning rays touched his skin. It was the beginning of a new day of possibilities, which meant hope.

A little smirk came across Charlie's mug. Then it got a whole lot wider. He took a long drag off his cancer stick and took a seat on the 800 lb. boulder many a Mehtar Lam soldier had sat on to contemplate matters. Charlie was up to something but he was taking another one's direction on the matter. Let it be known, he was one willing participant though. The ring leader was one Rod Martin. And it all had to do with a soldiers R and R.

Charlie had found out the night before that he was finally scheduled to go back to the states for leave. He shared it with his dad on Facebook. That started the cover up. "Did you tell your mom", said Rod. "No, you're the first to know", replied Charlie. "Okay, great", exclaimed Rod. "Let's have some fun. Want to"?

It didn't come to asking Charlie the question a second time. Charlie was all in. Rod took over the ringleader duties. If anyone was ever considered cantankerous, it was Rod. He loved a good joke. But he loved making something special too. And this was so much more of the latter. "When do you think you'll leave, and then how long will it take you to get here", Rod questioned. The two drafted a plan. At least a tentative one. Air travel delays were going to be the biggest factor in what they had up their sleeves. "Dad that sounds great", Charlie fired back. "But what if things don't go as planned?" "We'll figure it out. Trust me, son. We'll get past the ifs."

Two days later, Charlie began his journey home. It was going to be a long trip back. But it was sorely needed. He had some things to deal with. For now though, he could relax a little. But strange as that was, it wasn't what he thought it might be. He was still on guard looking right and left and sizing up his surroundings. Maybe when he got back in the states it'd be different. Then again, maybe not.

The big Boeing 747's wheels came off the ground at the Oshi International Airport in Kyrgyzstan headed for the United States. There was some applause, a few cuss words and also a collective sigh of relief. Over 400 soldiers looked down at a region with some disdain. Then they looked up. Some looking to the clouds. And some higher, much higher than that.

While Charlie was airborne, his brothers and dad were putting their finishing touches on a Homecoming. Eddie had done his part in saying he had a long weekend and wanted to come home again. For the life of her, Hope couldn't understand why. Dan and Rod took his supposed wishes and delivered up a story Hope bought lock, stock and barrel. This would get them to the airport with Hope believing they were picking up Eddie.

The wait was going to be forever. But if all went off as planned, it would be one for the Ages.

CHAPTER 55

Hope was dragging her feet a little bit. Her husband and sons were finishing their "ultimate" plan. She was in no big hurry to get ready to head to the airport. It looked like the 4 Horsemen were going to pull off one big piece of handiwork. Hopefully they wouldn't be called the 4 HorsesAsses. Surprises are one of life's greatest pleasures. One and a half hours away and counting. Rod grabbed a seat at the dining room table and started pounding away at his laptop keys. His post looked like this....

This might be my favorite journal posting that I've ever written.....gosh, what am I saying? Without question this is my favorite journal posting......you're coming home on leave!!!

When I finish writing these words, I'll hop in the truck and head for the airport to pick you up. It's been a long five days since you told me paperwork had been completed for your "leave" and when you finally are touching down in the states. What a journey. Afghanistan to Kuwait, to Dallas, then Chicago and then Des Moines. It's been even harder to keep this a surprise for your Mom! I can be sneaky at times....well, that's probably not the best word to use, how about I say creative as we put together a great "gotcha" moment? It will be emotional to say the least to see your mother "melt" when she sees you for the first time, in a LONG time. Heck, I'll probably do that when we connect at DM International.

During the last several days, mom has asked repeatedly if I've heard from you. I told her you were out on a mission and would be back on Wednesday or Thursday. My guess is, if she had to go much longer not hearing from you, she'd hop a plane herself to Afghanistan. So, these are a couple of thoughts I have as I get ready to head out.

First off, I want this to be a relaxing time for you. It's your two weeks and you need some rest and relaxation. Secondly, I hope we have some great one-on-one time that allows you to talk about anything and everything you'd like. And thirdly, help me to make you laugh and cut up. I want to hear that funny laugh of yours again!

I've heard about many soldiers whose leave time have turned into "nightmares" for both the soldier and his/her family. I'm sure there are preconceived thoughts as to what each wants to take place during those two weeks. I'm not going into this with anything other than your wishes and desires to be met.

In addition to your Mom and brother's moment, I'm most interested to see our dog Mason's reaction to hearing your voice. Our first Golden, Nala, was a smiler. Mason is getting better at expressing himself. I think he has a big grin stored up for you. He has missed you a lot. His, go-Mace-goes are prime for the snow covered yard. Oh.....yeah, sorry about that. I tried to hold off on the snow coming. I know you don't like it any better than I do. I'm sure you'll have to be happy with just starting up that new motorcycle and listening to it purrrrrrrrrrrrrrrrrr....and dream what it would be like to take it for a spin. Knowing you though, my guess is that on any warm day we get, you'll peel around the block, right?

Okay....I think I'm ready to shut this post down. It's been almost six months since we've seen you....and it seems like six years. I hope you remember me. I'll be the short little guy with a smile a mile wide and tears streaming down his cheeks. Welcome home son!!!!

Get ready for some tears from your family. And maybe even some shock and awe.....

YGG,

Rod

CHAPTER 56

"Come on Mom", Dan shouted. "Yeah, dear get a move on or we're going to be late", added Rod. Dan and Rod Martin were taking a chance. It wasn't all that long ago Rod had told his youngest son, you don't ever want to tell a female they're running late. You might win the argument but you'll pay for it later, Rod alluded. But today was unlike any other. If the two of them got in trouble, so be it. It was going to be worth it.

The three had just entered the carousel doors of the Des Moines International Airport. Both men had on their North Face Triclimate jackets. Dan's was a dark blue and Rod's was gray. Both had on blue jeans and black sneakers. They could almost have passed for twin brothers. Well almost. Hope had on a light taupe Eddie Bauer Astoria Hooded Down Parka with a pair of black designer Levi's and white Nike's. They were all dressed for warmth. There was a surprise about to unfold. Eddie Martin was on his way home for a weekend visit. Or was he? That's what Hope had been told. Hope describes the circumstances....

> **"Rod asked me about my experience of Charlie's coming home for Rest and Relaxation. It's a difficult thing for me to put words to. I have never been so surprised in all my life. What a beautiful thing for my men to have arranged for me. But at the other end of beauty was such emotion that I have no words to explain. But I will try and tell the story".**

"The Martin men did a superb job of secrecy. Total stealth. I however was restless as a bird caught down in a window well wondering when I would see Charlie again. I loved that Eddie wanted to come home again, but he was just home a short time ago and I knew a flight back would be quite expensive. I know he can't afford this, I kept saying to myself and to Rod.

Rod, Dan and I were on the way to the airport to pick up our penniless Eddie. The rascal was in on the setup from his barracks room in Maryland texting me all the while. I was engrossed in pounding out my messages to him, lagging behind Rod and Dan as we walked into the airport. 'Where should we meet you Eddie? Have you landed yet?' I was a one finger texter, never could get used to the flying thumbs method. 'Eddie? Should we meet you at the luggage carousel?' Dan breaks in, "come on Mom, would you walk with us, slowpoke?" "I'm coming. What's the big hurry?, I asked. I've not gotten a text back from your brother yet". I continued to look down at my phone, waiting as if a red light is taking its time at finally turning green. Then I heard it- "there he is!", Dan blurted. I looked up and got the shock of my life. My beloved, precious, priceless Charlie was walking towards us. I stopped dead in my tracks, turned white as a ghost and dropped my purse. Truly, I was speechless. This is where I can't put into words my thoughts or feelings. He carried his big military duffle and was dressed in full military attire. He walked up to me and I grabbed ahold of him like Mary and Martha must have embraced their brother Lazarus when Jesus brought him back to life. My heart was pounding and I could hardly breathe. There was a lump in my throat I could hardly swallow around. I held on to him like nothing I'd ever held before. My tears were running unashamedly. There is no way to describe the feeling of getting someone you love so much back into your embrace, fearing for months that you may not get that gift ever again. I'm sure Charlie wondered if I would ever release my hold on him knowing that he had a father and a brother waiting for the same gift.

In many ways, Hope was reborn that night.

CHAPTER 57

Rod was in the SUV with no particular destination spot in mind. First, he'd gone to Saylorville Lake, a popular recreation area north of Des Moines. He'd driven around the man-made body of water with his head in the clouds. Or at least it appeared that way considering his mind was way, way off. He had been amused at the throng of ducks that had been in flight throughout his drive. It most likely was exercise time before they went and settled their little fannies in the cold, crisp water. It was nearing 5 p.m. The big orange ball in front of his eyes was the setting sun. How marvelous, he thought. And in another way, how sad. Another day was coming to an end.

Martin was now heading west on Highway 141 towards the little town of Woodward. He noticed a few road signs along the way. It took him back to a time when he was a little shaver and a cute marketing concept one company had come up with. The thought was to space small signs in order so passing motorists could read them every so many feet. A few doozies looked like this. "If daisies / Are your / Favorite flower / Keep pushin' up those / Miles per hour / Burma-Shave" Or "He lit a match / To check the gas tank / That's why / They call him / Skinless Frank / Burma Shave" and "Angels / Who guard you / When you drive / Usually / Retire at 65 / Burma-Shave. Martin recalled it being a hoot when his family had come across the series of signs. Everyone had enjoyed reading the roadside signs. Continuing westward into the setting sun Rod came up with one of his own. "My son/ Is home/From the War/Now I Wish/There was no more/ Burma Shave. Heck he could be a writer for Burma Shave, Rod concluded. A darn good one. However, another mile down the road Rod came to his wits. Maybe it was the time of day. Or quite possibly the fact that his son was home got him back on track. He looked in the rearview mirror and then far down the road ahead before he made a U-turn to head back to Johnston. Reality was beginning to set back in.

For the balance of the trip Rod made some other conclusions. First, the surprise at the airport had been successful. Hope had been stunned to say the least. Her heart hadn't stopped but it might have skipped a beat or two. And most importantly, she wasn't angry how things went down. Seeing Charlie in front of her had been one of her best presents ever. Rod's other assumption had to do with his son Charlie. Ever since he could remember, Charlie had been an inquisitive one. He had a favorite word. One for just about every occasion. Just this particular morn, Rod was reminded as he read some words of inspiration and guidance. The resource came from "Daily Guideposts", a daily inspiration for Military families. He knew for certain how tremendously helpful it had been to the Martin family....in so many ways. It calmed the storms, it had given different slants to their struggles, but most importantly, it provided a sword and armed them for what the World had in store. The message of the day was spot on. Author Philip Zakeski gave some insight to the word "why".

Zaleski told about his young son, Andy, who asked the question, "why do we die of old age?" In reply, father Zaleski responded, "because when you get older and older, you get slower and slower, until finally you stop". Andy came back again, "why do we taste with our mouth?" "Because we have taste buds", Philip said. "Then do we have smell buds in our nose and hear buds in our ears?", Andy fired back. Dad countered with, "I don't think so". Then here it came............"Why not?", asked Andy. Dad made a quick discussion shift, perhaps knowing that Andy was in his "why" mode.

It appears that when Andy reaches that questioning mode, he has more questions than Dad has answers. Zaleski's wife suggested that every time these back and forths took place, she was reminded that every child has a "Why" chromosome.

As Rod entered the door from the garage into the Martin's house, he hailed, "Hi, maw". The friendly overture was directed at his wife who was busy in the kitchen preparing one of her favorite home-made pizza recipes. She raised her head from where she'd been concentrating on working over the dough and gave somewhat of a smile. Rut-row, Rod thought. "Something wrong?", he queried. "You could say that", she returned. "Charlie has been home three days now and we've seen very little of him. I don't know whether to plan on him for meals or whether he'll even be around. I kinda thought he might hang with us a little bit". "Yeah, well it is what it is, dear", Rod offered. "Who knows what's going on with him? We just have to give him space. I was thinking about him a little while ago how he always asked questions. Mostly "why". I don't see any of that from him. He seems pretty walled off. Or maybe I should say, checked out. At least he's home". The Martin's discussion was interrupted by their youngest son, Dan. He had been upstairs in his bedroom doing some homework and was now bounding down the stairs headed out to meet up with his older brother. "Probably won't be home for dinner, mom", he said. "Okay..... okay", she stuttered. And bam, Dan was gone.

Rod looked at his wife and shrugged his shoulders. "Oh Well dear. You and me, I guess, huh?", he added. Rod turned and dissolved into the living room near the TV. He turned on Fox News but it was more for background noise than anything else. That is until the headlines of the day were tossed out by a pretty blonde woman newscaster. She read flawlessly from the teleprompter. "January 16, 2010. The headlines. Today, a Los Angeles prosecutor urged a judge to deny Roman Polanski's request to be sentenced in a three-decade-old child-sex case without surrendering to U.S. authorities. While overseas, one of Al Qaeda's top military strategists in Yemen was reportedly killed along with five other militants in airstrikes targeting two vehicles in the country's northeastern mountains. And back home, wrestling with a multibillion-dollar budget deficit, Arizona decided to close nearly all of its state parks, including the famed Tombstone Courthouse and Yuma Territorial Prison". Rod dropped his head towards his lap. "Good golly", he said out loud. "Is there ever a slice of good news anywhere"? "And in the entertainment business, "Avatar" won a record-breaking six Critics' Choice Movie Awards, but it was the independent Iraq war drama "The Hurt Locker" that took home the best picture honors from the Broadcast Film Critics Association". "Nice", Rod spoke. "The Hurt Locker was awesome".

Rod's attention left the TV again when the commercials began playing. More often than not, they were a tune out factor for him. His thoughts returned to his son Charlie. He'd had a dream about him last night. Not about being in Afghanistan, but back home. Most likely it'd come from Charlie taking his Crotch Rocket for a spin. Iowa was experiencing a warming trend for January. The snow was nearly all gone and temperatures had reached 65 degrees during the daytime. Charlie had gone for a joy ride and put his motorcycle through the paces hitting 120 mph on Interstate 80. Considering there was still a tremendous amount of sand on the road from an earlier snow, Rod had considered this less than intelligent. In Rod's dream what was evident in nearly every aspect was the danger or risk involved by Charlie. Achieving an adrenalin rush was always the main goal. Rod had heard about these "highs" in some research he'd done on soldiers returning home. He'd never be able to understand it, but he wasn't all that surprised his son was living it out. But what about Charlie's dreams, Rod thought. Now that he'd accomplished his wish to be a soldier, what was ahead? Or did he even care to go there? If a person can't dream, what is there? There's no life and no hope, Rod reasoned.

There wasn't much more dreaming in the Martin household for the next 11 days. Time flew by. Charlie was packing in the downstairs bedroom for his return flight to the hell hole. Hope was in the room folding and pressing things into the crevices of his bag to take advantage of every square inch. She stole several glances at Charlie but he did not return the action. His focus was clearly on getting on the road and getting the goodbyes behind him. It was as if Charlie Martin had found a new home. Or at least a new place to get on with life. And it wasn't in Johnston. It wasn't in Iowa. And it wasn't even in the United States. "I think I've got everything", Charlie voiced. "Let's get out of here."

CHAPTER 58

Rod was bushed. Or maybe drained. One or the other. Or maybe both. All he knew was Charlie had come home on leave and now he was gone again. It was the next day and the blog beckoned. Before he forgot all of his emotions he sat down and pounded out these thoughts...

Yesterday morning we saw our son, Charlie, off at Des Moines International Airport as his 15-day leave concluded and he began his long journey back to Afghanistan. I must say, this time was a whole lot different than when his deployment began from Boone, Iowa on July 30th. At the summer send-off, we were surrounded by hundreds of other families all experiencing much the same as us. There were tears, red faces and quite a bit of sobbing. Yesterday, there were two soldiers (Charlie Martin and another boyish looking military type) leaving from Gate C-1. We were the only family present to say good-bye. How sad must that have been for the one all alone. There were moist eyes, a bunch of uncertainty, but nowhere near the same emotions as the summertime departure....at least outwardly that is. And the funny thing is.....I'm not sure why.

I'll let you in on a few things I think might be causing this "flat" response. Because somewhere among them is no doubt the answer. First off, it wouldn't have taken much for someone to see that our soldier wanted to be home and then again, he didn't. I'll bet he dreamed of getting back to seeing his friends, his car, his new motorcycle and the aspect of "home". But the other part of home, the one that meant involved conversations, connecting on a deep, personal level or one that dug deeper into his attachment of the surroundings of his family.... hmmmmmmmmm PN (Probably Not).

I asked Charlie what was the thing that he thought of most when he was on the 5-day airplane trip headed to Des Moines. "Home", he said. That shocked me, really, because that isn't what I saw. We asked two things of him while he was with us. A lunch with his grandparents and a videotaping at our church....that's it. The remaining time was all his. He could do anything he wanted. What my wife and I saw, or thought we saw, was a soldier who didn't want to get close to anything while he was home for fear.......

Five and a half months remain on Charlie's deployment. I think that's what many soldiers think about when they come home on leave, the time that's remaining. Makes me wonder if they come home, try and put on a good face, show everyone that they're the same "old" person, when in fact, they're not. And we're not. Most parents, spouses, siblings or grandparents could easily see themselves smothering a soldier with love during their leave. However, even though that's exactly what a soldier would like too, I'm slowly convincing myself that defense mechanisms override and walls go up. Kind of like, I would like that affection, but then I don't. Charlie texted his mom and I while he was awaiting his international flight at the Atlanta airport yesterday evening that he was having a hard time expressing his feelings regarding leave. He did Facebook some thoughts though. "Atlanta sucks. I wish I was either back home or in Afghanistan", he said. As much as that seems odd, I think the thought is, "no limbo, please". Either get me back home or back to work. So, you can see the thoughts are kicking in. And I'll bet he's still processing today as he nears his landing in Kuwait.

So, I have mixed feelings, for sure about "leave". On one hand, it's great to be able to touch and hug a person again that means so much to you. On the other, you know you have to release them to go back to a war zone for another half-year. One family that I've met through this deployment process has a soldier coming home in June for leave. Let's see, 15-day leave, then back to Afghanistan for three weeks and then back home. Now that will be tough!!. I've been told that with the number of troops deployed, the only way everyone could get leave was to space it out. Thus, some got real early leaves and others way late. With 4,000 troops, I'm sure scheduling leaves is a nightmare in itself.

More than anything....everyone's experiences will be unique when their soldier comes home for leave. Don't be too high or too low in your expectations. Perhaps the best thing you can do, is just be there for them. You can always process the moments later, just like we are now. There are roughly 181 days left....that will sure allow some time for you and I and our soldiers to process over and over. God bless us all with that.

YGG,

Rod

* * *

As his hands left the keyboard, Rod had this deep down feeling he wanted to cry. He choked a little bit. But that was about it. The tears didn't come. For now, the well was dry. 181 left. The finish line was not even in sight.

Hope embracing the moment before Charlie's departure

CHAPTER 59

Charlie moved in his seat for the umpteenth time. He simply couldn't get comfortable. He was about halfway to the destination of his home away from home. This trip was much different. Maybe that had something to do with his discomfort. It wasn't so much that he had any anguish about returning to Afghanistan, it was more that he was uncertain of where he was going to be located. Before he'd left on his R and R, Charlie had heard rumors of possibly going to another base to back fill some other soldier's time off.

Martin was in seat number 5 of a row of 8. Being smack dab in the middle, Charlie didn't have to get up every two seconds to let someone out to go to the bathroom. He at least had ample opportunity to ponder and dream. "I wonder what everyone's doing back home", he muttered out loud. The soldier in the aisle seat next to Charlie looked at him for a minute, not sure if he was talking to him or not. Martin stole a glance at the curious one, nodded his head and then went back into his little shell.

The two plus weeks home had not been exactly what he thought it would be. First off, time passed way too quickly. Secondly, it wasn't nearly as relaxing as he'd thought it was going to be. He'd hung around at a neighbor's house with his brother and friends for a good share of the time. Gotten a few rides in on his new motorcycle. And saw a few relatives. Spent a little time with his parents. And that was about it.

Before he knew it, Charlie was back at the airport with his folks, brother Dan, and a couple of high school friends. Despite knowing the potential dangers that awaited him, he felt no different than when he'd left the states the first time back in October. Some might call it a lack of emotion. Some stiff necked. And others suggest it was the military training he'd received. He didn't shed any tears. The voice was strong and unwavering. The only thing lacking was the lack of eye contact. Maybe that was the secret to keeping emotions in check. Whatever it was, Charlie had walked slowly onto the plane visibly unshaken.

Hope offered some additional thoughts of what she'd gone through with his R and R.

> Charlie will never know how our hearts ached for him while he was at war. Or even know how our hearts have bled for him since he has been home. Nor will we ever know what he went through. Or what he was going back into. The two weeks he was home were an odd experience of some relief, knowing he was safe at home. And yet a deep sense of grief, for me anyway, sensing Charlie was not able to really relax or connect with us. To do so would make the journey back too difficult I am sure. So he was distant from Rod and I in particular. I wanted to make him all his favorite foods and to see him lounging around the house and telling us about his experiences thus far. But that didn't happen. He kept himself distracted by being gone a lot. He never once slept in his own bed. Looking back on it, I do understand his need to keep his guard up. It must have been difficult to come home and yet not be able to feel all the comforts of home because it is but temporary. The grief I felt when Charlie left our shores again was also a shock to me. I slept, or rather laid awake, in his bed for many nights. I have never cried like I cried on those nights, gut wrenching, down deep, soul searching wailing. It was a good thing that his room was in a corner of the finished basement. It allowed me to

dump my pain somewhat in private. I went from being numb at the airport when we said our goodbyes to being so torn apart I wasn't sure if I'd be put back together again. It was only in remembering and really thinking about what I knew was true, that I found peace again. Charlie was not mine and not 'ours'. He was on loan to us, but he was God's. And God loves him even more than we do. I knew God would see him through even if it meant he would no longer be with us. I know this life is temporary and tomorrow is promised to no one this side of Heaven. Something could happen to any one of us whether we were at war or not. My focus had to get off of fearing for Charlie and on to trusting God. In this I found comfort and hope and that's what held me together. Our sons are all such gifts to me. Not just Charlie but Eddie and Dan as well. And they too belong to God and I have the privilege of having them on loan to me, to us. I hand each of them back to their Maker in whom I have such Hope. That hope and trust enables me to carry on. To fight my own fight. Hope Is A Weapon....with it I can get up and face whatever this life brings me".

Charlie looked down at his satchel on the floor of the big bird noticing the book his dad had bought him. It was a paperback written by Marcus Luttrell and Patrick Robinson called "Lone Survivor". Now seemed as good as time as any to take a peek at the pages. So Charlie began to read. And he continued to read. And read some more.

Little did Charlie know, but his dad was reading the book at the exact same time he was. Rod had started on Luttrell's book the night before Charlie left to return to Afghanistan. He was finding the subject, the approach and the tense moments something bordering on a suspense novel.

The story was of a 2005 Seal Team mission called Operation Red Wings. These specialists were deposited deep into the inhospitable mountains of Kunar Province to capture or kill a senior Taliban commander responsible for murdering Marines. But the assignment quickly becomes compromised when they're confronted by a family of Afghan shepherds who may or may not have been affiliated with the enemy. The Seals were forced with a decision, should they kill them or let them go? The choice wasn't black-and-white. The rules of engagement say one thing, their guts another. Tragically, the decision our government wanted them to follow sealed their fates. Soon they were pinned down taking fire, outmanned and outgunned. Here is an excerpt from the book:

"Afghanistan. This was very different. Those mountains up in the northeast, the western end of the mighty range of the Hindu Kush, were the very same mountains where the Taliban had sheltered the lunatics of Al Qaeda, shielded the crazed followers of Osama bin Laden while they plotted the attacks on the World Trade Center in New York on 9/11.

This was where bin Laden's fighters found a home training base. Let's face it, Al Qaeda means "the base," and in return for the Saudi fanatic bin Laden's money, the Taliban made it all possible. Right now these very same guys, the remnants of the Taliban and the last few tribal warriors of Al Qaeda, were preparing to start over, trying to fight their way through the mountain passes, intent on setting up new training camps and military headquarters and, eventually, their own government in place of the democratically elected one.

They may not have been the precise same guys who planned 9/11. But they were most certainly their descendants, their heirs, and their followers. They were part of the same crowd who knocked down the North and South towers in the Big Apple on the infamous Tuesday morning in 2001. And our coming task was to stop them, right there in those mountains, by whatever means necessary.

Thus far, those mountain men had been kicking some serious ass in their skirmishes with our military. Which was more

or less why the brass had sent for us. When things get very rough, they usually send for us. That's why the navy spends years training SEAL teams in Coronado, California, and Virginia Beach. Especially for times like these, when Uncle Sam's velvet glove makes way for the iron fist of SPECWARCOM (that's Special Forces Command).

And that was why all of us were here. Our mission may have been strategic, it may have been secret. However, one point was crystalline clear, at least to the six SEALs in that rumbling Hercules high above the Arabian Desert. This was payback time for the World Trade Center. We were coming after the guys who did it. If not the actual guys, then their blood brothers, the lunatics who still wished us dead and might try it again. Same thing, right?"

Unfortunately, Luttrell was the only one of four men on the mission to survive after a violent clash with dozens of Taliban fighters. Eight members of the SEALs and eight Army special operations soldiers who came by helicopter to rescue the original four were shot down, and all aboard were killed. Luttrell was then rescued by a group of Afghan Pashtun villagers who harbored him in their homes for several days, protecting him from the Taliban and ultimately helping him to safety, according to a New York Times story on August 9, 2007.

This is what Charlie was facing. And Rod wondered if he actually knew the historical importance of it all. Hopefully he did. If not, maybe the book could give him a better perspective. Charlie looked out the window of the C-17 and saw the ground below. He assumed it was Kuwait but he wasn't positive as he and the other 100 soldiers departed the flying machine. This was to be a short layover until orders were all set for a group to head to Bagram Airfield. But that wasn't the case. The old classic army line was about ready to rear its ugly head. Time to hurry up and wait. And wait. And wait.

CHAPTER 60

Two days later the call finally came. Wheels up for Jalalabad. Charlie's time spent at Bagram was both good and bad. He'd been able to continue reading "Lone Survivor" and caught up on some much needed sleep. This was Martin's third time at Bagram but the previous two had been in and out with no layover. Charlie asked a buddy of his, E3 Jason Sullivan, about the nuances of the area so he'd know where to go and what to avoid. "Part of my duties in Afghanistan was escorting NDS agents (Afghan's CIA/FBI ... kinda... ugh) from FOB to FOB. So Bagram being the 1 of 2 central hubs for flights, I got to stop there a lot", said Sullivan. "Now I only got to stay in the transient tents (probably like 300 people squeezed into a big tent) and once my unit managed to negotiate me into a two man room (which wasn't bad at all), so I'm not too familiar with the living conditions for personnel assigned to Bagram. Our unit's POC did have her own little room in a wooden building there. There are quite a few brick and mortar buildings, saw several huts too. Aside from that, there's pretty good roads, a good KBR ran chow hall, a HUGE (by Afghan standards) PX with surrounding shops and a bazaar". Sullivan continued, "There's Russian massage shops ....uh huh. There's also since my visit, a BK, Popeye's Chicken, Pizza Hut, Subway and Green Bean Coffee. I saw security forces doing airfield security and MPs driving around giving people "tickets". Too many tickets and they take away your GOV privileges (happened to our POC for speeding, lol). I thoroughly enjoyed it there. Oh...the Pat Tillman center plays movies 24/7 too! All in all Bagram is like a vacation inside a warzone".

Charlie had taken Sullivan's advice on several things. He saw a couple of flicks at the Tillman Center and got some hot brew at Green Bean Coffee. He had set down residence in the transient tents which was an adventure all to itself. 300 dudes snoring off-key was not blissful. It made for a restless sleep. That's why his daytime nap was a highlight. Sullivan had nailed his description to a T.

But there was a flip side. Bagram was a dangerous area. And getting more so by the day. In May of 2010 the Taliban proved just how fragile the area was. Here is what was reported. "In what appeared to be a new strategy of increasingly high-profile attacks, small groups of raiders tried to penetrate Bagram, in northern Afghanistan, killing an American contractor and wounding nine soldiers.

The choice of such a symbolic target and its timing — one day after six soldiers were killed in a suicide blast in Kabul — suggest insurgents are trying to strike at the very heart of Nato operations while international troops prepare for an assault on their southern stronghold of Kandahar. The sprawling base at Bagram is home to thousands of American troops and houses a notorious detention centre making it a key target for insurgents who appear to be picking targets that will generate most headlines. Bagram, known as "the other Guantanamo", has become a feared symbol of arbitrary detention and alleged torture in Afghanistan. The militants launched their attack, hurling grenades and firing machine guns. It continued for hours with sporadic rocket and small arms fire. Ten insurgents were killed, including four who detonated suicide vests", US officers said.

Charlie made the walk on the runway to the C-130. He and another 60 soldiers single-filed on the bird that would take them to Jalalabad before the last leg of the trip to Mehtar Lam by a Black Hawk helicopter.

Another 24 hours later Charlie tossed his bags down in the hut, bushed and happy at least to be in familiar surroundings. That was until he heard the old crony call, "Martin, get your ass up here. Where the hell you been?" There was only one voice that could be. E5 Thomas Gibson. Charlie had more than one dream while he was on R and R where the Sarge had been front and center yelling and screaming. Wow, Martin thought, dreams do become reality. Was that something he couldn't handle? No. Was it enough to convince him the Sarge was overboard? No. Was he glad there was someone like the old geezer leading his unit? Yes. And the bigger realization was, Charlie knew....duty was calling.

Charlie ready to roll

CHAPTER 61

Charlie was back in Afghanistan and in his state of "normalcy". Rod, on the other hand, was nowhere near that. Hope was a mess, at least inwardly. Dan was thinking more of Eddie coming home from AIT and not so much about family dynamics. The days had now turned into weeks since Charlie completed his R and R. The passing of time had not done anything to ebb the tide. Rod was still trying to make sense of his coming home. Initially he was upset with the lack of connectivity that took place between Charlie and the family. Then hurt feelings settled in. And ultimately, it turned into a slow, slow burn.

"Why do they even give soldiers time to go home?", he thought. Rod's best guess was, most R and R's end up this way. It was probably better if military personnel were sent to some remote island rather than going home, he thought. An even bigger question welling up inside the elder Rod was his wondering how many soldiers went AWOL rather than return to the war zone. Rod read up on the subject and found out some thoughts that helped bring him some understanding. He found out his range of feelings were very normal. He recalled how the family was so happy to get Charlie home. But along with that excitement came additional vibes of sadness or even madness about saying good-bye again. It had been a shear roller coaster of emotions. Very little discussion of Afghanistan had taken place among the family. Charlie had shown his brothers some disgusting videos of Afghan culture. It was probably a good thing he didn't share those images with his mom and dad.

Rod had not mentioned anything about one of Charlie's fellow guardsmen suffering misfortune while he was home. The information had come across the wires while Charlie was on his way to Iowa.

"Sgt. Brian Pfeiler became Iowa's first major casualty of the Afghan War this past Thursday when he stepped on a landmine while on foot patrol. Reports indicate that Pfeiler lost his right foot in the explosion. He is a member of Dubuque's Company D, 1st Battalion, 133rd Infantry Regiment Task Force Ironman. The Guard says the mine blast occurred in the eastern province of Laghman".

Rod blogged about Pfeiler's incident and gave a little of the sergeant's family insight.

"I was notified by the military Thursday morning about 8:40 (Iowa time)," said Kate, Pfeiler's wife of five years. "They said, 'I have some news to tell you. Your husband's been injured. He stepped on a landmine and had an injury to his right leg.' They told me he was stable." Okay, picture that for a minute. You're Mrs. Pfeiler and you hear the news...your husband has been injured. How do you react? What comes to mind? What words come out of your mouth?

This is what Rod and his family were struggling with. How do you react and what do you say and do you say it? That was the Martin's issue. Needless to say, Pfeiler's misfortune was sidestepped, but that was just the beginning. After a quiet couple of months in Afghanistan, things were quickly changing. Days after Charlie returned to the war zone came the worst possible news. One of his own had been killed Stunned and with a heart aching for a family he didn't know came Rod's blog post.

"What will happen is God's business. Remaining faithful, no matter what happens, is yours". These are the words that jumped off the page to me today in reading "Daily Guideposts....Daily Inspiration for Our Military Families". So it is with those thoughts that I share with you my impressions of the day of Specialist Shawn A. Muhr's funeral, Sunday February 6th.

As my wife and I made the drive to Coon Rapids, Iowa Sunday morning, I found myself hoping for a glimmer of sun, somewhere....anywhere. The day was gray, cold and a fresh snow fall blanketed much of the countryside. It was a somber day. A day for reflection and a day that we'd try to find out more about Specialist Muhr. And most importantly, it was a time to pay our respects for a job well done.

Arriving at Coon Rapids-Bayard High School, we were "drenched" in an array of U.S. flags. It was a humbling experience to enter the school through this patriotic doorway. As we crossed the threshold, we came face to face with a number of military personnel and Iowa's Commander in Chief, Governor Terry Branstad. The Governor's presence gave me comfort that one of our own had not been forgotten....that Super Bowl Sunday had not gotten in the way of our leaders taking the time to remember.

After signing the guest list, we made our way into the gymnasium where over 500 were already assembled. The mood was calm and quiet. At 1:30 p.m. promptly a young man from the Coon Rapids community opened with a very nice rendition of the Star Spangled Banner. He didn't forget the words and he didn't try to over exaggerate the song. He nailed it.

The service itself had several rough moments. The audio system had numerous failures and feedback issues. I found myself wondering if Shawn, the man they called "Ox", was being ornery, as he was known to have been over the years. Was he trying to get everyone's attention, one last time? I also found the music selections quite unusual for a young man of his age, 26. How did he ever develop a taste for Jimmy's Dean's "Big John" and Claude King's "Wolverton Mountain?" It had to be the sure country in him coming out. The final choice of music, "The Ballad of the Green Beret" provided the lead-in to recognition from his fellow officers and soldiers.

Maj. Gen. Rodney Anderson spoke on behalf of the 546th Transportation Company, 264th Combat Sustainment Support Battalion, 82nd Sustainment Brigade of Fort Bragg, N.C.. The Major used such words, as "loyal, larger than life, always uplifting, exceptional Soldier....and Awesome", as a means to emphasize the fact that his buddies will roll on in his honor. Major Gen. Anderson's words captured much about the man, Shawn Muhr. Other words were brought forth by one of his best friends, who wrote a poem that appeared on the back of the bulletin.

"OX"

Leaving my family and friends today

Shipped off to another place to stay

I was always there to help, always knew what to do ....I always knew that I was part of my Crew

It was always hard to leave my family behind But I knew that my buddies needed me on that line

I fought for your life, and so many others I fought for all of my sisters and brothers When I got into the fight

I knew what to do I was always on mission, that wasn't new Now I'm back home, glad to be home again Only this time, I won't be walking in

This trip home I will be laying down With all of my family standing around I know they'll be crying, and they are all so sad I never wanted them to feel this bad

They look so down, but they have love in their eyes Everyone knows, I'm going to the stars in the sky

...I'll never get to say, what I hope they know I'll be watching over them as they all grow

They will never forget me, and I hope they see How much I love them as they look down upon me

There was more love in me than stars in the sky Everyone knew me, as that big lovable guy

I know what I did was right

I never had a doubt Driving my truck was what my mission was about

A name is now called, a single bell rang Think about me, you can't forget my name Just keep your memories of me in a box. Don't ever forget me. I'm the big lovable "OX"

.....I'll miss you big guy!

Days before the funeral, I was talking to a military friend of mine who knew that I was going to attend Sunday's service. "Whatever you do", he said, "just don't stay in the shoes of Shawn's father too long". "You mean, go there, but don't stay there?", I countered. So I did. I put those shoes on in my mind and went there for a short period of time, then I jumped back into mine trying to put some perspective in the day. But it was then, that I began thinking of your shoes, and the ones over there...and there......and there.

I have a myriad of new questions. Some relative to funerals themselves and others surrounding the news coverage of our fallen soldiers. Today is not the time to delve into those other than to say, this. I appreciated the coverage the Des Moines Register gave Specialist Muhr's day. On the other hand, there was only one television station present at the funeral. As we walked out of the door of the high school, I asked the news reporter where she was from. "News Channel 8 in Des Moines", she said. "Thank you for coming", I responded.

Now, I've got to keep reminding myself, "What will happen is God's business. Remaining faithful, no matter what happens, is mine".

YGG, Rod

CHAPTER 62

Several days had gone by since Hope and Rod Martin had traveled to Coon Rapids for the funeral of Specialist Shawn A. Muhr. There had been little spoken between husband and wife since then. Perhaps there was a fear that in talking about death, it would place their son in harm's way. People have a tendency to think that way.

Rod was sitting in the living room of the Martins home. The TV was on blasting out sports stories on ESPN. Faithful dog, Mason, was nearby, fast asleep. The quiet time was interrupted by a cellphone. "Hello", said Martin. "Hey, Rod, Major Jenkins, here. You said if I run across a story to give you a call. Got some time?"

One hour later Rod put his phone down on his lap. His hands were sweating and his mind was racing a million miles a minute. The story the Major had just told him was beyond belief. Somehow he needed to write about it. The story needed some legs. After all, that's what Rod wanted his blog to represent. Slowly, he got up and went into the kitchen to grab a can of 7-Up. He was going to need some hydration for what was about to take place. Sitting down at the dining room table, the laptop power button was pushed. The following words were placed on his site.

A non-descript U.S. military vehicle pulled up to the modest Coon Rapids, Iowa home in the early evening of January 29th. The two military men in the car had received an assignment earlier that day, a difficult one to say the least. As both got out of the car, they took some deep breaths for composure sake and headed up the walk and into the garage where the side entrance was located. Inside the house were Vice Commander, David Muhr, and two of his American Legion Post 357 friends. The three were partaking in a competitive game of cribbage. Their plans that evening, after the friendly card game was a relaxing dinner and some further conversation. The sound of the doorbell interrupted the game. As Mr. Muhr made his way to the door, little did he know that on the other side of the door would be information..... information that would assure that the dinner conversation later that night would be one they had not experienced before. The major and chaplain readied themselves as the door swung open. They were the bearers of some news.... Specialist Shawn A. Muhr had been killed earlier in the day while on a supply mission in the Helmand Province in Afghanistan. They were there to deliver that message as respectfully as they knew how. All eyes met at once......as the Major asked, "Are you David Muhr"?

The names of the two military men are not of importance here. What I would like to impress upon you is how that day unfolded.....the thoughts along the way and the necessary "gifts" needed in relaying the death notification to Muhr family.

The United States Military is extremely experienced at delivering the death notification to the proper kin of a fallen soldier. During WWII and the Korean War, notification was done through a telegram. Hardly a respectful way. Years later, with the sheer number of fatalities from Vietnam and the Gulf War, the military began training their personnel to deliver the death notification in person. To date, 3,503 death notifications have been delivered to families of servicemen and women who died in Iraq and 1,475 in Afghanistan. If anything, this has become a "learned" process, one where compassion is of the upmost importance.

The early hours of January 29th were somewhat uneventful for the Major and Chaplain. All that changed at 12:20 p.m. when the cellphone call came from the Deputy Personnel Officer telling of a death in the Iowa Military family. Immediately, the problems of the day changed. In several hours, they were going to convey one of the most difficult and important messages of their lives. "I knew I was going to deliver some news that would ruin someone's day", the Major recounted.

Now, the important aspect for the two officers to remember was respect. It was the significance of the word that provided strength and composure. It began with the Class A uniform both took considerable time in preparing.....ensuring their dress was precise. Other preparations were taking place in their minds and some of those were of the prayerful variety. Prayer for the right demeanor, strength in the words to deliver and compassion to help direct the family in picking up the pieces. By 3:15 p.m. they were on their way to Coon Rapids..... albeit with a potential slowdown in the making.

The Army's policy is for the primary next of kin to be notified first and then the secondary next of kin. In this particular case, the widow of Specialist Muhr, Winifred Olchawa, who was at Fort Rucker, Alabama, was first on that list. As the Major and the Chaplain drew closer to Coon Rapids it was apparent they would need to divert their course. Not only did they have to wait on the news that the Ft. Rucker message had been delivered.....they now needed to avoid anyone detecting them. Two Class A uniformed officers in a government vehicle in a small town would certainly be easy to spot. For a little over an hour the wait continued, hidden next to a grain elevator in town. Finally, the message delivered call was received. At 5:45

p.m. the non-descript military car began its final course to the Muhr residence.

Minutes later, when the Major began his words to David Muhr, he said them with a sense of strength and compassion. "Mr. Muhr, I have an official message from the Secretary of the Army".......

A recent NPR program (National Public Radio) discussed the notification process from all sorts of angles. It spoke on the "sorrowful anger" that many experience when they are informed of their soldiers passing....it touched on how that moment affects everyone (officers and family) very deeply in so many ways.....and it spoke about the assistance to the family in the days leading up to the funeral and beyond. One of the officers interviewed mentioned, "there is no way to soak into the experience of seeing two soldiers in their Class A's coming to the front door.....and then to see that world collapse. Our faces will be locked together....the image of the news I just delivered".

P.S. My religious belief teaches me to feel as safe in battle as in bed. God has fixed the time for my death. I do not concern myself about that, but to be always ready, no matter when it may overtake me. That is the way all men should live, and then all would be equally brave--- Thomas "Stonewall" Jackson

YGG,

Rod

CHAPTER 63

It was hard to reset but both Hope and Rod were giving it their best. The past several days since Specialist Muhr's funeral had been difficult to process. Their collective hearts went out to the family. Deep down they couldn't imagine going through such an ordeal. The additional part of the story provided by Major Jenkins brought them closer to the situation than they could have imagined. But there was a ray of light about to help.

Rod was seated in a booth at the Johnston Panera. His trustworthy laptop was on the bench seat beside him. As he looked westward he saw a few patches of blue sky that were trying to break through the dark gray overcast. A smile broke out on his face which translated into motivation to write another military experience. This time it was going to hit home....the Martins home. He wrote…

> Our son, Eddie, snuck in just under the mark. Yesterday would have been the sixth month of his leaving for Basic Training and AIT (Advanced Individual Training). Only thing is, he avoided that distinction, if you can call it that, by arriving home late Wednesday night.....dressed to the hilt.
>
> February 9th will be a day he remembers for quite some time, I'm sure. He got up at 4 a.m. with the rest of his graduation buddies. Showered, cleared out his room, chowed....and headed off to an 8 a.m. graduation. In stark contrast to Basic

ceremonies, not many families were present. But that doesn't lessen the pomp and circumstance of the day or diminish the honors that were bestowed on the graduates. That remains.

I think back to October 21st of last year and Eddie's graduation from Basic at Fort Knox, Kentucky. Over 200 soldiers were acknowledged that day. The honor graduates received special recognition and one in particular spoke of the road ahead.....and the trials that will present themselves. "Stay guarded" was the message. I could only imagine how proud the parents of that soldier were. Shortly thereafter, the caps flew in the air signaling an end to the festivities. It was then, that soldiers went looking for friends and family. The image forever implanted in my memory is seeing the person I knew as my son, maneuver through the crowd to reach us. The aura surrounding him was different. Frankly I've thrown out words like changed, manhood, jaw dropping and a bunch more that I thought might fit. None have really expressed it all....it's been intangible.

Later that day, Eddie and his fellow soldiers boarded a bus to take them to Aberdeen Proving Grounds in Maryland for AIT. There they would begin working on their MOS (Military Occupational Specialty) as a Light-Wheeled Vehicle Mechanic. "From Day One, I had my eyes set on being an honor graduate", he reflected. He reminded me of an early Facebook post when he first arrived in Maryland saying that same thing. If only I could remember that.....

Because, he was. Distinguished Honor Graduate PV2 Eddie Martin. Has a nice ring to it, I must say. Now, I don't have to imagine what it must have felt like for the honor graduate's family at Basic, I know. What I now find myself trying to visualize, is if I had been there Wednesday, hearing his name announced and watching as he made his way across the stage. "If only I could imagine"......

What I won't have problems in remembering is his arrival at Des Moines International Airport later that evening. He purposely was the last person from his flight to head for the escalator. At the top, he stood in his Class A's, the same uniform he had on when he graduated earlier in the day. Most of the graduates chose to travel in their ACU's (Army Combat Uniform). Not this dude. He came dressed to the hilt. As he descended the steps you could see his pride growing the closer he got to us. If we couldn't be there for his graduation, then he'd bring it home to us. And I'm glad he did.

It has been a long six months. So much has taken place, changes have been happening so, so fast. Young men have had their lives altered. They've learned accountability, teamwork, responsibility and a whole lot more. As Eddie summed up, "I've learned to be a leader and how to be a better person in the future". Forty nine soldiers graduated from Aberdeen on February 9th. They are going to be the ones to lead us. I challenge them all to LEAD BOLDLY.

"Yea, though I walk through the Valley of the Shadow of Death, I will fear no evil: for thou art with me; thy rod and thy staff they comfort me"-Psalm 23:4

YGG,

Rod

Rod recalled shooting a glance at his youngest son as they left the airport terminal headed to the parking ramp. The smile on his face had been worth a million bucks. Dan had one of his buddies back and that was a good thing. Not only for him, but the entire family. There had to be a collective sigh from the Martins knowing one of their sons had navigated a military commitment and was now safe. When Dan had started the SUV, Rod had stated ever so loudly...."HOME, PLEASE!" And take your time. "Oh, one more thing. Dan, how's it feel to have your brother back?" The youngster slowly turned his head towards his Dad in the back seat. There was a smile on Dan's mug like he'd never seen before. He wouldn't say a word. Sometimes words don't do a situation justice. This was one of them.

Eddie in dress uniform

CHAPTER 64

Charlie stepped outside his new digs in Kalagush, Afghanistan. It was his first look at the FOB known for its beautiful scenic views. Not. He'd flown in with a small group of soldiers in a Blackhawk the night before. There was total darkness when they landed so he had no idea of what the location was like. Now he was getting his first images.

He took a long drag on the cigarette between his lips, dropped his hands to his side and let out a billow of smoke. This was going to be an interesting place, he thought. And more dangerous. A perfect fishbowl without the water. He followed up his previous drag with another longer draw on the cancer stick. Yes, his training as a Forward Observer was going to get a real work out here. There would be little down time.

The flight from Mehtar Lam the night before had taken roughly fifteen minutes. Had they convoyed in, it would have taken them around two hours. One road in and one road out. A graveyard for IED's. It was cold then and equally cold now. The winds made it seem even colder than it actually was. There wasn't any white stuff on the ground but it was apparent Old Man Winter was in the neighborhood.

The mountains all around the FOB were gigantic and colorless. Goats and shepherds sprinkled the ribbon trails that wound skyward. There was a wide surplus of cover for an enemy wanting to do harm for sure. Stuck in the middle was the base consisting of 70-80 American soldiers and an adjoining area for 30-40 ANA forces. It was small. A lot smaller than Mehtar Lam. Carved out and built up from the stone and sand valley, FOB Kalagush was and remains a front line defense against smuggling of drugs, arms, and insurgents over the Hindu Kush in Afghanistan. It was not uncommon outside the wire to see burka-clad women carrying loads of firewood accompanied by young men with large caliber machine guns.

Charlie looked off in the distance and saw an old friend Specialist Randy White coming his way. "Martin", he bellowed. "What the hell are you doing up here. I didn't think I'd see you again". "Dude", shot back Charlie. "Can't keep a good man down. Besides they said you needed a babysitter. So here I am." The two bear hugged each other and then broke apart for a look-see. Satisfied they both were alright, they continued in conversation. The subjects ranged from their R and R's, to girls to Kalagush and to the Taliban. The Specialist informed PFC Martin what their duties consisted of. Martin and White were the only FO's at Kalgush. That would mean they'd be working together a lot. There might be two missions a day they'd be going on. Sometimes overnight scouting of locations would be needed in an attempt to deny enemy movement. According to White the key thing was for them to stay active. "What ya think?", Randy asked. "Hmmm", began Charlie. "A little afraid. Yeah, that's it. Afraid, yet filled with joy". Throughout their talk, the two kept their antennas up. One thing everyone was told when arriving at the Gush was stay alert. Even more so at night. Red reflectors were used on many things producing light. Safety was a chief concern. Charlie raised his noggin to one of the towers overlooking the FOB. The wooden structure stood about 30 feet high and looked like it had weathered years of storms. "Those much help?", he inquired. "More than you'll ever know, dude", responded White. "More than you'll ever know."

Back in Iowa the day was coming to a conclusion. Rod was in the basement with the big HD box replaying a University of Iowa basketball game. He was staring at the screen but there was little being retained as the video bounced off his eyes. His mind was somewhere else. Father Rod looked down at his cellphone and read the poem another time. It was one suggested to him by a former soldier who had endured his time in the theatre. He'd said to Rod maybe there would be something he could glean from it.

by Alan Seeger

I have a rendezvous with Death
At some disputed barricade,
When Spring comes back with rustling shade
And apple-blossoms fill the air—
I have a rendezvous with Death
When Spring brings back blue days and fair.

It may be he shall take my hand
And lead me into his dark land
And close my eyes and quench my breath—
It may be I shall pass him still.
I have a rendezvous with Death
On some scarred slope of battered hill,
When Spring comes round again this year
And the first meadow-flowers appear.

God knows 'twere better to be deep
Pillowed in silk and scented down,
Where love throbs out in blissful sleep,
Pulse nigh to pulse, and breath to breath,
Where hushed awakenings are dear...
But I've a rendezvous with Death
At midnight in some flaming town,
When Spring trips north again this year,
And I to my pledged word am true,
I shall not fail that rendezvous.

Rod wanted to find out more about the poem. He was able to dig up some information on the poet, Alan Seeger. Seeger was an early-20th century American writer. He served in the French Foreign Legion during World War I. Seeger's poem was a favorite of President John F. Kennedy, who often asked his wife, Jacqueline, to recite it. For nearly 15 minutes Rod processed the words he'd read. In some respects they'd provided some understanding. In another respect, it brought to light the ever present reminder that death could happen at any minute.

Rod was pretty certain his son Charlie hadn't spent any great length of time thinking of losing his life. Maybe Rod would have to do that deed for the two of them. The longer Rod sat there frozen in time, the more he thought of the recent death of Specialist Shawn Muhr. He refrained from walking down that road. He closed his eyes, let out a big sigh and rose from the chair. His walk up the stairwell to the main level and then onward to the second floor was a little shaky. As he shucked his clothes and slithered under the sheets he muttered the words, "please God don't put that burden upon us. Please. Please. Please.

CHAPTER 65

It was Friday, the 18th of February. A day for celebration. Not so much because of the time of year, but because of whose birthday it was. Dan Martin was closing in on a big, big number. Today he hit number 17 on the calendar. Next year was the big one.

The smile on the Dan's face showed his happiness. As far as he was concerned it was party time. Not only was this one way to shelve the issues his family had been going through with Charlie's deployment, but he was celebrating his closeness to manhood. At least by society's standards. Dan looked around the table at the Outback Steakhouse in Ankeny. Smiling back were his middle brother, Eddie and his two parents. "Okay, big guy. Order anything you want on the menu. It's your day", Rod exclaimed. Quickly Dan's head dropped to the menu in front of him. Ever since his dad had told him they were going to Outback for his birthday dinner he had been salivating. He had his mind made up but seeing his choice on the list of food selections provided proof. "I'm getting the center cut top sirloin", Dan shot back. "How about you guys?" The tall, young and slender male waiter greeted the group and quickly surmised they were there to eat and then socialize. Dan being the center of attention ordered first followed by Hope's choice of the Victoria's Filet Mignon. Eddie and Rod went with the Ribeye. Minutes later the young slender male waiter turned and headed for the kitchen. Everyone had made their choice. It was now up to the cooks to provide a satisfying outcome.

Some two hours later the Martin's pushed their chairs back from the table. They were stuffed. Way beyond the appetite they'd come with. It had been a good night. Thankfully, for Dan, there weren't any party hats, streamers or waiters singing Happy Birthday. Rod leaned into Hope's ear and said, "wouldn't it be fun to be that age again and know what we know?" Martin's wife let out a squeal and Rod followed with a big belly laugh. "Yeah, if only", Hope replied. As the family made their way to the parking lot there was an ample amount of joking around taking place. It had been a night the entire clan had needed minus the hundreds of calories they all put down. Rest came easily when their collective heads hit the pillows an hour later.

Rod was up at the crack of dawn the following morning. He ambled down the steps in his dark blue pajamas. He scooted into the kitchen and started the coffee maker with some butter pecan grounds in the hopper. The aroma was a delight to his smeller. He quickly poured a cup and headed to the PC to check the internet for overnight news. After about five minutes, Rod was able to determine, at least by his own terms, that the world was still in operation. His day could now begin. Moving on, he clicked on his blog and penned some things he'd been thinking about, his oldest son, Charlie.

Dear Sonpo:

It's been quite a few days since I wrote down anything specifically for the journal about your deployment to Afghanistan. As I looked back, it was January 1st....far too long to go without sharing some thoughts. I'm trying to figure out why it's been so hard to write this, frankly I've been numb since you came home on leave and then went back to Afghanistan.

Maybe it's my way of thinking that the worst is past and that we are on the downward slide. Another part of me has wrestled with what this will mean when you do come home. How will you be affected by your deployment? What has this time meant in the manner of sacrifice for you and us? How will others view your commitment?

A little over a week ago there was a situation where a wounded Iraq Vet stood up at Columbia University and voiced his opinions on the military at a town hall meeting. Anthony Maschek, a former Staff Sgt. who was shot 11 times and received the Purple Heart bravely stepped up to the mike and issued an impassioned challenge to fellow students on their perceptions of the military. "It doesn't matter how you feel about the war. It doesn't matter how you feel about fighting", said Maschek. "There are bad men out there plotting to kill you."

The response? Some students laughed. Others hissed and booed. Some called him racist. All of this directed to a young man, 28, who spent two years at Walter Reed Army Medical Center in Washington recovering from grievous wounds. In all, the former Staff Sgt. suffered two broken legs and wounds to the abdomen, arms and chest in the Kirkuk, Iraq attack.

This disgusted me. We're not living in the 1970's. This is not the Vietnam era. I can recall the treatment our military men and women received during those times. I've also heard stories from former soldiers that leave you shaking your head. Stories like a soldier returning home and upon landing on American soil, threw away his military clothing in the airport restroom. Why? Because he knew how little respect he'd get if he wore the uniform. He knew the public's disdain.

So I wonder, where's the tolerance? Where is the respect Anthony Maschek should have been given? And would Maschek have been offered the same response if he had stood up and supported some political view or gay rights issue. If indeed Columbia University is an educational institution then they need to step up and educate here. Let's have those same students who booed, hissed or yelled insults, take to the mike and see for themselves what accountability means. Okay, I know that was a knee-jerk reaction. Perhaps the real answer lies in the Ivy League school taking the remarks of this "misguided" few for a lesson in tolerance and the freedoms we have...and guess who brought those to us?

Anthony Maschek must be a proud man. Thank God for that. His message went practically unnoticed by a group that can't see or hear particularly well. There are bad men out there plotting to kill us. If you don't know that by now, well...............

I don't question your commitment. I don't question your sacrifice. We can only hope and pray that situations like Anthony Maschek's pave the way for understanding. Understanding that as we look around us, the need for our military is growing. And along with that should be our respect and gratitude. Stay strong!!

154 days or 22 weeks to go however you look at it! Praying for your safety, son. Praying for you daily......

Love you,

Dadpo

"Speak and act as those who are going to be judged by the law that gives freedom, because judgment without mercy will be shown to anyone who has not been merciful. Mercy triumphs over judgement .-James 2:12-13

YGG,

Rod

Rod let out a long sigh. He'd gotten a bunch off his chest in his post. But he was left with one image that kept circulating in his thoughts. It was a pair of boots. Not just any pair, but Charlie's boots. He thought back to the time when his wife had brought a pair of Charlie's boots with the family to Fort Knox. She had insisted they take a picture of the family with Charlie's boots marking the spot that was missing him. She was onto something with her request. As usual, she was a step ahead of her husband. Rod went a little further with her idea as he recalled Eddie's remarks navigating the hills of Fort Knox. "If it wasn't for looking at the boots ahead of me and thinking those were Charlie's boots, I don't know if I could have made it through", said Eddie.

Rod recalled reading an article by David Feddes, "A Soldier's Feet". Feddes made the point that in spiritual warfare, a soldier of Christ must wear combat boots of peace. Sounds kind of like an oxymoron. How can war bring peace? How can the footwear of peace serve as combat boots? Well, sometimes the best way to enjoy lasting peace is to first win a war that gets rid of a constant threat to peace.

How about another illustration?, Martin said under his breath. Parents often times bronze their children's booties as a keepsake. Perhaps the military should contemplate doing the same thing when a soldier is being discharged. How fitting would that be, he thought. And then Nancy Sinatra's old tune came into his thinking....

> **These boots are made for walking**
> **And that's just what they'll do**
> **One of these days these boots are gonna walk all over you**
>
> **And he repeated it again....**
>
> **These boots are made for walking**
> **And that's just what they'll do**
> **One of these days these boots are gonna walk all over you**
> **Are you ready boots?**
> **....Start walkin**

Charlie sat on the corner of his bed. He'd just returned from the Command Center where he was able to connect with a few friends back home and read his dad's most recent blog story. He tugged at his right boot for some thirty seconds before finally pulling his foot to freedom. As he placed the boot in his hand next to the left one already in position on the floor, he chuckled to himself. He kind of felt like a fireman. His boots were always at his side ready for action. Over the years he'd heard his dad sing some funny song about boots. He didn't remember how the song went, but it had something to do with walking. Or walking all over you. Collapsing on the pillow Charlie reflected on his footwear. Tomorrow, he'd be getting a whole lot of walkin in. That's just what he was going to do.

CHAPTER 66

Hope and Rod were sitting in the comfort of their living room. Rod in the rocker and Hope snuggled with her feet under her on the long brown Ashley Danely Sofa Chase. They'd been conversing about a number of things over the course of the past fifteen minutes. Eventually the talk moved to something regarding their son's deployment, either directly or indirectly. This afternoon, the talk had taken a turn to Rod's blog and what the next topic might be.

"Anything brewing for a story idea, dear?", asked Hope. "I'd think you'd have any number of different ways you could go". "Well", stammered Rod. "Aaaah, yeah, kind of". He fired off some thoughts, but one had more substance than the others. It had to do with soldiers and their coming home on leave. Rod spoke at length about a recent TV report he'd seen about a soldier surprising his young daughter in her kindergarten classroom. "The response from the little cutie brought a tear to my eye", he offered. "She was totally shocked. Her dad walked into the room and she did a double take, or it could have been a triple take. When she knew it was her dad for sure, she came running into his arms. It was beyond priceless, if that's possible", Rod suggested.

Then there was the other side of the story. Several nights ago, there was a disturbance at a Des Moines residence. Seems like a soldier about ready to return to the battle front had gotten into an argument with his wife. One thing led to another. Alcohol was involved. A whole lot of yelling had taken place and the police had been called. Fortunately, it hadn't turned violent and no charges had been filed. But damage had been done.

"There's always the good with the bad", Rod surmised. Hope looked at things a little differently. "Not necessarily, dear", she suggested. "It doesn't have to be that way. It would appear that there is love in one of those situations and the other is lacking. It's not a good versus bad". Rod tried to digest the remarks and provide an immediate reply. But nothing came. Other than a smile. He was going to have to toss that thought pattern around a little more before responding. Actually, he decided to change the subject altogether.

"You know what, honey", he said. "I think I need to do a little research and find out who has been coming to the blog. There's a way I can track the hits on the site to see where they've come from. Maybe I can do a little yellin of my own. Although a whole lot nicer. What do you think?" "Sure why not?", said Hope. "Might be you'll find some love in some very strange places", she said with a smile.

Later that night Rod fired off this short post after a quick follow up through the blog tracker of countries on his site.

The internet is a unique creature. Sometimes I despise it and other times I marvel at it. But finally, curiousity has gotten the better of me!! I've got to ask a question now that we've been active with the blog site for over 4 months.

And here's why. We've had visitors from 30 countries to "My Father's Voice". Not 30 counties, not 30 states, but 30 COUNTRIES. In alphabetical order, here they are:

Georgia, Germany, Greece, India, Indonesia, Iraq, Israel, Italy, Japan, Malaysia, Portugal, Romania, Russia, Singapore, Slovenia, South Korea, Sweden, Ukraine, United Kingdom and United States.

***UPDATE 3/6/2011, 8 p.m. CST..Make that 31. Welcome United Arab Emirates to the mix. What's up?

Can you find yourself on the globe? Somewhere....you can find your location. But why and how? Those are a couple of questions that have befuddled me. How did you find the blog? What association to the military and God do you have? And what has brought you back time and again? I'm curious.....

I'm also inquisitive of the thoughts you leave with. So let me ask this question to you, whoever you are? What say you? Connect with us and tell us why. If you would rather not comment at the end of a story, then use my email address on the left side of the site and we can interact that way.

Curiousity killed the cat. I'm hoping that doesn't happen to me. But, my gosh, isn't this world we live in strange? Yet it is still something to behold.

Where in the World are You? And what are you up to and what are you thinking....I'd love to hear. If you're a soldier far away from home, then this is your pathway for the world to know your experiences. Let us know...the world is your stage. Just step right up!!

YGG,

Rod

Rod wrapped up the story and closed the lid. "Dear, all done" he yelled. "31 countries. 31. Go figure. It's amazing that we've had that kind of traffic. I'm shocked and you've had a lot to do with that. The two of us. As a team. Me the writer and you the editor. I wonder how we even got here", he concluded.

After a minute or two of contemplation, Hope offered her logic as she replied, "It's not a question of how we got here, it's where are we going?" That's the real question.

CHAPTER 67

The next morning, Rod was still in ponder mode. His wife, Hope, had posed a very direct question. One that he didn't have any answer to. "Where were they headed?" So much had taken place in their lives in the past six months to get them to their current spot. What lied ahead, though? Those words were an echo bouncing around in his head. Rod pulled up the zipper on his dark green North Face parka, turned to head to the garage and was startled by the buzz of the cellphone in his right front blue jean pants pocket. He pulled out the instrument and quickly answered, "Hello". It was his mother checking on Charlie first, the remainder of the family second. "I hope Charlie stays out of harm's way", said Grandma Martin. "There's been so much more activity going on in recent weeks that we're hearing about. That makes me concerned", she stated. "Amen to that", said Rod. "Keep me posted because I worry about him night and day", she followed up with.

Those final words from Rod's mother had not done much to solve his wondering issue. In fact, it might have taken it one step deeper. At times like these blogging, or in this case, journaling, was giving him some solace. After dinner that evening he sat down at the dining room table and fired up his laptop. It was time to write.

Dear Sonpo:

I've been struggling the last several days. I know that sounds selfish, but I have been. I've been wrestling with what to do with my future, our family's future. Where do we live? Do we move to another part of the country? All sorts of questions. And in it all, I'm asking God to lead. But it's hard being patient!!

Then I think of you, son. And I think of all the wasted energy I've exerted. It makes me wonder what your days are like. How the days run one into another and you have no idea if it's Thursday or Friday. Then I watch the news and see what's going on in Libya and Yemen.....and I wonder, is this ever going to end?

Earlier this week, my brother passed on an email that I've found myself thinking about quite a bit. It puts a lot of MY struggles into perspective. It might just do the same for you and others. I'll post this as a narration piece. The first part of the comment is the common occurrence In The World (ITW) and the follow up thought is about you and any Soldier (S).

(ITW)Your cell phone is in your pocket. You're looking at all the pretty girls.
(S)He patrols the streets, searching for insurgents and terrorists. He's told he will be held over an extra two months. So no leave now.

(ITW)You call your girlfriend and set a date for tonight.
(S)He waits for the mail to see if there is a letter from home.

(ITW)You hug and kiss your girlfriend, like you do every day.
(S)He holds his letter close and smells his love's perfume.

(ITW)You roll your eyes as a baby cries.
(S)He gets a letter with pictures of his new child and wonders if they'll ever meet.

(ITW)You criticize your government, and say that war never solves anything.

(S)He sees the innocent tortured and killed by their own people and remembers why he is fighting.

(ITW)You hear the jokes about the war, and make fun of soldiers like him.

(S)He hears the gunfire, bombs and screams of the wounded.

(ITW)You see only what the media wants you to see.

(S)He sees the broken bodies lying around him.

(ITW)You are asked to do something by your parents. You don't.

(S)He does exactly what he is told even if it puts his life in danger.

(ITW)You stay at home and watch TV.

(S)He takes whatever time he is given to call, write home, sleep and eat.

(ITW)You crawl into your soft bed, with down pillows and get comfortable.

(S)He tries to sleep but gets woken by mortars and helicopters all night long..

I must tell you son, those words are helping with my perspective. The next time I start complaining, I'll think of you and all the soldiers around the world who sacrifice for us minute by minute. I pray my attitude, my thoughts and ultimately my words provide evidence that I am put on this earth to serve..... not be served.

Philippians 2:1-4 If therefore there is any encouragement in Christ, if there is any consolation of love, if there is any fellowship of the Spirit, if any affection and compassion, make my joy complete by being of the same mind, maintaining the same love, united in spirit, intent on one purpose. Do nothing from selfishness or empty conceit, but with humility of mind let each

of you regard one another as more important than himself; do not merely look out for your own personal interests, but also for the interests of others.

Love,

Dadpo

The breath of air released from Rod's mouth signaled an end to the writing of the day. It had been therapeutic. Rod looked over at the pictures on the dining room hutch. There were ones of the Martin boys at various times in their lives. Aaaah, what memories. Charlie's military picture stood out. It showed a dignified, stern, handsome soldier. A proud individual.

Rod had to admit the longer he looked at the photo the closer he felt to his son. It made him wonder if Charlie carried any pictures with him. Wasn't that something all soldiers did?, he thought. The next time he talked to his son, he was going to find out. Afterall, isn't a picture worth a thousand words?

CHAPTER 68

The next day was busy time for Rod and Hope Martin. Rod had headed off to Hope to meet with a couple of acquaintances from the Hope@Work he'd done. It had been a good time to see some faces he'd thought of in recent weeks. It was with great interest that Rod could see each of them growing their faith and how work was a part of it all. But it was also emotional. Several of the group had cornered Martin at different times during the afternoon and told him how much they appreciated his help when things weren't going well for them. He'd seen more than a tear in their eyes. Heartfelt thanks went a long way, Rod thought. But it wasn't him doing the work. He was simply placed there to help facilitate things. The day had left him wiped out. Hope, on the other hand, had been on her feet most of the day doing retail at her "fun" job at the card and ornament store. It was work Hope truly enjoyed. In some sense it was her own little mission to help people find something for a loved one. When she did hit the home property after a long day, she was always ready to stop serving. More often than not, either Rod had to offer up a meal idea or everyone was on their own. Or it meant eating out.

When Rod opened the door leading into the Martin's house he could hear his wife in the kitchen. "What the heck are we going to eat?", she muttered. "There isn't a whole lot here.". Hearing her husband's arrival, she glanced over at the doorway. There with a big smile was Rod. "Okay dear.

Time to take a break", he exclaimed. "Let's go get some grub and take in a movie." "You're kidding, right", she questioned. "Nope. Let's go", stated the lifesaver.

A couple of hours later, the Martin's found themselves stuffed on a Felix and Oscar's deep dish sausage pizza staring at the movie placard at the Wynnsong Theatres in Johnston. They narrowed it down to Dear John and the Book of Eli. Eli won.

The story revolved around Eli, a nomad in a post-apocalyptic world, who is told by a voice to deliver his copy of a mysterious book to a safe location on the West Coast of the United States. To Rod, the story was fast paced with a race to the finish line, being the final prize. It was probably not the best choice in some respects for either one of them. By all accounts they should have chosen something with a little humor/romance. But at least it gave Rod another blog idea. When they arrived at home he headed over to his spot at the dining table, said goodnight to Hope and sat down in the stiff dining room chair to pound out another story.

We're on countdown for a lot of things in the world right now. Let's see, there are the Stanley Cup Finals, the upcoming NFL Draft, the Royal Wedding and of course, May 21.....Judgment Day, which will dissolve into the End of the World on October 21st. We'll see about the last mention. If I'm not mistaken, there is only one individual that knows if that's really going to happen. I'll just leave it at that. The countdown I'm most interested in is for the Iowa National Guard troops returning home from Afghanistan this coming summer.

It's been a long eight months of deployment thus far. For the soldiers, it's been a day by day exercise in peace keeping. And in recent weeks, another objective has popped up. Clear the Galuch Valley from north to south and establish a coalition footprint in the area which is a known insurgent stronghold and training area. Additionally, the plan was to eliminate insurgent forces, weapons and bomb-making materials in the Valley. For families, the days are full of uncertainty. What is most certain, is that soldiers are closer to the action than ever....and in harm's way. Here is an officer's take on the theatre of the long road back.

By The Grace Of God....The Homecoming

"When you're in a place like this doing the kinds of things required to be successful, for my soldiers every day is game day. One of my biggest concerns is that we become complacent," Col. Benjamin Corell said. Corell is commander of the 2nd Brigade Combat Team, 34th Red Bulls Infantry Division.

Corell offered some further insights. Charlie Co. is stationed at the Kalagush forward operating base in Nuristan Province and is part of 2nd Brigade Combat Team. Spc. Timothy Bagley of Brandon and Sgt. Eric Lindsey of Eldora, members of Co. C based in Iowa Falls, were injured when their vehicle hit an improvised explosive device, according to military officials. Their injuries were described as not life-threatening and both are expected to recover.

Corell said as the weather breaks in Afghanistan, snow melts and mountain passes open. "Insurgents have more freedom of movement when this happens so it's not uncommon to see an uptick in attacks. This is something we fully expected would happen as we moved into spring," Corell said.

According to Corell, soldiers conduct more than 150 patrols a week. Since the bulk of the brigade arrived in late October, troops found more than 40 pieces of unexploded ordnance, responded to 20 indirect fire attacks on posts and were involved in more than 50 small-arms battles. The number of seriously wounded soldiers has been low, Corell said, "and by the grace of God" there haven't been any fatalities".

Rod looked over at the calendar on the nearby desk. It read April 11th. It seemed like the finish line was in sight. The countdown was on

---

in every person's mind who was connected with the Iowa deployment. It wasn't weekly, or daily. In fact, if a person stayed quiet long enough you could hear it. Tick-tock. Tick-tock.

CHAPTER 69

The clock had not stopped as the night continued at the Martin household. Hope had settled in with a nice book. Rod had spent the night surfing the sports networks trying to find something of interest. He'd settled in on a Chicago White Sox game. Their ace, Mark Buehrle, was on the mound against the Oakland A's. It was a fairly enjoyable game, except the final outcome. 2-1 Oakland win in 10 innings. When that fun concluded, Martin turned to News Channel 8 to catch up on the latest news. He almost wished he hadn't. The news wasn't good. The remainder of the night was a toss and turnover special. Finally at 3 in the morning, he figured sleep was not going to happen so he headed for his laptop.

He sat for few minutes staring at the keyboard unsure of where to start. None of the clothes on his back were designer vintage. Everything about him and the moment was non-descript. Then the words came.

When I first saw the news last night my heart jumped...then it felt heavy and sad. Spc. Brent Maher, 31, of Honey Creek, Iowa became the first Iowa National Guardsmen killed in action since the group deployment some eight months ago. Specialist Shawn Muhr had been killed several weeks earlier, but he wasn't part of the 4,000 troops that originally deployed.

In an earlier blog I reported on the fortunate "Grace" our Iowa Guardsmen had received in their days in Afghanistan.

While this puts a spin on that assertion, I still feel we have been blessed to have suffered so few casualties. For the Maher family, I'm not sure they'd come to the same conclusion..... today. That's why it is so important for us.....all of us to think, pray and act as a support system for them in the days, weeks and months ahead.

I was uplifted to read a statement from the Maher family early this morning. Despite the suffering they are undergoing, they see the big picture. "Brent died doing what he loved, serving his country and protecting the freedom that we enjoy and providing the people of Afghanistan with the opportunity for freedom," the statement said:

Spc. Brent Maher:

Maher was killed when his armored truck struck an IED as he stood in a gun turret. "It takes an amazing amount of personal courage to get up and do that gunner's job every day", the Camp Dodge Public Relations Office related. Apparently, the bomb blew up under the armored truck in which Maher was riding during a patrol near the city of Gardez in eastern Afghanistan.

Three other soldiers in the truck were injured. They were identified as Sgt. 1st Class Nicholas Jedlicka, 31, of Council Bluffs; Spc. Justin Christiansen, 24, of Nebraska City, Neb.; and Spc. Dustin Morrison, 20, of New Market. Their conditions are not known at this time, but Hapgood said they would be transferred to a hospital in Germany. The four guardsmen were stationed at Combat Outpost Dand Patan, a location next to the border of Pakistan. They were members of B Company of the 1st Battalion of the 168th Infantry Regiment based in Shenandoah.

Maher is survived by his wife, Brenna M. Maher, of Honey Creek; daughters Kaitelyn, Elizabeth and Hannah Rose, and a son, Matthew Douglas, 8, all of Niles, Mich.; his mother, Cheryl L. Tyner and step-father Mick Tyner, both of Essex, Ia.; a brother, Greg Maher, of Biloxi, Miss.; and grandparents Roy and Wilma

McGraw, of Essex, Ia. He was preceded in death by his father, Matthew Maher. Funeral arrangements are pending for the Maher funeral.

Back on the battle front, I'm sure there is a different set of emotions being experienced by Iowa National Guard troops than there were just a week ago. Our servicemen and women will remain steadfast in the duty they've accepted. Missions will continue.....ambushes will also be a part of the day...... and of course IED's will remain in their hidden traps. My prayer would be for safety in these next months. The loss of one life is one too many to have to endure......

YGG,

Rod

Please God no more....

....but a day and a half later Rod was back at his laptop with the following story.

It couldn't have come at a worse time. As many in the state of Iowa are still trying to come to grips with the death of Spc. Brent Maher, today, we hear the first details surrounding another soldier's death.

National Guard officials have scheduled a 7 p.m. news conference today at Camp Dodge in Johnston. They haven't said what the subject is, but there has been confirmation through a relative that it will concern the death of Don Nichols, a 2009 graduate of Waverly-Shell Rock High School. Nichols was a member of the Iowa Guard's 1-133rd Infantry Battalion. Nichol's mother, Becky Poock, was notified of her son's death Wednesday night.

Earlier we spoke of the countdown to homecoming for the 4,000 Iowa troops that deployed to Afghanistan. Those were to be special times. Now, we need to be specially guarded in our thinking. Iowa Guard officials had warned of increased insurgent action this spring. Looking back, perhaps we all "distanced" ourselves from the danger our soldiers face each day, into a false sense of security.

I teared up seeing the story mentioning Nichols death. I can't help but think selfishly of my son today. I'm tremendously proud of him for his sacrifice and commitment to duty. This has been a hard week for anyone connected to military life. First, the thought of withholding pay to our soldiers because of a government shutdown and then two deaths. Our anxieties are going to continue, I fear. With the end of deployment in sight, forces seen and unseen will be rearing their ugly heads. Now, we need to pray.....

We are hard pressed on every side, yet not crushed; we are perplexed, but not in despair; persecuted, but not forsaken; struck down, but not destroyed.-II Corinthians 4: 8-9

YGG,

Rod

Easter was eleven days away. Many would be reflecting about something in their lives. For three Iowa families, the upcoming Holiday was going to be a difficult one. Rod and Hope made the journey for both of the recent funerals. It had been so surreal. Where would HOPE begin?

Flags lined the highways in Waverly, Iowa honoring Specialist Don Nichols as he was laid to rest

CHAPTER 70

Dan and Eddie were being their usual selves. Silliness was on their docket as they made their way out the door to connect with some friends. Rod found this a little agitating. He was a kid once so it was easy for him to remember what growing up was like. Very few cares in the world. Mention the word seriousness and there was generally a blank stare. But there were also times when decorum should be exhibited. This was one, Rod thought. But even his actions left a little to be desired.

"Damn it", shouted Rod. "Honey, I'm really at a frazzled state right now." He picked up a little red stress ball off the couch and tossed it at the far living room wall. He looked over at his wife who was curled up on the couch. She seemed stoic in her response. "Look at the horrible things going on right now. The tornadoes last night in western Iowa were just terrible".

Martin was referring to a report from the National Weather Service where they confirmed 10 tornadoes in Iowa from the 27 that were reported in the Midwest.

The most severe struck Mapleton in Monona County in western Iowa around 7:20 p.m. Authorities say it destroyed or damaged more than 100 homes and injured more than a dozen people, but there were no fatalities. Still, 600 people were displaced.

"Then add the death of Specialist Nichols to it all. It's kinda overwhelming", he stated. Still, Hope remained calm. "How can you just sit there and not have any of this seem to bother you?", he asked. "I know I said a couple of weeks ago that I'd found my niche with writing the blog by being able to provide hope. But, crap...I'm not the Hope Doctor, ya know".

Thirty seconds of silence was broken by Hope's emphatic words. "No you're right, dear. You're not the Hope Doctor. But you can be the Hope Messenger. Can't you?", she inquired.

The look on Rod's face was like someone had slapped him. Hard. He reeled back a little bit on his feet and dropped his eyesight to his loving wife. He'd been corrected. There was no other way around it. Hope had found the proper words for just the right time. "Why didn't I think of it that way?", Rod asked. "That's why I'm here", she related with a bigger than life smile. "Now take a deep breath and be the Messenger you can going forward."

Rod collected himself and his thoughts and sat down in the living room rocker. He kind of liked the Hope Messenger title. But one thing he wanted to be careful with, if he was going to continue his work, he was not about to give false hope. There was enough of that around. If it wasn't our politicians throwing out platforms they'd never followed through on, then it was our doctors giving us remedies that were never meant to cure our ills, but rather just to treat the symptoms instead. And not to forget, religion with the glut of televangelists preying on financial security. Yes, Rod determined. He'd avoid that type of hope like the plague.

Leaning back in the chair Rod closed his eyes. The last few minutes had helped immensely. He felt refreshed. Maybe even cleansed.

He reached down to the right of the rocker and picked up his laptop. He hadn't connected with his son in days. There was no time like the present. There had been no discussion between the two of them since the recent troop deaths in Afghanistan. Rod recalled Mrs. Guinta's words before making a connection. "Don't ask a lot of questions". He checked his

Facebook messages and saw a note from Charlie that he was headed to BAF. The following dialogue occurred.

> **Rod-April 14, 2011 at 7:03pm CDT where u been??? What is BAF...call when you can...miss you!!!**

> *Charlie-April 14, 2011 at 7:13pm CDT*
> I had to escort enemy POWs to Bagram with a couple other guys and I've been gone since the 9th and I'll prolly be gone for 2 weeks or so but I'm not sure. I won't be able to call until i get back to Kalagush.

> **Rod-April 14, 2011 at 8:14pm CDT**
> So you're in Baghram for a couple of weeks? What are you doing there? I think Marty Huff is there, will you be able to see her? Can you connect with us via facebook much then?

> *Charlie-April 14, 2011 at 8:15pm CDT*
> I just said what I was doing. Watching POWs until they get them processed and what not. And no I won't be able to see her. I don't have like any free time at all. And I'll try to get on when I can.

Rod now had an idea of what Charlie had been up to even if he'd had to ask the question twice to understand. Watching POW's. Now that would be interesting, he thought. And dangerous too. All in one. When a person feels like a caged animal who knows what they might do. Rod felt Charlie had the situation in hand. After all, he was experiencing every part of combat possible.

The quiet was broken by the ringing of the doorbell. Rod stared for the longest time before lifting himself out of the chair. It was like he was trying to see who was on the other side. The doorbell rang again. "Coming", Rod yelled. The nervousness in his voice said he would rather not. Still he turned the knob and the creak of the door echoed so eerily...

CHAPTER 71

As Rod slowly opened the door, there was both relief and humor. Humor quickly took over. Standing ever so stately, was the Martin's neighbor from across the street, Al Collins. Collins, who stood about 6 foot 4 inches had on a blue flannel shirt, blue jeans, Red Wing work boots and looks of a three day old beard on his mug. He was holding the runt of Hope's cat contingent, the three-legged Peanut. "Morning", said Al. "I'm glad you didn't say Good in front of that", replied Rod. "Because what you're holding in your arms wouldn't imply that." They both laughed. "My guess is she made her way over to your house again", inquired Rod. "Yup, she can't seem to remember she lives here when she gets out". What they were doing today was something they had done time and time again. And as always, Collins would bring the cat back home. Always. Just once, Rod thought, he wished he'd keep her. But Hope would have none of that. Dang cat had more lives than Carter had pills. Even getting caught in the garage door years ago and losing a leg hadn't slowed the thing down. She was always into something. "Thanks, I think", said Rod. "Next time I won't answer the door though, okay?" Collins smiled and shook his head and sauntered back across the street. Rod closed the door and slowly let the cat down to the floor. He closed his eyes for a minute and said a little prayer under his breath. "Thank God it was nothing more than Peanut", he murmured.

These last several weeks were something entirely new to most of the Guard family. Some had deployed before but for most it was foreign territory. In most people's fears were thoughts of having someone they loved die. And that image was now all too real. Rod had been reading some on-line material in recent days in hopes to better understand the why's. And this is what he had come up with. Don't focus on the fear of losing your soldier, but on how blessed you are to have them.

Sitting down in front of the laptop keyboard he wiped his mind as much as he could. He wanted to focus ever so intently on a message, a hope message he wanted to deliver. Here is what his keystrokes delivered.

A NORMAL PERSON HAS 1,000 WISHES. A SOLDIER ONLY HAS ONE, TO COME HOME SAFE.

This phrase came from Sgt. Sonja Titus of Ankeny, Iowa who is stationed in Afghanistan via a Facebook post Friday morning. Considering what the "families" of the Iowa National Guard have been going through this past week, those words couldn't have been more appropriate.

Last July, over 4,000 Iowans and several hundred Nebraskans were deployed to Afghanistan, the largest in Iowa National Guard history since World War II. The safety of these soldiers has been a thought all have embraced since the day they departed. It doesn't matter if it's been hopes, dreams, wishes or prayers we've all been desiring the same thing Sgt. Titus mentions, a safe return home for every soldier. Now, we know that's not possible.

In recent days we've lost these two, fine guardians of our constitution.

"When something like this happens, it's a reminder for other families that it could be any one of us ... getting that call," said Darci Ritter, Family Readiness Coordinator for the Waterloo-headquartered 1st Battalion, 133rd Infantry. "This is

a hard time", Ritter said. "It seems like the walls are tumbling down." But there is HOPE.

In Eastern Iowa, a community banded together to help the families of the two fallen soldiers. Folks who've never met either soldier are stepping up to help. From a KGAN-TV report came this information. "Volunteers covered a table inside Regina High School in Iowa City with baked goods Friday night. Imagine if every muffin, every cookie on that table were a toothbrush, or a sock. That's basically what the group Iowa Troop Pantry does. Volunteers raise money for basic supplies to send to troops overseas. But Friday night's fundraiser was even more important because all the money went to the families of the two fallen heroes: Specialists Maher and Nichols.

"Those guys are our family, our family's hurting," says Mike Tyson, one of the directors of Iowa Troop Pantry. Two Iowa soldiers killed in one week. Both leave behind families, children, wives, struggling to cope and a community unsure of how to help". One community did, though. Now we need others to follow their lead.

Encouragement is also coming within the ranks of other deployed families. Here are a couple of comments.

The first is from Tonya Rosol...."My son, Lt. Justin Foote was on foot near the vehicle when the IED was detonated. He is the platoon leader for this scouts/sniper platoon. We are grieving the loss of Donny and praying for the gunner's recovery. My son escorted Donny's body back to Bagram along with the injured gunner where he will wait for Donny's brother who is in another part of Afghanistan to arrive to take Donny home to his family. God Speed to the brave men and women. Life is so fleeting".

And from Mark Johnson...."My son, Spc. Jacob Johnson was 2 trucks behind Don's. Jake went through Basic & AIT at Ft. Benning with Don, drills, NTC and the same squad in Afghanistan. We talked to Jake shortly after the incident and he said he carried Donny to the chopper. My heartfelt sympathy goes out to the family and Chelsey. I can't imagine what they are going through and how their lives have changed forever. God bless them and God rest Donny at peace in Heaven".

And lastly from the parents of Spc. Nichols fiance, Marvin and DeAnn Bliss....... "As Chelsey's parents we'd like to extend our thanks to all the 133rd families and friends that have reached out to Chelsey. She is a strong woman with a strong family and friend base. We will make it! Our thoughts and prayers go out to all the family members of the 133rd and their soldiers on their SAFE RETURN HOME".

YGG,

Rod

As you can see, Hope is prevalent. And more than anything. It's a weapon not to be taken lightly.

CHAPTER 72

The rock of the Martin family sat in her familiar command post. The over-sized chair had seen much wear and tear over the years. Still it was comfortable. Hope sat with her eyes closed cupping her hands on an amaretto delight. It was one of her favorite coffee brands. She was soaking it all in as a means of inspiration.

The past several weeks had been one of tragedy and pain. But it also had been a time of tremendous community outpouring. The loss of the state's soldiers had not gone unnoticed. Hope wondered where her men were at mentally during this period. Heck for that matter, she wondered where she was. It was time to turn to her trusty prayer support, Martha Townsend. Over the course of Charlie's deployment, Townsend had been strong in her vision and wisdom. Hope reflected on the relationship of the two jotting down some thoughts in her journal

"There are times in life when God provides for us through the presence of another. All week I have been held up by the prayers and encouragement that have come to me through Martha. Martha was someone who came along at the perfect time in my life like sunshine after a rain. We met through a class we both took at Hope. The sweet thing we both looked forward to most in our relationship was getting together and taking our needs and our thanks to God. And now was a time that I was thankful to have her strength, faith and encouragement.

Dear Hope,

I am thinking of you and want you to know that my prayers are going up for you and your family. I am so grateful for Charlie's service and I simply cannot imagine what you are going through right now. Remain strong and confident in the Lord for He shall bring you through, of this I am certain.

"I look up to the mountains. Does my help come from there? My helps comes from the Lord who made the Heavens and the Earth. He will not let you stumble; the One who watches over you will not slumber. Indeed, He who watches over Israel never slumbers or sleeps. The Lord himself watches over you. The Lord stands beside you as your protective shade. The sun will not harm you by day nor the moon by night. The Lord keeps you from all harm and watches over your life. The Lord keeps watch over you as you come and go, both now and forever.-Psalm 121

Remember, God has your every need-past, present and future fully covered. Remain undivided in your devotion to Him-receive everything you need from your indwelling Lord. If you ever need to talk, I am here!

Love, Martha

Several days later, Hope got another message from her strong arm of support. This time she was reading it straight off her email.

May 9, 2011

My heart feels like I should keep praying for a "miraculous turn of events! So this is what I'm praying for. I'm praying and believing for that miracle!

Miraculous turn of events...

Miraculous turn of events...

Miraculous turn of events...

Miraculous turn of events...

Miraculous turn of events...

Miraculous turn of events...

Miraculous turn of events...

Miraculous turn of events...

Miraculous turn of events...

Miraculous turn of events...

Miraculous turn of events...

Miraculous turn of events...

Miraculous turn of events...

Miraculous turn of events...

Miraculous turn of events...

15 times she typed out the words. Hope wasn't sure what this meant, but she was sure of the power behind the words. So much so that she printed the message out, cut out the 15 sentences that read, "miraculous turn of events and she put it her purse where she would have it with her always. And she looked at it often, smiling and marveling and wondering. Martha later told Hope she had no idea why she felt so strong about that prayer. But she did. Perhaps time would tell what it meant. But for now, Martha and Hope would lean together on the presence of their Lord and rest.

As tough as these days were for Hope she still felt she and Rod were in this together. The talking, the praying and the tears kept them close. As far as Eddie and Dan went, well she wasn't quite sure where they were with things. Sometimes a person gets so washed over with their own survival (so to speak) that they don't quite see much else.

Not wanting to escalate fear in her sons' she didn't really confront them much about how they were handling things. And with Eddie in the Guard as well there was the fear of him having to deploy. That was a place Hope didn't want to go in her thoughts. And Dan and Eddie probably didn't want to think about that possibility either. One day at a time, that was enough on any of their plates.

CHAPTER 73

Hope's mind-set and wisdom regarding their family's deployment got put to an early test. The day before Easter 2011 should have been a joyous one. In many ways, for the Martins it was. The family had spent a majority of the day making salads getting ready for a family dinner at Hope's parents. They were looking forward to the anniversary of Jesus' resurrection. However, late in the afternoon came a notification that would offer a threat to her assertions. This time there was an imaginary knock at the door. The news had come from an overnight press release.

Rod sat hypnotized at the dining room table. He was wrestling with two words. Fear and Hope. He wished he didn't have to battle these thoughts out. But there was really little choice. When he finally was able to construct some words to the situation, his fingers began hitting the keys, pounding out another blog.

> **This is going to be a short post, but I pray one that hits you right between the eyes and straight into your heart. You see, I'm way past the heart broken stage....my heart is bursting. Last night we received word of the death of Staff Sgt. James Justice of Grimes. Justice was killed by enemy small arms fire during combat operations on Saturday, April 23, in Kapisa Province, Afghanistan at approximately 10 a.m., local Afghanistan time. Wounded in the attack was Spc. Zachary Durham, 21, of Des**

Moines, Iowa. Both soldiers were assigned to Troop A, 1st Squadron, 113th Cavalry, Camp Dodge, Johnston, Iowa.

That makes three Iowa National Guard soldiers we've lost in the last ten days. We've also had countless wounded. Which leads me to this thinking. We need prayer in a big-time way. And here's why...

There remains somewhere in the neighborhood of two months left for our guard troops to maintain their mission objective in Afghanistan. Two months doesn't sound like much, but when you break it down into days....it sure is. 60 days.... that's alot.

What is tugging at my heart today is the need for a prayer vigil. Why you say?

BECAUSE PRAYER CHANGES EVERYTHING......

I'm not sure how a prayer vigil can be put into action. I've never done one before, but I know people, you know people who know other people........ We need to do this, not only for our soldiers but the families of Spc. Muhr, Spc. Maher, Spc. Nichols and Staff Sgt. Justice. God is at work today searching for "hearts that want to work for him". If you've wondered before how you can serve the kingdom, here is an opportunity.

YGG,

Rod

Shutting down the laptop, Rod had come to a conclusion. In reality, hope is fear's biggest enemy. The two can't live together. Standing in the kitchen, Rod took a long swig from a glass of cherry Kool-Aid. His beverage of choice kept him young and helped him conjure up some lines from a movie from many moon ago, "City Slickers". It went like this:

Curly: "Do you know what the secret of life is?
[holds up one finger] This.
Mitch: Your finger?

296

Curly: One thing. Just one thing. You stick to that and the rest don't mean s***.

Mitch: But, what is the "one thing?"

Curly: That's what you have to find out".

"Hmmmm", said Rod out loud. "I think I know the secret. In fact, I know I do".

CHAPTER 74

It was hard to determine the exact reason for the uptick in Taliban activity in Afghanistan. It could have been the warmer weather. There was even the suggestion that the Muslim fundamentalist group knew there was going to be a changing of the guard in the coming months. Or maybe they wanted to make sure the Taliban name was not forgotten. Regardless of the reason, a fairly mild deployment had drastically changed.

Rod and several volunteers were continuing their work on a Prayer Vigil that was becoming reality. Little did they know what was ahead. Shortly after Rod's feet had hit the floor on the morning of May 2nd, he had been in scurry mode. His cellphone had provided the information that planted him in front of the television soaking in everything he could. Osama Bin Laden, the founder and first leader of the Islamist group Al-Qaeda, was killed in Pakistan by United States Navy SEALs. Many, many Americans were rejoicing on this day.

After more than an hour of being captivated by the news of Bin Laden's death, Rod headed to the dining room table and fired up his laptop. He hit his Facebook site and posted a quick message to his son.

Rod MartinMonday, May 2, 2011 at 9:20am CDT how you doing today?

Charlie MartinMonday, May 2, 2011 at 9:21am CDT So on the plus side Osama is finally dead thanks to the Navy Seals, that

could be good and bad but only time will tell. On the downside... The truck I was riding in today hit an IED... it was such a big blast that it picked the 30 ton truck off the ground spun it in a 180deg turn and blew off the whole front end. We found the motor and front end minus one tire 300ft in front of us and the other tire was 600ft to the west in a river and there were parts that were even further away than that. Good news is that I'm safe, just have a headache the size of Texas and I'll probably be sore tomorrow. The guy in the passenger seat got medevac'd out on helicopter, messed up his back and the gunner had some cuts on his face but other than that were all good.

Rod MartinMonday, May 2, 2011 at 9:23am CDT Praise the Lord!!

Charlie MartinMonday, May 2, 2011 at 9:24am CDT Yea no kidding.. it had to happen the day Osama dies out of all days

Rod MartinMonday, May 2, 2011 at 9:24am CDT Just the 3 of you in the truck

Rod MartinMonday, May 2, 2011 at 9:25am CDT you have no injuries other than your headache? Did you go have a doctor check u out?

Charlie MartinMonday, May 2, 2011 at 9:26am CDT Nope Im all good. I had to go have a traumatic brain injury test with the medics and I passed so they let me go.

Rod MartinMonday, May 2, 2011 at 9:27am CDT how many trucks were part of your group?

Charlie MartinMonday, May 2, 2011 at 9:29am CDT

5 US trucks and 3 ANA trucks. After it happened we had to wait for about 3 hrs until EOD could come do a post blast analysis and they brought a wrecker so we could tow it back. I got some pics Ill send ya tomorow if I have time

---

Charlie MartinMonday, May 2, 2011 at 9:33am CDT Well dadpo gotta run. Im gonna try to get some sleep hopefully. Its been a long day. Ill talk to you guys later on tho! Love you guys!

Scenes like this from IED's are all too common in Afghanistan

When Hope came home that afternoon, she quickly began a conversation with her husband that lasted well into the early evening. Not only was Bin Laden's death shocking, they both surmised it was going to ignite hostile feelings in the region. Both were in agreement of that. Of greater concern was the IED Charlie had hit. Over the years, he'd blown off times when he had been hurt. Was this one them? Even the answers to Rod's questions seemed a little disjointed. Later that night, or actually early the next morning, Hope sat composed in front of Rod's PC. Her brain was working a million miles an hour. She simply had to get her message out. Thus...

Hope MartinTuesday, May 3, 2011 at 3:32am CDT Hey Love, It is 3am and I am wide awake, of course thinking about you and all of our Soldiers. I heard about the escape from what could have been deadly. I give God thanks for covering you and shielding you. Your Dad and I are doing all we can to ramp up the spiritual support you all need to get through these last weeks. The battle is not only against the physical enemy but spiritual enemies as well-or maybe even more so. You must therefore fight this battle in both the physical and the spiritual realm. You must pray any time you can against the enemy forces of darkness. Out loud if you have time alone. I encourage you to pray as such-"I might be only one man but I am also a child of the King. And because I am His I carry with me the power that is in His shed blood on my behalf. And in His name and underneath His blood I pray against all of the spiritual forces of darkness that are at work. May the plans and purposes of God Almighty go forth and prosper. And may the hold of the power of darkness lose it's grip. Oh God go before us, with us, and behind us. Be our shelter and may our battle be Yours. We need your presence and we ask this battle to be fought in your strength and might and for Your sake. The Lord rebuke you Satan and all of the angels at your side. Protect us Lord and keep Your armor on us always. The helmet of Salvation to guard our minds and give us the mind of Christ. The breastplate of righteousness to guard our hearts. May we not lose heart in the battle and may our hearts hunger after You oh God. The belt of truth around our waist. Give to us the truth Lord that we might be quick to see and discern our enemies in wisdom. The gospel boots of peace on our feet. Protect our steps and direct our path. The shield of faith. Increase our faith oh God to extinguish the darts of our enemies and last but perhaps most important-the sword of the spirit, which is the word of God. Bring your word to our minds Lord and may we know it and trust it. It is our sword and every Soldier needs his

301

weapon. Your word says escapes from death belong to you. It says You are our strong tower, our refuge, our strength. Cover us in Your armor." That's also my prayer for you and I hope you will take time to pray whenever you can. It is a powerful weapon. I thank God you are safe. Please let me know how you are doing right now. How you are feeling from the blast- your head and body? And also how the other two Soldiers are doing. Call when you can...I love you so much Charlie and we are right there with you every second. Our hearts never leave you nor the presence of God on your behalf. God is at work. Your Dad is sensing Him move and is starting a prayer vigil for you all. I am right there with him. We will keep you posted on it...Mompo

The next morning Rod found the message his wife had sent their son. The words were written so eloquently. He was proud of her. Old Hopester had hit a home run. Rod checked back in with Charlie moments later.

Rod MartinTuesday, May 3, 2011 at 10:18am CDT hey kiddo

Charlie MartinTuesday, May 3, 2011 at 10:18am CDT hey dadpo

Rod MartinTuesday, May 3, 2011 at 10:19am CDT how u doing today?

Charlie MartinTuesday, May 3, 2011 at 10:20am CDT not too bad. jus been hangin out today and recoopin. theres a mandatory 24hr off period after an IED. but i have 2 missions tomorow so it wasnt really much of a break caus i would have had today off either way.

Rod MartinTuesday, May 3, 2011 at 10:34am CDT wow. how's everyone else in the truck? just the three of you?

Charlie MartinTuesday, May 3, 2011 at 11:03am CDT their good. the guy who got medevac'd is coming back tomorrow and no there was 7 of us in it

Rod MartinTuesday, May 3, 2011 at 11:03am CDT seven!!! where were you?

Rod MartinTuesday, May 3, 2011 at 11:04am CDT what type of vehicle is it called

Charlie MartinTuesday, May 3, 2011 at 11:05am CDT yup. the driver, truck commander who is in the passenger seat, the gunner, and 4 of us in the back. it was an RG31. if it would have been a MATV which is what we usually ride in, we would have all been dead.

Those last words remained on the screen for many minutes. Rod sat there for another ten minutes awaiting some more conversation. But nothing came. In Rod's mind, whoever came with up with the saying, "silence is golden", should think again. This was far from it.

CHAPTER 75

There hadn't been a lot of discussion in the Martin family regarding Charlie's close encounter. Maybe not talking about the danger Charlie had escaped in the IED explosion would somehow make it less truthful, Rod reasoned. Hope said little but it was obvious Charlie was in the forefront of all her thoughts. She had taken a pair of Charlie's old army boots to work and kept them under her desk. It just made her feel closer to him, like to have a little piece of him with her. She tried to message her son via Facebook as often as she could. Rod and Hope continued with their commitment to attend the funeral service of any military member who had given their life during the deployment. They made their way to Manning to pay their respects to Staff Sgt. Justice. A day later, Rod filed this blog story.

> I drove by the sign on Highway 141 west of the Woodward, Iowa exit for the second time in my life, at least that's what I recall. It's not a very big billboard, if that's what you want to call it....and it's about as simple as it gets. The letters stick out on the white background, but oh, how they make their point. "Prayer Changes Everything" is the message. Short, simple and right to the point.

I had a number of thoughts going through my head as I was driving westward, but the sign changed it all. Not only did I forget what was on my mind.....I started thinking about the Justice family and the support and prayers they needed in the loss of their son, Staff Sgt. James Justice. So I prayed. Did that change the fact that I was headed to a funeral......no. But I think it played a large part in the 2,000 plus people that showed up. I'm sure there were others praying for that same result.

Which leads me to THE PRAYER VIGIL. I've talked about a prayer vigil for several weeks now. Quite frankly, there have been some disappointing times as I've tried to rattle the bushes and make people aware of the need. And then there have been the victorious times where people have offered encouragement or support. Through the highs and lows, I've received an education that helps put frustration into its proper perspective. Have you ever heard the phrase, "I'm a slow learner?" Living proof...I am. Where I'd like everyone to support this vigil or attend, it's just not going to happen. God will direct those that he wants to help in the event's success and those that he wants to show up. No more and no less. I'm only helping deliver that message. So here goes with the details to date.

Location: West Side of the Iowa State Capitol in Des Moines, Iowa

Date: May 15th, 2011

Time: 2:00 p.m.

You might be asking yourself, why should this prayer vigil matter to me? Well...it's not just for the safety of our soldiers in their "countdown" days, it's for the deployed families who are struggling with a myriad of emotions. Let me put it this way. Last summer when the 4,000 troops deployed there were tears and much more. That lasted for some time. Then a numbness emerged where acceptance of the mission became more real. But now, its back to the emotional stage. Phone calls and doorbell rings are taking on a different set of tones. Should I answer that? Does it carry bad news? Let's pray not.

May 15th is also a day where you can individually learn how to pray specifically for our troops....and what to pray for in regards to the end of deployment and family concerns. It's also about taking the messages heard on May 15th and returning to the communities around our state. Some just need direction. I think you'll see that in evidence a week from Sunday.

Next week, I will be placing a link to a 24/7 calendar on the MFV blog where you can register for a one-hour block of time to pray specifically for our troops/families. No matter your situation (short/tall/old/young/disabled) you can pray and hold yourself accountable by reserving a time slot. Our hopes are to extend that through July 4th.....and maybe beyond, if the need is there. Visitors from over 60 countries have come to "My Father's Voice". We want you to pray as well. Your reason for coming to the blog and praying might be overwhelming in itself.

So you see, the event on the 15th is only one little part of the whole picture. All I know is....the Holy Spirit is moving and he is asking us for PRAYER like we've never seen before. Does Prayer Change Everything? Come next Sunday and find out.

YGG,

Rod

P.S.

The time is now. Time was of the essence. I've read once some thoughts on prayer that Rick Warren had written. This might shed another light.

"Do you ever wonder if prayer really works? You're praying about something and Satan whispers to you, "This is a waste of time. Forget it! Who do you think you are? What do you think you're doing? Don't waste your time." Prayer works because God is in control. The basis of all miracles is God's sovereignty. Why does He do one and not another? Because God is in control. We have to trust His wisdom and His goodness . Ephesians 3:20 says, "God is able to do far more than we would ever dare to ask or even dream of, infinitely beyond our highest prayers, desires and thoughts or hopes."

Prayer can do whatever God can do. His resources are available to you. Twenty times in the New Testament it says, "Ask". It's encouraging to know that things that are out of my control are not out of God's. I may not be able to change a situation, but I can pray and God can change it.

Those are some powerful words.....and oh so truthful. That's why I'm sharing them with you as we approach our Sunday Prayer Vigil at the Iowa State Capitol. Come and be a part of it. It begins at 2 p.m. on the west side of the Capitol in the area they call the West Capitol Terrace. In a day or two, I will share with you the people who have offered their gifts to this day. You'll be amazed how God has moved in bringing the right people to us. Realize I don't have time to send you a formal invitation, but know you're on my list. And by the way, if you have some reservations or you don't know how you'd get there, check with your friends or neighbors. They've got the same invitation. So, why not come together?

Today and in the coming days, You and I may be the only message of God's love, grace, and forgiveness that people hear and see. Remember that. And remember that....simply because our troops and their families are so, so deserving of this day, where as one, we can stand and raise our hands to the heavens in appreciation and asking for their safety and protection.

YGG,

Rod

CHAPTER 76

Rod Martin glanced at the bathroom mirror as he got out of the shower. It was the day after the Prayer Vigil. He was physically exhausted. Yet the reflection bore none of that impression. Martin couldn't put a finger on it. The past nine months had changed him. In a truer sense, God had changed him. He was more convicted in his Christian walk than ever. When he'd first given his life to the Lord, he'd lost friends that didn't understand his way of thinking. As he sized himself up he saw the reflection of a man ready to take his commitment to the Lord another step deeper. One last look, a brush of a dark brown lock with his hair brush and he bounced down the stairs ready to put down in words an impression of something far more important than him.

The Prayer Vigil had taken place on Sunday, May 15th, with a sufficient amount of seeds being planted. Only God knows how many. The underlying take away for Rod and many of the people that took part was the importance and timing. Would there be a miraculous turn of events? And if so, how long would it take to happen. Rod thought. The next day brought forth a shocking encounter. One Martin shared via his blog site.

Your physical senses are incapable of judging whether a seed is alive or not. You cannot see, feel, hear, smell, or taste the life in a seed. There is only one way to prove a seed is alive -- plant it.-Believers.org

The words above speak so much truth, but as human beings we often times get in the way. How do you know the power of the seed you plant? You don't. You might not ever know in your lifetime....but that doesn't mean you don't plant it. I have a myriad of thoughts from Sunday's Prayer Vigil that was held for the Iowa National Guard troops and their families. Foremost, though, is this. We heard God Ask....We Obeyed..... and We Planted Seeds. And those seeds will multiply. I think of the thousands who heard and saw the radio and television reports of the event. And then I think of the outreach we can have in placing parts of the vigil on You Tube. That's where we're feeling directed. Yes, our seeds can have far reaching effects. But it takes us to act on those promptings.

Case in point, this morning, I'm coming home from picking up my son, Eddie. We pull in the driveway and get out of the car as our neighbors are leaving their house. "Saw you on TV last night, wow, that was great", the husband said. I could say I was taken aback by his comments, but that wouldn't even begin to put the proper wordage to it. I was blown away. For over two years now, we've lived next door to these people. They hardly ever say anything to us...or any other neighbor for that matter. When they come home, it's in the garage and down with the door, immediately. We've tried to connect with them despite some outbursts....like our dog venturing into their yard, one of our cats killing a bird near their bird feeder and our teenage kids noise and cars. Not once have they mentioned the yellow ribbon around the tree in our front yard, around the mailbox or on a post at the front door. Not once, since our son deployed to Afghanistan in July of 2010. Not once.

And then there it was. The neighbor man says, "my son flies for a commercial airlines and takes soldiers back and forth to Kuwait. When will your son get back?" And the dialogue was off and running. Coincidence? Not hardly!!! There have been other conversations as of late and I know there will be more. That's the neat thing.

"A reporter asked me after the Prayer Vigil if I thought it was a success. "It's not up to me to say", Rod said. "I know the people that God wanted to be there, were. Maybe I can put it into an even better perspective. On that Sunday we invited people to come to a session...kind of like a recording session. People sang, they spoke, they prayed. I do know the ones that attended the vigil were moved deeply. I had more than one of the performers mention the "longing" expression of comfort many in the crowd displayed. Yes, the Holy Spirit was there front and center".

Now, the message is being taken forward through those that experienced the day firsthand, those that heard and saw it on the radio and television news and then the ones that will see it on YouTube and on Facebook and through My Father's Voice.

Back to a comment I made at the head of this post. There is only one way to prove a seed is alive -- plant it. So what's next?

The seed of the word is planted in our heart, then the water of the word keeps it alive. In the Bible, 1Corinthians 3:6 says "I planted, Apollos watered, and God's life makes it grow. For our soldiers, know that people are loving on you big time. You are in their thoughts and prayers. Just know that there are more today than yesterday and they'll be more tomorrow than today. Rest in that.

YGG,

Rod

CHAPTER 77

It was Friday, the 20th of May. The weekend was finally in sight. Five days since the Prayer Vigil. Hope and Rod Martin were still soaking in all the elements of the previous Sunday. Hope was continuing to be on the lookout for a "miraculous turn of events". What did her friend Martha's prayer mean? She wasn't sure but her eyes and ears were moving to and fro trying to pick up any sense of truth. It was early evening in the Martin household. Hope was sitting on the living room couch with her faithful cat Bubba Bruise on her lap. In her hand was the cellphone that had been busy for the last hour. If it wasn't for conversation, it was texting. She was reaching out to anyone that could shed some light on Martha's wisdom. For now, she was coming up empty. "I wish I knew", said Hope. "Maybe I'm looking too hard", she mentioned to another friend. "Just be still", her friend encouraged her. "Be still?" Hope replied back

Those were the last two words Rod heard as he and Mason stole their way out the garage door. They were headed for Terra Park and a walk among the bushes and trees. It was a beautiful evening in Hawkeyeland. The temps were hanging in the low 70's, there was just a subtle hint of a breeze and the skies were heavenly. The red wisps of the clouds merged into breathtaking orange. Spectacular was even an understatement. It was as if there was a rage against the dying of light. Rod felt moved to tell his four legged friend what he thought of the scenery. "Mason, you ever seen anything so awesome?", he inquired. Rod looked down half expecting an answer from the canine. While he didn't answer back, the Golden did the unexpected. Mason stopped, looked up at his master and gave a little smile followed by an eager wag of his tail. Mason knew. And Rod knew Mason knew that he knew. This was certainly not the time to call it a night and head home. Just to their right was a big old rock. One perfect for sitting and soaking in the day. "Come on buddy", Martin exclaimed.

Over the course of the next fifteen minutes Rod sat and stared. For a brief time he was back at the Prayer Vigil hearing Ms. Guinta's words. Rose had given a beautiful prayer that day. Then he tried to visualize Charlie in Afghanistan. His day was about to begin. May 20th had been one of the best days Rod had lived in a long time. What type of day laid in store for his son? The best? The worst? Or somewhere in between? He thought back to the Facebook message he'd gotten yesterday.

CharlieMartinThursday, May 19, 2011 at 11:31am CDT just got back from a mission, I got sick and threw up twice while we were walking and climbing in 110deg heat. Im thinking about going and getting an IV in the morning since I'm dehydrated now from throwing up all the liquids in my body

Rod didn't keep with the thought of Charlie for very long. Not that he wasn't concerned. He was. Sometimes it was better not to hang on every word. So he moved on. Next, he saw images of his family from a number of years ago when they lived on an acreage outside of Indianola. Those were some fun times, he thought. He smirked when recalling Eddie racing his motorcycle along the edge of the pond, hitting a dip and going head over heels to a face plant. It was an image straight out of "America's Funniest Videos". It was funny and scary at the same time. The accident could have been severe. When the young cyclist finally got the dirt out of his mouth so he could talk, everyone realized he was going to be alright. Then the hoots and hollers began. Aaahh, what a memory.

The barking of a dog in the distance broke the ambience. Mason tuned his ears up full throttle. Somebody was causing a ruckus. And a tail-wagger was signaling a notice. Mason listened a little longer and coming to a conclusion that things were alright, he looked at Rod. It was time to continue their walk.

Later as man and dog sat on the front porch, Rod tried to figure out how many days were left in the Guard's deployment. As he counted the number off in his head, he also noticed his heartbeat seemed to echo a soldier's march. Left, left, left, right, left. He came to the realization it had to be around 60 days. That is unless something drastic happened. 60 days. Less than 2 months and less than 8 weeks. No matter how you looked at it, it still was a long way off. The light was at the end of the tunnel. But way, way down there.

Rod thought it might be time to bring a little fun into the Martin's lives. What could he do to take some pressure off the family? Memorial Day Weekend was around the corner. Maybe a trip to Lake Ponderosa would help. A little boating, fishing and swimming never hurt. As Rod reached the front door he had convinced himself that he had come up with a solution. Lake fun, here we come. Martin reached into his pants pocket and dug out his cellphone. He punched in the familiar digits. "Hello, Mom", he fired. "Rod here. Remember me?"

CHAPTER 78

The chuckle at the other end of the phone call was one Rod liked to hear. He talked to his mother every Sunday evening. Most of the conversations started with something to get her to laugh. Grandma Martin has a cantankerous chuckle. And Rod pushed the envelope as much as he could to hear that sound. "You're something else", of course I know who it is, Ray", she returned. "Funny mom, funny", Rod fired back. The balance of the talk focused on the family and eventually turned toward Charlie. Once Rod had updated her on the goings on, he called it a good night. "Night, Mom. Love you", he let slowly roll off his lips.

Rod sat down at the dining room table somewhat satisfied in the direction the family was going. He flipped up the lid on his PC and started churning out some thoughts. Two hours later he was still glued to the dining room chair stuck in exactly how he wanted MFV story to turn out. This is going to have to wait, he thought. The timing was important. Rod shut off his computer and made his way up the stairs into the bedroom. The moon was shining ever so brightly. It was three days removed from a full moon. Its brilliance was nowhere near the setting of the evening sun but it was glamorous unto itself. As his head hit the pillow, Rod said a prayer he hadn't uttered in a long, long time. Why it came to him tonight, he wasn't sure. Under his breath, he started, "now I lay me down to sleep. I pray the

Lord my soul to keep. If I should die before I wake. I pray the Lord my soul to take." Moments later he was in la-la land.

The next day Rod kept busy watching his Chicago White Sox throttle the Los Angeles Dodgers in an inter-league game 9-2. Mark Buehrle went seven innings in getting his fourth win of the year. Both teams were 21-26 on the season. Neither would be playing come autumn. Of that, Rod was certain.

Saturday morphed into Sunday morning. Rod had not yet completed his story. Now feeling somewhat guilty he realized he had to churn something out. He sat at the table in his PJ's. Rod's day outside the house wouldn't start until he had completed the blog job. Another hour later. He published the following.

> I've got to ask you a question....and I hope you'll be honest with yourself. I'd like to inquire of all the soldiers, the families, the relatives, the friends.....all of you, collectively, How ya doing? How ya doing knowing that days are dwindling down in the deployment of your soldier with the Iowa National Guard Troops that deployed to Afghanistan in October. How ya doing with any news item that hits the wires? How ya doing after you hang up the phone talking to your loved one? How ya doing after a Facebook correspondence runs dry and there is nothing more to say? How ya doing with those restless nights of sleep not to mention any bad dreams you have along the way? How ya doing during the waking hours, during work time, during activities that used to be of great enjoyment to you......are you finding your mind wandering all over the place? And how ya doing in sharing your struggles along the way with people who have checked out on you.....you know the ones that were supportive at first, but give you the impression that you overreact far too much? Now, I ask you again, "How ya doing?" And don't tell me the stock answer... "fine".

I'll share with you where I am. Maybe that will help. I'm tired, I'm wore out and I'm exhausted. I can't wait to get our son off the soils of Afghanistan and on his way home. My wife feels the same way. We just want him home. I'm sure leaving Afghanistan is a pretty common mind-set amongst the troops as well, at least what I've been able to view from general attitudes of soldiers I know. They're exhausted too.

So how about joining forces? You, me, our soldiers our friends, our family, etc. When I said I was exhausted and you could be too, that doesn't mean were down for the count. We're still breathing and operating in this universe. Here's my suggestion to you. You can take it or leave it....hopefully, you'll take it. Even though I'm exhausted that doesn't mean I can't pray. I've prayed more in the last six months than I might have in my entire life. And that's been a good thing. In addition, I've found out how to pray better. That's been awesome as well. Last Sunday, we held a Prayer Vigil for the Iowa National Guard Troops deployed to Afghanistan and their families. I saw another way to pray. I can pray, you can pray, we all can pray for our troops. This past week we had four soldiers from the 133rd, my son's unit, injured in another IED blast. Did the prayers from the Prayer Vigil make a difference? Would the injuries those four soldiers endured have been more serious had we not been fervent in prayer? I don't know....but I do know prayer is a mighty force. We're that close to getting the troops home. We're exhausted, no doubt. But we're not done quite yet, we can all keep praying.

YGG,

Rod

CHAPTER 79

Memorial Day Weekend came and went. It had been a fun time for the Martin family. Not just the immediate Rod Martin gang, but the lake-style part of the family too. There had to have been more than fifteen bodies sharing ski time, swimming, fishing and most importantly, eating. The weather was fantastic and a great time for everyone. But it ended all too quickly and Tuesday, May 31st meant a return to the grind and reality not to mention the worry. The worry. It never went away for long.

The next ten days Hope had done her best to keep the family on the run. There had been movies, a couple of long walks and a real strong effort to just keep busy. Finally it caught up with Rod after getting a message from Charlie. A scary message quite frankly. His blog report on June 11th said as much...

> **May 25th, Seventeen days ago, the Ironman Battalion of the Iowa Army National Guard was involved in a firefight of hellacious consequences. For sixteen of those days, our son, Charlie, who is part of the battalion, kept the story inside. At least inside Army walls. Yesterday, he told me a reporter had been by for interviews and a story would be forthcoming regarding a significant battle. Despite giving me some of the details the following story was certainly an 'Oh My God' experience with**

a miraculous turn of events. The story comes from Pat Kinney, who is a reporter for the Waterloo-Cedar Falls Courier.

WATERLOO - A tale of courage under fire has been received out of Afghanistan involving soldiers of the Waterloo-headquartered Iowa Army National Guard battalion. Members of the Guard's 1st Battalion, 133rd Infantry Regiment - the "Ironman Battalion" - lived up to their nickname in the recapture of the Afghan town of Do Ab, Nuristan province, in heavy fighting with entrenched Taliban insurgents on May 25.

After being pinned down for more than an hour by unrelenting mortar and machine gun fire in an exposed helicopter landing zone, the soldiers fought their way to a livestock compound that offered a defensible position. They provided cover fire for a second wave mainly made up of friendly Afghan forces. Supported by assault helicopters and Air Force fighter jets, they drove off the enemy and retook Do Ab, a governmental center similar to a county seat, according to soldiers' accounts. The 60-soldier force - 42 "Ironmen" and 18 Afghan nationals - sustained no casualties while killing more than 100 Taliban.

While the 1/133rd, part of the 34th "Red Bull" infantry division, has seen combat throughout its eight months in Afghanistan, the May 25 operation was the heaviest fighting experienced to date. It was one of the "most significant engagements the Red Bull has been involved in since World War II," Guard spokesman Maj. Mike Wunn in Afghanistan said. "We had many points through the day where luck was on our side. Our guys did an outstanding job, which led to all of us coming home," added 1/133rd battalion commander Lt. Col. Steven Kremer of Cherokee. "It's just amazing to me, it's unbelievable everyone came out," Kremer said.

The soldiers were members of the 1/133rd's headquarters and headquarter company, as well as Charlie Company, and the battalion mortar and sniper teams. The sniper team was headed by Staff Sgt. Jeremy Buhr of Waverly.

Intelligence reports indicated the reinforced Taliban had seized Do Ab. The 1/133rd's mission, Kremer said, was to assess the enemy strength and determine how large a force would be needed to deal with the insurgents. The Guardsmen flew in on two Chinook helicopters in a fairly confined landing zone, the only flat area in the rough terrain around Do Ab.

They discovered the enemy strength soon after landing. Guard 1st Lt. Justin Foote of New Hartford, formerly of Evansdale, 1/133rd reconnaissance platoon leader, said an air burst from an enemy rocket-propelled grenade exploded over one of the Chinooks as it took off, and the fight was on. "The whole (landing zone) erupted into fire," Foote said. "From every point of high ground, from every piece of defensible fighting position the enemy were in, it pretty much rained down - all types of weapons, small arms fire, machine gun fire, RPG fire and enemy mortar rounds." Soldiers would take cover behind rocks for protection, only to be subjected to fire from another angle. "You were taking fire from pretty much every direction," Foote said.

The experienced Taliban were dug in up to their chests in the rocky fortifications. The two Chinooks had landed 300 meters apart, under such withering fire it took the Ironmen an hour to consolidate their divided force. Noncommissioned officers moved back and forth in the open, exposed to enemy fire, to coordinate their soldiers' efforts. But the Ironmen, at this point in their deployment, know their jobs well in such situations, said Maj. Aaron Baugher of Ankeny, senior ground force commander during the operation, and Sgt. Edward Kane of Portland, Ore., an interstate transfer soldier serving with the 1/133rd.

The Ironmen mortar and sniper squads and supporting Black Hawk assault helicopters laid down suppressing fire on the north side of the landing zone. That allowed the entire force to finally move to defensible positions. The Black Hawks also sustained heavy damage from the Taliban fire, but survived the fight.

The force leaders on the ground decided to head for the shelter of the compound of defensible livestock buildings rather than take a narrow and exposed road directly into Do Ab, especially after a friendly Afghan police force the Guardsmen were to meet up with did not show.

With the assistance of Air Force personnel, the soldiers called in F-15 and F-16 fighters which dropped 500-pound bombs on the enemy positions - some within 200 meters of their own. Apache helicopter gunships also arrived to help take out the Taliban positions. When more Chinooks arrived with additional Guardsman and Afghan nationals, the Ironmen already on the ground provided covering fire. When a thunderstorm prevented additional troops from being brought in, the decision was made to move into Do Ab under cover of night. We own the night," Kane said.

The Ironmen and their Afghan allies had moved into Do Ab by sunrise, which comes at about 2:30 to 3 a.m. there. By that time the Taliban had sustained enough casualties they had withdrawn from Do Ab. The Ironmen eventually made contact with the Afghan police. Do Ab was deserted upon their arrival, but within four days of retaking the center, children could be seen playing in the street again. Kremer noted the entire battalion was involved in supporting their comrades in the field at Do Ab, gathering and flying in ammunition and supplies throughout the operation, among other tasks.

Guard soldiers once took supporting roles in previous deployments. But Kremer said the engagement at Do Ab illustrates that the Guard troops can perform alongside their active-duty counterparts, and his citizen soldiers are well suited to the task of winning the peace as well as the war by rebuilding the Afghan community.

"We do everything the active duty Army normally does - combined action with local military, Afghan national army, Afghan national police - we're out doing everything they do," Kremer said. "Government development, security - we're doing it all. And we bring a certain skill set, because back home we're school teachers, and police officers, firefighters, and carpenters. We understand community relationships." The "Ironmen" said they may be back in Iowa in about six weeks.

After reading this account, my heightened thoughts began to settle into place.....slowly into some sort of focus. Here are my impressions. (1) I'm so thankful our U.S. and Afghan soldiers were injury-free. (2) I was awestruck in the courage that was exhibited. I know this is their job. That still doesn't downplay the actions. (3) I began to think of the "other" side. The bad guys. Somebody's son, husband, father, brother, or another relative name or someone's friend died. Over 200 Taliban were killed. And that saddens me. (4) Remind me, why are we in Afghanistan anyway?

Several weeks ago, Rosemary Giunta, mother of Staff Sgt. Salvatore Giunta prayed for our enemies during the prayer vigil we held for our Iowa troops. "Let them know you God", she said. "Give them a hunger to know you".

"You have heard that it was said, "Love your neighbor and hate your enemy"...But I tell you: Love your enemies and pray for those who persecute you"--Matthew 5:43-44

YGG,

Rod

Rod closed the lid on his computer knowing this post and the words that brought it to life would not go away any time soon. Little did he know, just how much. This was truly a MIRACULOUS TURN OF EVENTS!

CHAPTER 80

It was a day in the lower 80's in Johnston, Iowa. It was June 17, 2011. Two days before Father's Day. It had been a stinker of a day. Isolated thunderstorms had spoiled much of the outside activity. But off to the west, Rod was seeing a smidge of blue sky. This was the break he and his trusted buddy, Mason, were looking for. Walk time.

As Rod passed by the oval mirror hanging behind the over-sized couch he caught a glimpse of his reflection. It caused him to stop and gander. A little smirk crossed his face. "Wow, I don't have much hair, do I", he thought. It had been a couple of months now since Martin had said to his wife, "give me a buzz cut. I want to look like the boyz do. Freshly shorn", he had demanded. It was like his days growing up in Hampton, Iowa. Short-cropped hair. He hated it then and he wasn't fond of it now, but....

"Come on dude", said Rod. "Let's get a walk in. Rod didn't have to suggest it twice. Seconds later the two were headed down the maple tree-lined street. When they reached the park area some two blocks from the Martin's home, Rod came to an abrupt stop. Staring right at him was one of the most magnificent rainbows he'd ever seen. He starting counting. There was red, orange, yellow, green, blue, indigo and violet. Seven all total. Could there be any more?, he thought. He grabbed his cellphone out of his pocket and googled number of colors in a rainbow. When it popped up 7.

Martin smiled. "Seven, the number for completion. Only you God. Wow!! Only you", he mouthed to himself.

Martin let Mason off his leash so he could enjoy the fresh smells among the damp grass. His nose was working overtime. While the Golden Jet was doing his thing, Rod decided to let his mind do some of its own. His memories went to a little less than a week ago when word had first come out concerning the Battle of Do Ab. All he could think of was an old Clint Eastwood movie from 1992, entitled, "Unforgiven". There was a scene in the movie where Eastwood was talking to a young gunslinger who gave the impression he'd killed a number of men. In truth, he hadn't. Having just taken down his first, Eastwood offered this advice.

"It's a helluva thing to kill a man. To take all he's got and all he's gonna have". Rod couldn't shake off these thoughts. What must it have been like to face the long firefight that had taken place...then to see the carnage that was left? Martin surmised, "I can only think how bad that would be". Then almost as quickly as he'd thought that, he followed it with, "actually I can't. How could I?"

In recent days, Martin had read as much as he could get his hands on regarding the Battle of Do Ab. Just this morning he'd come across an article from Staff Sgt. Ryan Matson. The final paragraphs were neatly etched word for word in his mind.

"The Recon Platoon provided cover for the commandos and American forces while they cleared the Do Ab District Center. After a final burst of enemy resistance, the battle ended.

"They (Task Force Red Bulls) got fire for about another hour and a half, maybe two hours after that, and then there was total silence," Baugher said. "We found out later ... the remaining insurgents had broken contact and fled. The Apaches, and AC-130 gunship had dropped a final heavy

series of bombs, causing them to finally flee, and preventing additional attacks."

"We spent the next two days securing the district center and doing some patrols through the villages. Not a single shot was fired during that time."

It has been a long year of fighting the enemy for the soldiers of Recon Platoon. But there is one thing they could all say definitively about the battle at Do Ab.

"Nothing was comparable to this," Foote said. "Nothing.

Mason's barking brought Rod's focus back to the here and now. The dog had a rabbit cornered under a big evergreen tree. "Mason", Martin yelled. "Come on boy, let's go home. You don't need that rabbit". The skies were darkening again. The rainbow was giving way to another shower. The two of them shot down the street to Martin's house. As the skies opened up, Rod and Mason hit the garage door. They had escaped without a drop of rain on them.

Later that evening Rod was sitting in the family room recliner with his PC on his lap.

He had been forwarded a video clip from one of the producers at their church. It was a video made when Charlie had been home in January. It was a back and forth video from father to son. Charlie talked dangers of his job and actual happenings in Afghanistan and Rod shared his emotions when he heard of his son being injured. It had been a tough video for Rod. He couldn't help but choke on his words when discussing his love for his son. Soon, some 15,000 members of the congregation would see it first-hand. Humbling to say the least....but also a piece where it was easy to see the importance of what Father's Day should be all about.

As Rod replayed the video several times over, the song, "Watching Scotty Grow", popped into his head. He remembered hearing it for the first time on the Johnny Carson Show while he was in high school. Mac Davis had been the talent. Bobby Goldsboro had released it years earlier, but Davis had written it. His rendition left nary a dry eye.

> **There he sits with a pen and a yellow pad. What a handsome lad.**
> **That's my boy**
> **BRLFQ spells mom and dad**
> **But that ain't too bad**
> **That's my boy**
> **You can have your TV and you nightclubs**
> **And you can have your drive in picture show**
> **I'll stay here with my little man near**
> **We'll listen to the radio biding my time and Watching Scotty grow**

Just thinking about the song again, caused a tear to drop from Rod's eyes. Davis had captured the whole father-son relationship in such a great manner. It might have been the first time Rod had ever thought about that correlation. As the tune continued to play in his head he chimed in singing like he was in the shower with no one in ear shot.

> **Say a little prayer before I go**
> **Me and God**
> **Watching Scotty grow**

And then ever so slowly Rod let the remainder out. He made sure each word had the right emphasis. Like he wanted God to hear the words. He repeated the lines another eight times.

> **Me and God**
> **Watching Scotty grow**

Rod sauntered into the kitchen and made a bologna and cheese sandwich, grabbed a big handful of Cheetos and a bottle of water. He slowly crept up the stairs, ate his snack and slid into bed. It was only 9 p.m. But it felt like midnight. The rest of the family was out of the house. Probably just as well. Rod shut his eyes hoping to find some rest. Scotty's song continued to play over and over and over, kind of like counting sheep. The images of Charlie came quickly. First was his birth and Rod exclaiming, "look at the size of those hands", then his first steps, his first solo bike ride, the hilarious picture as a 7-year old in shorts and knee-high cowboy boots dressed in his football uniform and then the last flash….in his combat attire. Rod had seen Charlie grow so much over his 20 years, he wanted to see more. But the light had turned to darkness. It was all Rod could do to keep his eyes open until there was no more.

CHAPTER 81

Charlie Martin brushed some of the Afghan desert off his jacket and looked in the mirror hanging in his hutt. He knew he felt tired, but he had no idea he looked that way too. If there was a look beyond tired, he was the perfect poster child. Some of it was caused by lack of sleep, some by the stress of the continual threats he was under and most likely there was the weather. Day after day it had been over a 100 degrees. With low's in the high 90's. The 70 pounds worth of gear soldiers carried around wasn't much help either. If ever a person wished for snow this might be the time. The grass had to be greener on the other side of the hill, Charlie thought.

The days were running their course for the National Guardsmen that had deployed late in the summer of 2010. There were already rumors of some people hearing when they'd be headed home. Charlie wasn't among them. As he was walking along the sand-packed soil headed to the communications center he began to think of home. Aaaaah. Home.

Charlie settled in front of a computer and went to his Facebook page. Seconds later, his dad's message hit the screen.

> **Rod MartinSaturday, June 18, 2011 at 10:15am CDT what u doing?**
> **Charlie MartinSaturday, June 18, 2011 at 10:16am CDT not too much. just got back from a mission.**
> **Rod MartinSaturday, June 18, 2011 at 10:16am CDT long one?**

Charlie MartinSaturday, June 18, 2011 at 10:16am CDT not too bad.. we left in the early afternoon.

Rod MartinSaturday, June 18, 2011 at 10:17am CDT not many of those left hopefully

Charlie MartinSaturday, June 18, 2011 at 10:17am CDT hopefully so, prolly at least 3

Rod MartinSaturday, June 18, 2011 at 10:18am CDT about every other day

Charlie MartinSaturday, June 18, 2011 at 10:18am CDT yup. but my platoon sgt is going to jalalabad for a day or 2 so i might have to pick up his mission one day

Rod MartinSaturday, June 18, 2011 at 10:19am CDT everyone packed

Charlie MartinSaturday, June 18, 2011 at 10:19am CDT for the most part.. some of my stuff is already headed back to the US.

Rod MartinSaturday, June 18, 2011 at 10:20am CDT where is your computer at?

Charlie MartinSaturday, June 18, 2011 at 10:20am CDT with me.

Rod MartinSaturday, June 18, 2011 at 10:20am CDT so maybe we can skype when you are in Wisconsin

Charlie MartinSaturday, June 18, 2011 at 10:20am CDT it depends if i have internet there or not but hopefully yes

Rod MartinSaturday, June 18, 2011 at 10:21am CDT i see. let's hope. I think Eddie will be there when you are. He leaves July 8th for Fort McCoy

Charlie MartinSaturday, June 18, 2011 at 10:22am CDT for what? AT for 2 weeks?

Rod MartinSaturday, June 18, 2011 at 10:22am CDT yup. He is at Camp Dodge now.

Charlie MartinSaturday, June 18, 2011 at 10:23am CDT ahh i see. thatd be cool if i got to see him there! are you sure hes going to mccoy and not ripley?

Rod MartinSaturday, June 18, 2011 at 10:23am CDT thats what he told mom last night. we can double check

Charlie MartinSaturday, June 18, 2011 at 10:24am CDT sweet. well hopefully its mccoy. thatd be cool!

Rod MartinSaturday, June 18, 2011 at 10:24am CDT oh yeah

Charlie MartinSaturday, June 18, 2011 at 10:24am CDT what are him and Dan up to today?

Rod MartinSaturday, June 18, 2011 at 10:25am CDT Ed is at camp dodge, Dan sleeping and working later

Charlie MartinSaturday, June 18, 2011 at 10:25am CDT ahh i see! nice nice. man i cant wait to be home

Rod MartinSaturday, June 18, 2011 at 10:26am CDT i hear you.. hard to stay patient

Charlie MartinSaturday, June 18, 2011 at 10:26am CDT yup that's for sure

Moments later, the two Martin's ended their discussion. The only thing seemingly left was time. Which meant the Waiting thing. Rod turned from his chair at the dining room table and looked out the window. The day was slowly winding down in Johnston. Charlie's was barely underway despite his early morning mission. Rod looked up at the stars and contemplated. What was his son's biggest hope right now? Charlie had said he was ready to get home. Was that his biggest Hope? What was any soldier's hope at this point in their mission? Was it staying alive?

Rod took a deep breath and slowly let it out. Yup, he thought, Hope is one of the most important mental traits in life. For Rod, his family, for all the 4,000 who deployed and their families and loved ones the day was right around the corner for their return. Or so everyone hoped.

CHAPTER 82

The Martin's were up early and on their way to church. Each of them showed the signs of a less than sound sleep from the night before. The ride to West Des Moines was pretty much in silence. Eddie and Dan were putzing with their phones, of course. Rod and Hope were in their own thoughts. Rod was visualizing the video that was going to be shown about his relationship with Charlie. How would that come across to his fellow church goers? Would it make the point he wanted it to make? He was certainly hopeful it would. His wife was thinking more about the lack of sleep the night before. She'd taken several knees to the back from her husband. After the third time, she got up and headed down to Charlie's room. Sometime after 3:30 a.m. she had finally drifted off.

The service turned out to be a special time. Pastor James Kinchen's message hit home. Relationships were special, he said. And fathers to sons were especially so. The video of Rod and Charlie turned out to be a hit. Rod had numerous people seek him out and offer their thanks for the words he and his son had shared. On the way home, Rod's cellphone went off. After a short conversation, Rod hung up. He turned to his wife then looked back at his sons. "Charlie's coming home", he said with great joy. "He's coming home!".

Ten minutes later he was parked in front of his laptop and filing the story he had been waiting to share for quite some time.

Finally!!!! I just got off the phone with our son Charlie who gave me a second day of "great" news. Yesterday, he sent me a message concerning our relationship and how it's grown this past year. It was the best present a Father could ever hope from a son on Father's Day. Much of the change in our relationship has come due to his deployment to Afghanistan. It hasn't been all bad. For sure there have been some tough moments. But it's time to put Afghanistan in the rear view mirror.....at least that's the best possible wordage I can paraphrase from Charlie's comments.

Perhaps as soon as twelve hours from now (Monday at 11:25 A.M. CST) Charlie will be hopping on a helicopter with a number of other Iowa National Guard buddies......headed HOME. Or at least the first leg of the trip. I will write more about Charlie's trip at a later date. More than anything, I don't want to jeopardize any of our troops as they begin this "pulling out" process. I know that I'm speaking for a great number of people today who have prayed faithfully for our troops safety. Don't stop now y'all. Keep 'em coming until all of the Homecoming's have been completed in Iowa. That day is coming, you know.

Anyway, I wanted to share this good news we got today. It will be even sweeter when we hear his voice telling us he's at his next stop back. To be continued......

YGG,

Rod

The next few days sped by. The entire family was pretty wound with excitement. Even though his final destination might be a month away, it was an indication that he was leaving a dangerous part of his mission. When Rod had taken a few moments to let things sink in further, he decided to put forth another blog post.

I was headed to a meeting the other day, just traveling down the highway when all of a sudden I had this feeling come over me. Where am I? and that was followed quickly by, where am I going? For the life of me, I had no idea. For what was most likely only a few moments, I was lost. My brain was in a complete freeze, but like I said, it didn't last long. It was however, a scary feeling. Ever had that happen to you? This wasn't the first time it's ever come upon me and strangely enough I had someone tell me about a similar experience for them just days before. Something tells me we aren't the only two going through this.

Hopefully, it's not the first stage of Alzheimer's, but if it is, we'll just have to deal with it. For now, I'm going to chalk up the experience to brain overload. That's the best excuse I can think of. I think back about 11 months ago when the first of the sendoffs took place for the 4,000 Iowa National Guard troops. Gosh, that seems like years ago. Long.....years ago. This time period has brought about changes in us all. Some for the good and some not so good.. One thing for sure is, we are remarkably different than before.

Sgt. Brian Pfeiler comes to mind. In early January, Sgt. Pfeiler became the first known casualty among the Iowa deployed. Jeff LaPage, father-in-law of Sgt. Pfeiler wrote a letter to President Obama that says so much about the character of our troops and their willingness to sacrifice.

President Barack Obama
January 17, 2011
Mr. President.

My son in law, Sgt Brian Pfeiler from Earlville Iowa who is attached to the 133rd Iowa National Guard station in Afghanistan was recently injured. He stepped on a land mine while on patrol and lost the lower part of his right leg. This happened on 06 January. He is now stateside recovering at Brooks AFB in San

Antonio, Texas. Please note that this is his 2nd deployment with his unit. He previously served in Iraq where he was also injured. Brian is alive today because of the bravery of one man, Sgt Elijah Wright of Janesville Iowa who was along on patrol when Brian was injured. Thanks to Sgt Wright's extreme heroism, his wife Katie and 3 year old daughter Madison will have been reunited with their husband and father. I am writing to you because I would like to see Sgt Wright receive some kind of award, medal or recognition for his bravery in getting to Brian quickly and saving his life. He is a brave and heroic young man and he is our angel. As Brian's father in law, I am forever in Sgt Wright's debt for what he has done and would like to see him recognized for what he did.

Regarding Brian. He is recovering well physically from his injury. But he has a deep sense of guilt for being injured and feels that he somehow let his unit down. He also feels like he somehow failed in his duty. In speaking with my daughter, his wife Katie, she says that he keeps apologizing as if he did something wrong. Mr President, right now, Brian could use some words of encouragement. Could you please let Brian know that he has nothing to apologize for and that he did not let his unit down?

Thank you Mr President,

Jeff LaPage

Could you Please let Brian know that he has nothing to apologize for? That was Mr. LaPage's request. How about we all get on our hands and knees and pray for Brian because he has nothing to apologize for? That seems like the proper thing to do. That should help in his healing process..... "Therefore whoever humbles himself as this little child is the greatest in the kingdom of heaven."-Matthew 18:4

Sgt. Pfeiler's humbleness in his duty, frankly, is not unusual. We see it time and time again. However, its experiences like Brian's that will be a focal point for the returning troops. Many will come home with guilt in the injuries they've sustained, the things they've seen and the things they've been asked to do, all in the Line of Duty.

Early this week we began hearing of soldiers embarking on a first leg of their return home. Some have reached that destination while others are still in the "wait" mode. It's time to put on a different hat and educate oneself in helping make the reintegration process a successful one for you and your soldier.

On another note:

On July 8th and 9th, my wife and I will be part of a panel at the "Parents of Soldier's Retreat" in Pella, Iowa. Additional panelists will be Rosemary Giunta, mother of Staff Sgt. Salvatore Giunta, Dale and Rhonda Jordal and Dan and Judy Merchant. Each of us will bring a little something different to the table. Chaplain Michael Crawford and the Third Reformed Church have worked together to put together a meeting that will focus on issues like, "Expectations and Adjustments". "What will my soldier be like after?....?" and "A parent's concerns and how to deal with them". You need to be the parent of a soldier, but not necessarily an Iowa National Guard soldier to participate.

Time will go quickly now so it's important to not sit idly by. Look for meetings such as the one I described. Call your local Family Readiness Group and get some information. Be aware your knowledge and support will go a long way in smoothing the transition process, not only for your soldier, but for you. It's imperative to get headed in the right direction......TOGETHER.

YGG,

Rod

CHAPTER 84

The days started falling off the calendar. Much of it had to do with the Martin's busy schedule. Top on the list was preparing the community for the homecomings of the Guard. Hope was integral in the array adorning Lake Point Circle and Pioneer Parkway in Johnston. There hadn't been a total count of how many trees were wrapped in yellow ribbons but there was a ton of them. Many of the townspeople knew the significance. Others were clueless. "What the heck are the ribbons doing wrapped around all the trees?", they'd ask. Sometimes it opened up a conversation for Hope and Rod to explain Charlie's deployment. Other times the sheer ignorance of people left them shaking their heads. "Where have these people been the last 10 months?", Rod would ask his wife. "How can you live and work in this town and not realize what's going on with the Guard members that deployed last year?" It was the frustrating interactions that brought on some things Rod was struggling with. Dreams and nightmares.

"Sleep? What was that?", Rod mumbled to himself more than once throughout the day. It seemed most days were like that as the July 4th weekend came into sight. The dreams focused on the actual homecoming and how Rod hoped they'd play out. The nightmares were more along the lines of the problems Charlie's group had leaving Afghanistan.

Rod rolled over in bed in a sweat. He wanted to curl up to his wife but the heat of the night and his damp t-shirt ruled that out. He needed cooling off. He looked up at the ceiling of shadows cast from the quarter moon on the big ash tree in their back yard. A new moon was going to be rising. Maybe that was some of the reason for the strangeness, Rod thought. All had to do with some sort of delays in the flights home. Rod hoped not. He continued looking at the ceiling or perhaps he was simply looking up. After several minutes his eyes shut down and another set of waves swept through his mind.

Rod was imagining he and his wife at the Parent's Retreat. It had been an extremely difficult time. Since the Martin's were part of the program, they were asked a host of questions. Some caused the two of them to re-think what their thoughts had been in the past months. Maybe this coming home wasn't going to be as smooth as they'd imagined. Rod sat erect in his chair. Stone-faced. The question had just been put forth by the mother of a soldier returning from Boone, Iowa. "So if your soldier can't integrate into civilian life. If he is suicidal. How am I going to handle that?", she inquired. Rod spent the next five minutes offering his thoughts and information he'd been provided by assistance groups. "Bottom-line. Don't give up on your soldier", he offered. "You are most likely his only support line to getting this thing figured out." There was a smattering of applause. Then it grew louder and louder. Rod looked down at his trembling hands. Somehow he'd made it through the Retreat without breaking down or shedding a tear. Then he heard the noise. His dream came to an abrupt halt.

It was the same noise he'd heard when they were in Kentucky for Eddie's graduation. Or it sure sounded like it. It grew more distinct. It couldn't be, he thought. Rod was clueless as to his whereabouts. Where was he? Part of him was afraid to open his eyes. The curious part wanted to make sense of it all. Slowly he opened his left eye. Staring at him was a bird on a rotted limb on the ash outside his window. It was singing and singing and singing. "Wow", Rod spoke ever so quietly as he opened his right eye. "It was the same dang song. It has to be", he reckoned. Could this be the same bird Rod had heard outside the Martin's motel room window when they had attended Eddie's Basic graduation? "Nah, couldn't be", Rod thought. Maybe the feathered creature was from the same family. The song was spot on.

Thankfully, this wasn't a nightmare. What was the reason for these thoughts?, he wondered. What the heck was going on with them? Maybe they were a precursor to the upcoming Parents Retreat scheduled for the next weekend.

The moment was interrupted with the sound of a marching band in the distance. Rod could hear the Johnston High School band playing "Stars and Stripes Forever". "Damn", said Rod. "What time is it?" " I think the 4th of July Parade is making its way down Pioneer Parkway. Honey, get up", Martin sounded off. "We overslept". The covers flew off the bed. Hope was exposed in her stars and stripes shorts and white t-shirt. She was ready. The scurry lasted all of two minutes before the two of them flew out the front door with lawn chairs in hand. Nothing was going to stand in their way of honoring their country. Especially not today.

The parade was nicely arranged. It was as if the Johnston community had put a special spin on the 2011 parade. The Martin's best guess was the Guard's deployment might have played a part.

Over the next couple of days and nights, Rod and Hope prepared for their retreat involvement. Some of the dreams and nightmares Rod had endured were now going to become reality. There were two days on tap for great back and forth between parents and military personnel. The day finally had arrived. The Martins headed for Pella, home of the Tulip Festival and wooden shoes.

The Retreat had been an exhausting one. Good. But exhausting. When the Martin's returned on Sunday afternoon, Rod snuck off to the deck and plopped his PC on his lap. Under a bright blue sky he posted the following on "My Father's Voice".

This weekend, my wife and I took part in a Parents of Soldiers Retreat at the Third Reformed Church in Pella, Iowa. We came away with some much needed information regarding our son Charlie and his return from deployment to Afghanistan this past year.

Hope and I were part of a panel that shared a parent's concern and how to deal with the issues both family and soldier will encounter in the coming weeks and months. A central theme that prevailed was the importance of prayer, not only on the safe return of each of the 4,000 soldiers, but the significance of continued importance in the reintegration process. Each soldier will encounter a new battle, much different than what they've experienced the last year. The enemy will be foreign to them. Some will struggle with depression, others with "normalcy" and some will disdain stupid people asking them questions......errr, let me rephrase that. Some people asking them stupid questions. Did you kill someone? What did that feel like, are not appropriate questions. It was suggested by one parent an opening line could be...."Welcome Home. We're so glad to have you back. You probably learned an awful lot during your deployment, what were some of the duties you performed?" At that point the soldier can either say a little or say a lot depending on their comfortability. That sounded like a good plan to me. After all, many of these Guardsmen have seen things, experienced things they may or may not want to share. If you can think in simpler terms of offering your mere presence and listening ears that would no doubt help. Be a friend, not a pest and not an intolerant soul.

At the end of the day on Saturday, Colonel Steve Altman informed the group of the procedure of reintegration, processing and Homecoming Celebrations. Colonel Altman said the first of the troops landed at Fort McCoy on Thursday. Another plane landed on Friday and one is due to land Sunday. That's the great news. It would appear the first of the Celebrations will be taking place on Sunday, July 17th. I'm not sure of that location. What's that mean for our son? Initially, we had information passed onto us for a Welcome Home on Thursday the 14th. That's not going to happen. It appears the Homecomings will coincide with the touchdown of each group at Fort McCoy. So as an example, if your soldier lands at Fort McCoy on the 13th....plan on roughly 7 days before your Celebration.

Disappointed? For sure. We are not unlike any other parent, spouse or relative. The days can't go quick enough. I did talk to Colonel Altman after the Retreat and asked him of the logistical nightmare that exists in getting the troops home. He was quick to agree with my statement. Despite the frustrations and our longing to put a big bear hug on a soldier, the National Guard is following an insistence to process each soldier properly. And that means a lot of things, but most important, medically. So much like Atlantis experienced on Friday, we are in a holding pattern. T Minus 7 Days and Counting. When mission control gives the okay....we'll resume the COUNTDOWN.

YGG,

Rod

There had been two questions presented to Rod that he answered to the best of his ability. He wasn't sure he was completely honest. Or was he? He guessed he'd have to find out. The first was, "how would you handle your son coming home with serious issues from his IED incident?" And, "what part of your son do you think you lost from his experiences?" "Those were tough", Rod recalled. In both instances, he said, he'd have to take things one day at a time and ask for grace and patience. Rod glanced at the yellow ribbon flapping in the breeze around the oak tree in the Martin's front yard. The end was near. Rod looked down at this computer and as he published his story he was quickly overcome with a selfish thought. July 16th was his birthday. What a great present that would be. Charlie returning home from war on his 60th birthday. "That wouldn't be too much to ask, would it", he uttered.

CHAPTER 85

Moments after closing the lid on his laptop, Rod heard his wife yell, "Dear, come in here, quick!" Whenever he heard those words, he knew he was either in trouble or she needed help. For sure, he knew he needed to react right away. As he entered the bedroom, he saw his wife staring at the high definition set on their dresser. She didn't look up at him as her full attention was on the tube. The scene was from Camp Dodge. The subject was the death of two more soldiers and the wounding of another.

When the video piece concluded Rod looked at Hope and emitted a sound he'd never heard his body make before. It was if he were bellowing in pain. It lasted for a full five seconds. Suddenly, he yelled, "Damn it". And then louder, "Damn it". He whirled and picked up a ballpoint pen off their night stand and tossed a fast ball into the far corner. The pen sprayed into pieces. And then he rolled off the same words again in quick succession. "Damn it, damn it, damn it". He turned to leave the room as Hope spoke in a manner of calm, "Dear. Settle down. Settle down". But Rod was having none of it. "I just need to be by myself for a while", he responded. "I don't know if I'm more hurt, angry or afraid. All I know is, this is, this is..... CRAP". Rod hustled up the stairs into Eddie's bedroom and threw himself on the queen mattress on the floor. His thoughts went in a hundred different directions. After an hour of staring out the window at the clear blue skies some perspective came into view. He kept hearing the voice, "stay the course, for them and for you". After another five minutes of thought, he slowly got out of bed.

Martin made his way across the living room and opened the front door. He stepped out on the deck and looked down the yellow ribbon lined street another time. The image of these symbols of life and hope was something he couldn't get enough of. Sometime within the next few days there would be soldiers seeing that same sight. The image raised his hopes. The song, "Tie a Yellow Ribbon around the Old Oak Tree", flashed into his mind. Then a smile came across his face. "Thanks, Tony Orlando. Thanks."

Tony Orlando's song always comes to mind when this image appears

As Rod closed the door on the outside world He made a straight line for his computer and a second posting of the day.

"When they were filled, God said unto his disciples, gather up the fragments that remain, that nothing be lost". -John 6:12

Several writings ago, I spoke of "picking up the pieces". Today and for many more days, there will be questions and thoughts regarding the deaths of our two latest soldiers. Why did they get so close to returning to their families and friends and then lose their lives? I don't know. But God does. I rest in that fact and that there will be rays of sunshine ahead......

From an ecstasy standpoint came news today of several Homecoming dates. A release from the Iowa National Guard follows:

"Community Homecoming Ceremonies for three Iowa Army National Guard units mobilized as part of Operation Enduring Freedom, will be held on Thursday, July 14 in Cedar Rapids, Boone, and Johnston. Local officials and Iowa National Guard leadership will participate and the public and media are welcome and encouraged to attend these homecoming ceremonies. Here are the units and details:

Cedar Rapids-11:30 a.m., Prairie Point Middle School gym, 401 76th Ave. SW Company C, Brigade Special Troops Battalion, 2nd Brigade Combat Team, 34th Infantry Division, Iowa Army National Guard (approximately 50 Soldiers)

Johnston-12:30 p.m., Johnston High School gym, 6501 NW 62nd Ave.

Company B, Brigade Special Troops Battalion, 2nd Brigade Combat Team, 34th Infantry Division, Iowa Army National Guard (approximately 50 Soldiers)

Boone-1 p.m., Boone High School gym, 500 7th St.

Selected Soldiers from Headquarters and Headquarters Company, 2nd Brigade Combat Team, 34th Infantry Division, Iowa Army National Guard (approximately 85 Soldiers).

Additional Soldiers from this company will return later in July-date and time to be determined".

The celebrations that are listed above will be full of tears and hugs and an outpouring of love.....and one of relief. But, not all have been so fortunate. To date, we have lost 8 soldiers since our National Guardsmen deployed last summer. We experienced all sorts of emotions, but none more truthful than agony and ecstasy. But know this, through it all, God has been with us...

YGG,

Rod

CHAPTER 86

"These last several days have been crazy, but even with that it sure seems quiet at the homestead with Eddie gone", Rod suggested. "I know what you mean", responded Hope. "And it's not simply cooking for one less person either."

Eddie had left days before. On Saturday, while his parents were in Pella at the Parents Retreat, he had left for Fort McCoy in Wisconsin for Guard Camp. When Eddie realized he'd be gone for his annual two-week outing, he had talked of how awesome it would be if Charlie's group flew into the same camp for "deprogramming". The odds were not that great. Rod and Eddie had conversed in the early morning hours on Saturday while he ventured north from Des Moines.

> **Rod Martin**Saturday, July 9, 2011 at 7:04am CDT what doing?

> **Eddie Martin**Saturday, July 9, 2011 at 7:05am CDT Leaving camp dodge right now. U

> **Rod Martin**Saturday, July 9, 2011 at 7:07am CDT how many in your truck?

> **Eddie Martin**Saturday, July 9, 2011 at 7:14am CDT Two. Just me and sgt edwards. We are taking 41 trucks though

> **Rod Marting**Saturday, July 9, 2011 at 7:15am CDT I see the picture on Facebook. 41 trucks????

Eddie MartinSaturday, July 9, 2011 at 7:17am CDT Ya. That pic-ture is the one I'm driving.

Rod MartinSaturday, July 9, 2011 at 7:19am CDT u found out where u are going for flood relief and when yet?

Eddie MartinSaturday, July 9, 2011 at 7:22am CDT Nope. It's the army. U never kno till last minute. And it would be the mizzou river in council bluffs

Rod MartinSaturday, July 9, 2011 at 7:23am CDT k. better let you drive safely. let us know when you get there. Love u

That was the last communication they'd exchanged. Rod looked over at the calendar hanging on the kitchen wall. It read, Tuesday July 12th. Martin strolled over to the laptop and lifted the lid. Some of the action was out of boredom, another sense was to see if Charlie had found out anything on his return to the states. There was one message and it didn't take Rod long to decipher it. It read

Charlie MartinTuesday, July 12, 2011 at 6:52 M CDT
To be at McCoy tonight. Tell Eddie

Well, the unbelievable had happened. Charlie was coming into Fort McCoy, the same Fort Eddie was at. The two would have their own homecoming days before the rest of the family. Maybe. Rod was beside himself. Finally, finally he was going to be on American soil again. Rod typed a short message to Eddie. Short and to the point. One he knew would surprise the heck out of him.

Rod MartinTuesday, July 12, 2011 at 7:54am CDT Charlie should be halfway to McCoy. Maybe get there around 8:30 tonight

Rod's engines were now on fire. He had a whole heap of thoughts running through his mind. If anything he wanted to stay the course and think of all the celebrations around the state and the various highs and lows taking place. He wanted to put a name and a face to any soldiers that were experiencing either type of emotion. He looked over some notes he'd taken down from an interview with a soldier for the right occasion. This time was as good as any. Here's how the story went.

I want you to meet a soldier. A soldier with a name that speaks loudly of toughness and strength. A name seemingly destined for the military. He goes by Doak. Sgt. Doak Keller. And yes, if that conjures up a John Wayne image, it should. His mom's side of the family loved that old western hero. Until recently, he was leading a unit of Iowa National Guard troops in their peace keeping efforts in Afghanistan. That is or was until May 18th when this report came to us.

Four Soldiers from the 2nd Brigade Combat Team, 34th Infantry Division, Iowa Army National Guard, were wounded when their vehicle was struck by an Improvised Explosive Device while conducting combat operations in Afghanistan on Wednesday, May 18.

Sgt. Doak Keller, 23, of Cedar Falls, Iowa; Spc. Jason Wayne, 21, of Cedar Rapids, Iowa; Spc. Frank Winslow, 26, of Rowley, Iowa; and Private 1st Class Tank Walker, 18, of Tama, Iowa, were transported to medical facilities at Bagram Air Field in Afghanistan.

A 2006 graduate of Dike-New Hartford High School, Doak is the youngest of three siblings. His parents are Randy and Trudy Keller of Dike, Iowa. Sgt. Doak , who has been home for some two weeks, will be returning to Fort Leonard Wood, Missouri in early July for continued rehabilitation from his injuries.

The following is a conversation with Sgt. Doak Keller. These are his words as he rehabs from wounds he received that day. It's our chance to experience a small fraction of Sgt. Keller's life and it also enables the opportunity to appreciate his willingness to serve.

MFV: Tell me how you decided to choose the military as a way of serving your country?

Doak: I was 17 and making bad decisions and needed to do something with my life. I knew I wouldn't make it if I didn't change something, so I joined the Army. I always wanted to be in the military when I knew my grandparents were. Army on my Dad's side and Navy on my Mom's.

MFV: What has been the most eye-opening experience to your decision?

Doak: The most eye-opening experience is pretty tough. I talked back once at basic training and I learned my lesson right then. Also, the first time in combat also opened my eyes up and made me realize don't take things for granted and don't regret anything you do.

MFV: As a young leader (Sgt.) what are some of the challenges to your job?

Doak: Challenges of the job are always learning new things and listening to everyone but having the mentality to lead your guys without regrets or second guessing yourself. Always being able to make a decision and sticking with it.

MFV: First time deployed? If not, tell me about the first and then this one? What feelings did you have when you hopped the bus and headed for Mississippi?

Doak: This is my second deployment but the first one was to Kosovo on a peace keeping mission and a lot more laid back. I was really excited when I got on the bus to go to Mississippi because after I joined the military I wanted to go somewhere and serve for what I joined for.

MFV: What was the general reaction of the Afghan people to you and your men when you patrolled?

Doak: They always made it seem like they liked us but some pretended and worked with the enemy when we weren't around. They got the best of both worlds, help from opposite groups.

MFV: Did you have any close calls before your IED incident?

Doak: I had a couple of close calls. I heard bullets go by sometimes but nothing too bad there because the Taliban were just shooting because they got paid to. I was on the opposite side when a mortar round landed on our helicopter landing pads. That was probably the closest feeling of the terrible impact and sounding like it was right behind me.

MFV: Thoughts on the IED incident.

Doak: I always wondered why it was our truck when three or four others went by it and we had one truck left behind us. That is about all of the how's and why's.

MFV: Final assessment of your injuries?

Doak: My injuries were fractured inside ankle bone, possible torn Meniscus in my right knee, fractured TI or C1 Vertebrae and I got my left forearm hit on some stuff and other scratches.

MFV: Did you sense something before the incident?

Doak: I didn't sense it but the whole time in the country I kept telling our medic that I would be the reason he got his combat medic badge and I was one of the reasons, haha. Also after switching drivers we kept saying we were gonna hit an IED. Just bad luck and a bad coincidence.

MFV: I'm sure you hated to leave your unit and men. Tell us about that bond.

Doak: The bond between soldiers is stronger than anything I've ever seen. You know for a fact they will risk their lives for you and know that they will always be there for you no matter where you're at. You can talk to them about anything. I hate being in America when my men are still there because I hoped that they would send me back and I don't feel like I should have left them behind.

MFV: Have you been able to stay in touch with your guys?
Doak: Guys in Afghanistan write me and they're on Facebook and the guys in the IED blast keep in touch with each other.

MFV: What do you miss?
Doak: Honestly, I miss everything...even the bad days because all the guys were still together and going through it together.

MFV: How is rehab going?
Doak: I have to get my knee checked out and just routine check-ups on my ankle. Everything is healing good and they say I will make a 100% recovery.

MFV: I'm sure you heard of the firefight the 1/133rd was involved in where over 200 Taliban were killed on May 25th. What was your reaction to that?
Doak: I think it is great. The 1/133rd has and always will be a strong and proud Brigade. If they want to overrun where we are at they'd better be ready because brothers have each others back and no one is gonna let them take it for free.

MFV: You mentioned you might not be able to attend the Homecoming Celebration. Thoughts?
Doak: I recently found out I most likely will be, but if I wouldn't have been able to, it would be pretty devastating not seeing the guys come back.

MFV: You received the Purple Heart. What does that mean to you?

Doak: The purple heart to be honest doesn't mean much to me. I know someone who was hurt worse but didn't get one and I did.

MFV: Would you do it all over again?
Doak: Yes, I would do it all over again.

I asked Doak what word described his pre-deployment and he said, "anxious". Then I asked for a word that described his deployment and he said, "bored, haha". And lastly, I asked for a word that spoke to his arrival stateside due to his injuries.... and he said "unfair".

If that doesn't sound like a true soldier ......one even old John Wayne would have been proud of. Thanks, Sgt. Doak, for a job well done.

YGG,

Rod

This was but one of thousands and thousands of stories from the deployment of 2010-2011. But, there would be many more to follow now that soldiers were coming stateside. Rod was banking on somehow his two sons could meet up at Fort McCoy. But one never knew what regulations might keep them apart. If they were able to connect, Rod thought, how awesome would that be. Purely, simply a God thing. And not a coincidence.

CHAPTER 87

The odds of the two Martin boys being at Fort McCoy was no longer in question. Before it actually happened, Rod and Hope had figured there was no way. Now that they were on the same camp grounds, would they be able to connect? Who knew? That might be another thing all unto itself. Still, Eddie figured he might as well try. He went to one of his superior officers, Sergeant Krol and explained the situation. Much to his surprise, the Sgt. said, "we'll make it work one way or another". Two days later on Thursday, the 14th of July, Charlie Martin strolled into the Fort McCoy PX. Waiting was his younger brother, Eddie, who hadn't laid eyes on him since he left on his deployment nearly a year ago.

Eddie had been anxious about their meeting, curious what he'd see in his brother. When their eyes met, Eddie felt a little welling up in his chest. His eyes were showing moisture in both corners. Charlie's remained dry and far away, though. The hug between the two was pretty one-sided. One full of emotion. And one hardly at all. That was Charlie's side. After a less than eventful embrace, the two parted. A faint smile showed between them. "How you doin, bro?", Eddie questioned. "Fine", Charlie fired back. "Fine". Conversation was strained and minimal. Still Eddie could sense Charlie was happy they'd connected. They spent about an hour and a half talking about a lot of surface stuff. Nothing with any substance. At least it was a beginning, Eddie thought. From outward appearances Charlie looked good. What was underneath was a mystery. As their time ended, they agreed to check with their superior officers to have another chance to talk. Saturday was their target day.

Two days later, Hope, Rod and Dan finally completed lining the Johnston streets with yellow-ribbons. After a long afternoon of work, their efforts were all wrapped up. The Martin's had received word yesterday that the Homecoming for Charlie's group was scheduled for the UNI-Dome on Tuesday, the 19th. Today was now the 16th of July. Rod's birthday. And while he was feeling blessed in putting another number on the board, a part of him was a little discouraged. "If only the Homecoming had been three days earlier", he muttered. But it was only a small sentiment. His bigger desire had been filled with having Charlie back in the states.

Eddie and Charlie weren't able to make Saturday work for their reconnect, but they did on Sunday. It would be their only other chance before Company E, 334th Brigade Support Battalion saddled up the convoy and made their way to Cedar Falls, Iowa. Their meeting was much like the first. Charlie was walled off. Eddie tried as he could to loosen him up. When they went their ways after an hour, Eddie was left with the lingering thought. Was his brother alright? Charlie had shared with him that in one of his briefings at McCoy, a doctor had questioned Charlie's thinking. Like maybe he wasn't in his right mind. Charlie said he was offended by the guy's remarks. He didn't say a whole lot about it other than that.

Eddie (L) and Charlie hookup in Wisconsin

Eddie laid on his cot that night playing back his time with Charlie. It was a typical Wisconsin summer evening. The temperature, 81 degrees, nearly matched the humidity, 88%. The wind was nearly non-existent. 4 miles per hour. It was perfect mosquito weather. And in Wisconsin that meant big Daddy's. Despite the continual scratching of bites, Eddie tried to focus. But his mind was somewhat disoriented. In trying to come to a conclusion, he wondered what kind of reception awaited his parents and younger brother. They had reached the final days of countdown. Finally. They felt they were ready for just about anything. The three of them simply wanted Charlie back.

It hadn't been a good night of sleep for Eddie. He still didn't have an answer in regards to Charlie and the reception his family was going to receive in a matter of days. Would they see the same Charlie he did? He hoped not.

Charlie spent Monday at McCoy going through more tests and observations. He and most of his soldier buddies were tired of all the poking and prodding. They were ready to leave the place and it couldn't come soon enough. When Tuesday morning came, 95 soldiers herded themselves onto four chartered busses headed to Iowa. It was a little after 8 in the morning.

The drive was long and boring. At least from Charlie's perspective. What was Charlie thinking as the busses rolled southward? Was he picturing what type of Homecoming that was going to take place once they arrived on the UNI campus? And who from his family and friends might have made the trip? Most likely those thoughts didn't exist.

Roughly half-way into the trip, the busses crossed into the state of Iowa where they were met by a slew of Patriot Guard and AMVET motorcycle riders. The two groups were going to provide an escort the remainder of the way to Cedar Falls. About noon, the soldiers and cyclists arrived at the Dome. Ever so slowly began a buzz in the stadium. Word had it that the group was outside. Suddenly, the cyclists revved up their engines and the large overhead door was rolled up as the guests of honor marched in.

The noise was deafening. Loud motorcycle engines being revved to their max mixed with applause, whistling and cheering. There were also a whole bunch of tears and smiles. The journey back was complete.

CHAPTER 88

The hootin' and hollerin' continued for some time. The hundreds of family members and friends wanted the 95 soldiers on the floor of the Dome to feel their love and appreciation for their service to country. Hope looked around soaking everything in. What a moment! Her grin said it all. Rod surveyed the slew of Charlie's supporters who had made the trek to welcome him back. The crew included Rod's mother, brother, sister and their families. Hope's brother, sister and her family. And there also was a lifelong buddy of Rod's, John Jefferson, that the boys thought of as an uncle that had showed up. Jefferson had been so involved in the boyz growing up years having had no children of his own. The boys were somewhat of a 'fill in' and Jefferson loved them dearly. Lastly were the parents of a soldier that Rod and Hope had met when attending the Parents Retreat weekend. The longer Rod looked at his son standing at attention the bigger the lump in his throat became. A half-smile contained his real emotion, that of swelled pride.

There were many more stories developing within the crowd. Prior to the ceremony, Savannah Kirby was overheard saying she wouldn't cry. But as much as she tried, tears flowed at the first glimpse of her husband, Spc. Jack Kirby of Dubuque. Days of watching other homecoming ceremonies, and nearly a year of anticipation, was too much. "I knew my day was coming sooner rather than later. I'm really excited," Savannah said. Several commanders spoke to the crowd. It would have been monumental if anyone could have recited what words they'd said. The crowd was waiting, much like the countdown of a clock at an athletic event. The end couldn't come soon enough. Finally, the unit was dismissed and the onslaught began.

Rod couldn't wait. He bee-lined down the steps onto the floor of the facility and made a mad dash towards his son. When he reached Charlie he put his whole soul into wrapping his arms around him and giving him the biggest hug he could muster. But there was no return. Charlie was stiff as a board. To be more exact, it was like hugging a telephone pole. The response was one Rod hadn't figured on receiving. One by one the other members of Charlie's support group arrived on the scene. Rod stepped back and let them have their time. "I was as rocked as a person could be", Rod later recalled. Typically, when someone greets you in the manner that I did you hope to receive some love in return. Charlie wasn't open to any of that. He wasn't rude per se, simply flat and emotionless."

Hope was lost in her own sea of thoughts and emotions. She was relishing the comfort of having Charlie back, where she could see him, touch him and hear him. She had asked Charlie what his thoughts were as he stood waiting in formation in front of the stadium crowd. "It was a whole lot of waiting", he offered. "Days and weeks of waiting to finally be over with". "What else?", she asked. "Relief to be home I guess. Plus wondering about what's next, what do I do now?", he pronounced. Hope wondered the same thing….what now? But then her thoughts reverted back to the present. "He's home, he's home, oh thank God he's home", she thought. For now, she rested in that.

It's accurate to say the Martin's had envisioned a different scenario. Maybe one like the Kirby's mentioned earlier. Savannah said she almost ran people over to get to Jack. The reunion was worth the wait, the couple said. "I don't even know how to describe it," Spc. Kirby said. "I'm looking forward to so many things. Spending time with family, going to a friend's house and golf.....and just enjoying life."

After a half hour of picture taking and chit-chat most of the entourage decided to take their conversations to a restaurant in Cedar Falls, Tony's La Pizzeria. Another hour and a half of small talk trailed off to a look at the clock on the wall. It was time for people to head home. That was not the case for Rod, Hope, Dan and Charlie. They had one more stop to make during the trip back to Johnston. Several months previous, Charlie had asked his Dad to see if he could locate a Golden Retriever breeder in Iowa. Rod had been up for the challenge. He'd found a rural breeder in Dows, Iowa who recently had a litter of ten born. The breeder told Rod considering the puppy was for a returning veteran, he would let Charlie have the pick of the bunch.

Charlie seemed more at ease around the puppies than he had at the Homecoming. Maybe a dog's presence in his life could help Charlie, Rod thought. There was a little guy that stood out from the rest, one Charlie ended up choosing. Charlie was going to have to wait for his little package to come home. The little Golden was a little over 5 weeks old and too young to leave his mother. Charlie would have to return for his newly named friend, Barrett.

Charlie's new companion and security blanket, Barrett

The remainder of the trip home took a little over an hour. When the Martin's pulled up in their driveway, Charlie was the first one to exit the vehicle. Another hour later after dropping off his bags and taking a shower Charlie was out the door. In his mind he must have been on R and R because he went AWOL for two days, whereabouts unknown. Hope and Rod didn't ask any questions. Their parental instincts told them better. It had been a long, long road HOME. Charlie had earned some space.

Rod sat down at his laptop for one final story of his son's deployment. He was still reeling from the Homecoming experience. There were several times he wiped away tears as he tried to explain the moment. He'd tried as well as he could to catch the situation. Not only for him, but for anyone else who would ever go through this. He pounded on the keys hoping that each word had more emphasis than the one before it. It was the best therapy he could come by right now.

"Hey, where are you going Soldier?", the Sergeant asked. Stopping in his tracks, the Private felt the heat begin to well up inside. Gosh, how he disliked those words. It implied he had no direction in his life, as a matter of fact, it made him feel like a kid all over again. Was he wandering into an area he shouldn't be? No, it was some burly dude trying to prove a point. The Sergeant was the one in control of the situation.

I don't have any facts to present, but I'm sure this type of an exchange happens far too often for most soldiers. However, if one is ever going to move up the promotional ladder, they'd better learn command and respect. So, they answer back, the best way they know how. "Going to the bathroom, sir", the soldier states. But underneath, one wonders.....

Four days ago, we welcomed back our oldest son from a year-long deployment to Afghanistan. Thankfully, he is back on U.S. soil. At least I think he is, from what little we've seen of him. He's been on the go day and night, night and day. Anywhere other than home. As a parent, you'd like to sit down and have some meaningful conversation of his past year's experiences. But that happening appears to be one that will take place later rather than sooner. And that's been frustrating. Certainly we want him to re-connect with old friends and reintegrate into society, but it appears to us, his methods closer portray a man on the run. Not necessarily from any one person, but the authority thing. We haven't put any boundaries on his return...after all, he's almost 21 years of age. But trying to find some reason for his actions led me to think of this. Is he trying to avoid the question, where you going? or maybe what are you doing? I wonder. I know I would. We haven't asked either of those questions.

I think maybe it might help to pose some statements and then some questions. I know I'd like to see the picture a little more clearer, how about you? One mother told me yesterday she feels safer with her soldier in Afghanistan than she does with him back in the States. That caught me off guard, yet when I thought about it further, it definitely made some sense. She further related that when her son was at work overseas, she knew what he had going on. At home, there were far too many other things taking place, namely girls and partying. Another parent suggested in the little time they'd seen their soldier home, he appeared in a word they could only describe as.... scattered. And then yet another family wore the facial expressions of disappointment as they talked about their soldier. Had there been a real intimate reconnection yet between them? It appears not.

So are parents and spouses expecting too much too soon? Maybe......Is the battle line already being drawn that separates, "you don't know what I went through and what I saw" to someone that wants to be there if only as a "pair of ears".

I'd like to offer some thoughts that are going through my mind today. It might hit home with you. It might at least cause you to stop and think, regardless if you are a parent or a soldier. For my wife and I, this past year has been the most difficult year of our lives. Hands down, the toughest. While our son was performing missions on an average of nearly one per day, we were struggling to maintain our faith, our hope and somehow provide a "stiff" upper lip. We were to be cheerleaders when it was the furthest thing from our conscience, yet somehow we had to go there. Our role was to provide a "mind's eye to home" for our son. I think we did that the best way we knew how. Did we shoot a gun or encounter an IED? Were we ever ambushed? Did we encounter an enemy far too hard to trust? I think you know the answer to those questions. No, no and no. However, most family members faced a different type of battle. Maybe it was financial. Or the children couldn't cope with a parent being gone and they became depressed, school grades suffered and behavioral issues cropped up. Perhaps it was loneliness thinking no one could understand what they were going through. Simply, it could have been lack of support.

Whatever the case, both parties have endured a tremendous amount this past year. It hasn't been all bad, though. There have been some unique stories of Hope and Faith and PATIENCE. And that's where I think we are right now. We need to be in PATIENCE mode. Both soldier and family member.... steadfastly asking God to give each of us the right words for understanding, and for each other.

If we follow God's lead regarding this time in our lives, I don't think any of us will have to ask the question....the one our soldier doesn't want to hear and the one we don't want to ask....."Where are you going"?

"My child, do not forget my teaching, but let your heart keep my commandments; for length of days and years of life and abundant welfare they will give you.

Do not let loyalty and faithfulness forsake you; bind them around your neck, write them on the tablet of your heart.

So you will find favor and good repute in the sight of God and of people.

Trust in the LORD with all your heart, and do not rely on your own insight.

In all your ways acknowledge him, and he will make straight your paths.

Do not be wise in your own eyes; fear the LORD, and turn away from evil.

It will be a healing for your flesh and a refreshment for your body".-Proverbs 3:1-8

YGG,

Rod

Rod pushed back from the table and looked outside. In the distance was a super blue sky with nary a cloud. It was a glorious day. One only God could design. Rod took a deep breath in and slowly let it out. "We've come a long way", he said under his breath. Then he filled his lungs again. This time appreciating everything he could. As he was releasing the air out of his mouth he quickly stopped. The realization hit him full force. "We're not done", Rod stated with a tremendous amount of certainty. "I thought we were finished with this journey, but we might have only just begun. Wow".

A WRAP

The Martin's saga did endure. Over the years, Eddie and Charlie had moved to Colorado Springs together. Eddie ended up staying. He'd found a job that morphed into a perfect position for him as Master Technician for an auto repair shop. He loved the mountains and all they offered. Charlie moved back after a year and a half with his girlfriend, Shirley and her daughter, Cheyenne to Johnston. Months later, they became pregnant and they had the Martin's first grandchild, little Ali. Dan was employed as an electrician and was working towards his journeyman's ticket and was really finding a niche for himself. Rod and Hope were nestled in their Saylorville ranch home. Things had smoothed out for the family in many respects.

It was Labor Day 2018. Rod was the first to rise in the Martin household. Today was to be the end. It had been roughly 17 months since beginning the book project. 'Hope is a Weapon". The labor of loves' final chapter was to be written. Despite a lot of foot dragging, Rod had finally decided to write an account of the family's experiences of deployment. It might have taken longer to write the book than Rod had first thought. But considering he was writing nights and weekends, not so bad. He hadn't been in any hurry. Still the process was daunting.

This was going to be a long day. So he figured he best get started early. He plopped down on the hard wooden Mission chair and raised the lid on the laptop. His fingers quickly went to the keys. After a short while

Rod raised his head and looked at the beautiful sunrise in view through the kitchen window. The blues and yellows were stupendous. Rod's mental make-up, though, was not. He needed a pick me up. Strolling into the kitchen he located the coffee maker and the Keurig on the counter top. He had a quick decision to make. Which would be easier? After a little argument with himself he chose the Keurig, stuck a container in the cylinder and pushed brew. Thirty seconds later he picked the coffee mug off the burner and added a small amount of Hazelnut cream.

He then ambled over to the dark brown love seat and settled in. He had one more thing to check before getting back to his writing. Grabbing his cellphone he scrolled down to Fox News and came across some political junk that took up most of the news....until he saw the continued heart breaking news from the Middle East. The headline said it all. The story provided the details.

"U.S. SERVICE MEMBER DEAD IN AFGHANISTAN FROM APPARENT INSIDE ATTACK"

"A U.S. service member was killed and another was wounded during an apparent "insider attack" in eastern Afghanistan on Monday, according to a statement from U.S. Forces Afghanistan. The sacrifice of our service member, who volunteered for a mission to Afghanistan to protect his country, is a tragic loss for all who knew and all who will now never know him".

"Crap. Crap. Crap", repeated Rod. "Triple crap". Rod felt sick to his stomach. Somewhere in the States there was going to be a knock on a parent's door. The news would be the worst possible. Their son had died in action serving his country. When would this ever end?, Rod thought. Ever? He sipped a couple of times on his brew hoping it would give him some answers. None came. What did come was an aftertaste he'd never experienced before. He put the coffee cup down and closed his eyes. Maybe answers would come this way. They didn't. Seconds after the lids closed he fell off into never-never land.

Within minutes there appeared an image in front of Rod's eyes of a slumped man leaning over a desk pounding away on a laptop. "What the heck?", Rod mumbled. "What's he doing?" The dream continued. Rod snuck up behind the fellow and peered over his shoulder. He could see something that looked like a letter on the screen. Looking closer he was startled by the opening line. The letter was being written to him.

Dear Rod:

You've no doubt heard some of the best therapy there is, is to write a letter to express your inner-most thoughts of a relationship and the effects from it. I wanted to write you this letter so you'd have it for a keepsake. Something that you can look back on with pride.

First off, writing a blog and then a book of Charlie's deployment and how it impacted the family was incredible. Be humble with that knowledge and honor. Not everyone could have done such a thing.

Remember what the most interesting thing you took away from this journey was? How about that Father's Day Facebook message Charlie sent you?

Dadpo---

I just got onto your blog and read your latest entry and I loved it. Every word of it. I'm so thankful to have an awesome caring dad like you. Even though we've had our times where we haven't gotten along so well and used to be far apart, I now feel that we have closed that gap and we get along pretty well! We've both come a long way since those days where we would just yell back and forth.and I feel that this deployment is a pretty dang good reason for some of it. Granted I'm young and still have a lot left to learn, I've noticed some big changes in me since I've been gone.

-Sonpo

Rod, take the words Charlie wrote to you and cherish them. They may be some of the most honest words he's ever said to you. Right now, of your sons, you'd have to place Charlie third on the totem pole as far as closeness. Eddie was first, Dan a close second (he was a lot like Charlie) then Charlie. Someday all three will be at the same level. Just wait.

Hope has mentioned to you several times how sad it is to read the things you've written. And you've always said. "Dear, it's not all sad. It's life in its most serious form. We've had a whole bunch of good times along with the bad".

Do you recall your most impressionable moment of the deployment? Remember when you surprised Hope at the Des Moines International Airport? She thought she was going to meet Eddie and you surprised her with Charlie as the package. The look on her face said it all. Love and shock all in a nice package. There might be nothing sweeter than a military person coming home and surprising their loved one. That one was one for the ages.

So where do you and the family go from here? Here might be a good road. So many of us put the carriage before the horse when we're merely seeking the faith needed to be healed. Did you know that hope precedes faith? Little is taught about hope, but it is another foundational key to faith. If you don't have hope, you won't be capable of having faith.

Hope was your rock throughout these times in more ways than one. Not only in your wife, Hope, who stood tall with her words and actions, but the other kind. Whatever that word means to you is what you have to hold on to. The license plate you saw in South Carolina in the Spring of 2018 said it all. "While I Breath I Hope". Hope is your lifeline and a means to arm yourself against all odds.

Make Hope your Weapon.

Hope all is well,

Rod

Rod looked closer at the man at the laptop. His eyes squinted as he tried to focus on the individual. Who the heck is he?, Rod wondered. He squinted again until a voice began calling his name.

"Rod. Rod", the voice beckoned. "What are you doing, honey?" Hope continued shaking her husband in the love seat hoping to bring him back to the living. "You seemed like you were in a trance. You'd smile and get serious and smile again. What were you thinking?", she questioned.

"I must have fallen asleep after reading the story about another soldier's death in Afghanistan. I was trying to get things in order to finish the last chapter in the book but there must have been something in the cream that put me to sleep. I saw this guy writing a letter to me in a dream. It was wild". "How heartbreaking for another soldier to have lost his life", said Hope. "How did that translate into your dream?" "I'm not sure exactly. I think it brought the whole deployment thing into a clearer view and how much we have to be thankful for with Charlie's safe return. To think where Charlie has come since he first got home. He is starting to figure things out. I trust he keeps doing that".

Rod lifted himself out of the chair and headed to the dining table for the last "Hope is a Weapon" time. He turned on the laptop and moved his mouse over to the draft area of his folders. He clicked on "A Wrap". "Wow", Rod yelled. "There's already something written here". He turned to his wife. "Did you get on the computer and write something? ", he questioned. "No", she stated defiantly. "Come on", Rod smiled back. "You had to".

Something didn't set right with Rod. When he'd written the letter to the editor concerning his son's deployment he knew the words weren't his, but from a higher authority. All he'd done was provide the keyboard work. But this was decidedly different. The words were on the screen but Rod had no idea how they got there.

"I hope you're not accusing me of something", Hope said returning his smirk. "Well......" he shot back. "The chapter has been written for me.

At least I hope it was." Rod quickly saved the draft making sure the words didn't jump off the screen. He didn't remember writing the letter to himself. Could he of done that? He wasn't positive. All he knew was, the words were there.

He slowly turned to his wife beaming. "I'm done", he announced. "The book is finished. I only hope the one thing people can take away from this project is some understanding of deployment and the sacrifices not only the soldiers make but their family and friends as well.

It all comes down to hope. We could go without food for awhile, maybe we could go without water for a few days, but we can't even go a few seconds without Hope.

We've had people come to the blog from 98 countries. Maybe it was for some form of Hope. I have no idea. But for some reason we've made an impact. Our journey will continue but this stage in our lives is complete. Right, dear?", he said.

"If you say so, dear", she replied. "I was hoping you might write a sequel." "Ahhhh, not so fast my dear", Rod replied. "Before I give you an answer let's head to the movie theatre. That's where God seems to talk to me best. Who knows what he has in store?", offered Rod. A big smirk crossed Hope Martin's face and she replied, "he does….that I'm certain of. All you have to do is respond."

Rod shook his head. "Women. You seem to have all the answers. Maybe someday we men can be as smart as you", he countered. And with a sly smile of his own, he added, "'I can only Hope."

ACKNOWLEDGEMENTS

To My God. Who through him all things are possible.

To my mother, Mary Ellen Kelling, whose spirit was with me through-out this entire process; to Lt. Colonel Doug Houston for his wisdom and patience; to author David Baldacci, whose bevy of novels gave me the courage to write a book in the first place, to J.D. Faraq for his simple ABC's of Salvation. And to Pastor Rick Warren who penned the following words.

"The deepest level of worship is praising God through the pain, thanking God during the trials, trusting Him when we're tempted to lose hope, and loving Him even when He seems distant.

At my lowest, God is my hope. At my darkest, God is my light. At my weakest, God is my strength. At my saddest, God is my comforter".

PARTING THOUGHTS....

Hope is a powerful weapon indeed. And it goes hand in hand with faith. But hope and faith in what, or who? It's like the motto we see at Christmas that says, "Believe". Believe what? These are very big questions and they deserve true answers. Without solid answers life has the power to chew us up and spit us out. We need hope, without it we die. And what is to die? The end? That's it?

God has written eternity in our hearts and made everything beautiful in its time (Ecclesiastes 3:11). We instinctively know there is something more. Death really is better understood by the word separation. Physical death is to be separated from the body. Spiritual death is to be separated from God. Physical death comes to all of us. To stay in spiritual death is a choice we make (unless of course we are too young or lack the ability to understand). What is LIFE then? If death is to be separated, life is to be united, our dead spirit reconciled to God. A new birth. In relationship with God we find hope, faith and life. There we can live beyond circumstances because there's so much more than that. And that is the good news, the gospel. The word gospel actually means Good News. What is the good news?

God came to us in Jesus, knowing full well that he would suffer greatly and be killed by his own creation. His grave today is empty for death could not hold him. He lives! And the same power that brought him back to life is there for all of us. How? It is ABC simple.

A is to admit we need him and to realize we have missed the mark, so to speak. Our many wrong choices and bad decisions have separated us from God.

B is to believe that he came to us in Jesus…that he died and rose from that death. And that he is coming again to set all things right. He will make all things new.

C is to call upon him. Don't settle for just "believing". He longs for relationship. He gives hope, faith and life even now. And HOPE IS A WEAPON!!!

The Brothers Reunited

ABOUT THE AUTHOR

John Kelling was a graduate of Minnesota State University, Mankato. His field of study was broadcasting and journalism. He later went on to work for WHO Radio in Des Moines, Iowa in various capacities of their sports programming. In addition, Kelling worked in TV production for various groups, most notably, ESPN, Fox Sports and the Big Ten Network. In 2003, he launched an eight-state sports network for a Midwest cable company. In recent years, he was a blog writer for a number of sports outlets. His blog on his son's deployment to Afghanistan led to this writing endeavor.....

UZBEKISTAN
TAJIKISTAN
STAN
Amu Darya
TAKHAR
Raghist
Yangi Qala
Khamyab
Imam Sahib
Dasht-i-Archi
Mazar-i-Sharif
Qala-i-Zal
Khwaja Ghar
Jurm
Sheberghan
Kunduz
Bangi
Khostak V.
Chardara
Khanabad
RYAB
Aliabad
Ishkamish
Astana Baba
Sheram
Samangan
Baiseqal
Sar-i-Pul
Dand-i-Ghuri
Puli Khumri
Qarae
Mirshadi
Almar
Bayanan
BAGHLAN
Khwaja Kinti
Qaysar
Kohistanat
Shakh
Tala wa Barfak
Dara
Duab
Charsada
Balkhab
GHIS
Charikar
Askin V.
Jawand
Murghab
Bamyan
Tagab
Ghalmin
Dawlatyar
Hariud
Panjab
Kabul
Surkh Rod
Chaghcharan
Tangi V.
Azra
Shahrak
Pul-i-Alam
GHOR
Nili
Kharwar
Charkh
Saghar
Pasaband
Helmand
Ajristan
Kulalgo
Sangan
Ghazni
Zurmat
Baghran
Gizab
Syabaghal
Tebla
Khost
URUZGAN
GHAZNI
Charchino
Khas Uruzgan
Kakar
0 km
0 mi
Nawzad
Deh Rawud
Tarinkot
Musa Qala
Nawbahar
Kajaki
Nawa
Sangin
ZABUL
Ghorak
Maruf
Kandahar
Spin Boldak
Registan Desert
Dishu
Shorabak
LMAND
Registan
Approximate Terr
Situation on Octo
Govern
Taliban
"Islami
Mixed